OUTSIDE CBI

OUTSIDE CBI

JOGINDER SINGH

GYAN

GYAN PUBLISHING HOUSE

NEW DELHI-110002

OUTSIDE CBI

ISBN : 81-212-0658-8

Published in *2001* in India by
Gyan Publishing House
5, Ansari Road, New Delhi-110002

Lessertype Setting at: Kamal Printing System, Delhi-92

Printed at : Mehra Offset Press, Delhi. *Phone* : **326 85 74**

Contents

Acknowledgements

I would like to thank, first of all the characters, mentioned in this book, who, by their very existence and interaction with me, made this book, possible. I have tried to portray them in their true colours, according to my perception. God forgive me, if there has been either an exaggeration or an under portrayal. If there has been one, it is only due to human frailties, to which I am as much subject, as any other fellow human being.

Preface

This book narrates about my life and how a village lad, with no public school education, became a police man, a bureaucrat, and ultimately reached the post of Director of the Central Bureau of Investigation. The man who would not bail out anybody, at the cost of the law of the country and his conscience. Thus resulting in out of the inconvenient job, by the politicians in power. The country is not as yet ready to wage a battle against the corrupt. It is for this reason, that many corrupt people still manage to be at the centre stage. The vote bank politics, caste, religious, regional exploitation and manipulation have enabled some scum of the society to remain on the top. Bureaucracy, being the backbone of the Government can no doubt play a vital role in keeping malpractices under check. This book is an attempt to portray partially, the problems of the common man and common civil servants and how to tackle some of them. Every body has his unique experience. There are more than one methods of dealing with problem. I cannot say that my method was the best. There is a Mahabharat in the life of each one of us. What is required, is to give a chance to Lord Krishna (our conscience) to guide us. I would have liked to give more details and more incidents. But even one thousand pages would not be enough. A balance had to be struck, between the bulk and what the readers would like to digest, in the limited time, at their disposal.

Eventhough I have tried not to be didactic, I have sought to comment on certain persons and situations. This book is intended for the young administrators, and the general public. It is open to each segment of the society to cull out, whatever it wants. India is what Indians are going to make it. Nobody is going to help us. We can make India of our dreams, by doing our best, in whatever field, we are working. Islands of excellence, created by each one of us, would go to make this country, whatever we want it to be, rich, vibrant and a place, "where the mind is without fear". Occasionally, the book may appear to be flippant, but serious incidents are humorously presented to break the spell of boredom. Working on a book is a Tapasya or a penance. Behind every spectacular success, there is a lot of sweat, perspiration and unspectacular work. I hope it will prove to be worth the labour put in.

Last but not the least I would like to thank Mr. B.P. Garg and, Mr. Amit Garg, Directors, Gyan Publishing House who showed interest in bringing out this book in such a short time.

Joginder Singh

1

Sweet and Bitter Memories

Everybody has sweet and sour memories of his/her childhood. When we sit quietly, several pleasant and unpleasant memories, come in our minds. Sometimes we enjoy them. Occasionally painful incidents disturb our mind. I also have similar recollections of my life. I belong to a middle-class rural family. I did not go to any public school, for the simple reason that my parents did not know what a public school was. Agriculture was not a good commercial proposition for us, the farmers of Punjab, until the green revolution made it towards the late 1960's. Real prosperity arrived in the lives of farmers only after hybrid varieties of seeds were introduced.

I was born in a place called Khajurwala, on 12th October, 1939. I have some claim to royalty, but I have no supporting records. Most of the sub-castes are named, after a place or place of the origin like Barnala, Jalandhari, Dhillon, Gill, Longowal, etc., who at one time, must have belonged to that particular area. My sub-caste is Punchi. Very likely my fore-fathers, who at one time were royalty, in Poonch in the State of Jammu and Kashmir, were driven out from there. It happened in the late eighteenth century, at the time of the conquest of Kashmir, by Maharaja Ranjit Singh. My father, Mahant Kartar Singh was the Lambardar or village headman of Khajurwala located in District Montgomery (now renamed as Sahiwal in Pakistan. There, he was the only person who had passed his Matriculation (or tenth standard, in the year 1936. My grandfather, Mahant Natha Singh, was a carefree person who believed in living life to the full. He was almost disinherited by my great grandfather, Mahant Devi Dass, who passed over, most of his land, and the village headmanship to my father. My grandfather had a happy-go-lucky attitude. He used to drink heavily. He had a number of mistresses, apart from three wires. But my father, came under the religious influence of a Sadhu, Bawa Charan Dass. This Sadhu, was responsible, for inculcating a religious bent of mind in him. Bawa Charan Dass also used to enjoy his drink in the company of my grandfather, with *kababs* and chicken. My father never touched liquor, till well past middle age and that too as a medicine. Bawa Charan Dass, wore the traditional, saffron dress of a sanyasi. In the eyes of this sanyasi all the religions were same. At time of prayer, he would render salutations, to all religious leaders, including that of Garib Dassi sect, and including my forefathers. He would tell the interesting and educative stories from *Ramayana* and *Mahabharta*. He had a good following in and around of Khajurwala and the nearby areas. He also had a controlling influence in the Dharamshala Garib Dassian, Hardwar. He would collect wheat, rice, flour from the rural folks, for feeding the devotees in Hardwar. Since he did not press his demands and left the offerings to the discretion of the givers, he was quite popular.

My recollection of village Khajurwala, which I saw 53 years back, at the age of eight, can naturally be a blurred one. But I remember the big banyan tree. Beneath this tree was the place, where the village lasses used to dance. It was also used as a school with a single teacher called, Maulvi Sahib. The teacher used to beat and punish all students. He would put a pencil in between the two fingers and press it, in case the homework was not done. Since I was the son of the village Lambardar, I was spared any punishment. But he was quite harsh and abusive to the poorer class of children. My maternal grandfather Lala Bahadur Chand used to live in Kanganpur, at a distance of 20 km. from our village. Once in a while we would visit him in our family tonga. The tonga was the only means of transportation. All well-off families had their own tonga, the horse driven carriage to take them around.

Kanganpur was the nearest railhead. The only other place I visited was Kasur. We went there by train, to see my uncle, late Rattan Chand (husband of my mother's elder sister, Sheila). He was an advocate. It was a new world there, when I saw the moving and talking human beings on the screen. It was almost incredible at that time and was my first exposure to the world of cinema. At that time I was only six-years-old. This sight, as also water running out of a tap, was too much of a unique experience, for a child who had never seen any miracles like these. When I was sitting with my father in the room of the Station Master, at Kanganpur. I saw a railway official using the phone. When the bell rang, he picked up the old style receiver and spoke something. After a few minutes, he went out. Just then the bell rang again. While sitting on the chair, I turned my mouth towards the phone and said that Babuji was not there. The ring stopped and after some time again it rang and I said in Punjabi, *"Main pehlai thwanu akhya hai Dauji aethey nai hain"* (I have already told you that Babuji was not there). But it had no effect and it kept on ringing. I kept on wondering, as to why the stupid fellow, is unable to understand simple Punjabi.

My father always showed reverence to my grandfather, no matter how drunk he was, which was most of the time. My native village, Khajurwala, could boast of only a primary school. I was studying in 4th standard with Urdu medium, while the national movement against the colonial rule was at its zenith and the country was about to secure independence.

My father, was the first and only owner of a first radio in the village, working on a dry battery. It was tuned to Lahore Radio Station only. It was the star attraction, for miles together. I somehow felt that somebody was sitting inside the box and speaking or singing whatever came on the radio. The use of loud speakers, at the time of fairs, for passing messages, hundreds of yards away, was another wonder. It excited a lot of curiosity and this remained the talk of the village for months together.

The National Movement

The national movement won. The British decided to grant independence, to India, on 15th August, 1947. My parents decided to go to Jagadhri, (now called Yamuna Nagar in Haryana) to my maternal uncle, Jaswant Rai Babbar. The plan was to go, from there to Delhi, to witness, the independence celebrations on 15th of August, 1947. Before leaving the village, my father as the village Headman, deposited about Rs 10,000, in the government treasury as the village land revenue. With only Rs 400, we left for Jagadhri where my uncle had taken up a job after his B.Sc. It was never, the intention, of my parents, not to go back. They had thought, they would go back, after the trouble of partition was over. So five of us, my father, my mother (Lajwanti), myself and my two sisters (Sarla and Manjit) landed at Jagadhri on 2nd August, 1947. At that time, my sisters were hardly four and three years old while I was eight. They, as well as I, did not know the difference between Delhi and Jagadhri. We arrived at Delhi and stayed with another uncle, Balwant Singh, who had joined as an inspector in some department, probably Food and Civil Supplies. He had married my father's younger sister, Hakim Devi. (She was a sister born from the second wife of my late grandfather, Amar Kaur). It was usual to practice polygamy in the early years of the twentieth century. The practice of monogamy in India, has seriously been accepted only after independence. Some people still practice polygamy. The government rules demand only monogamy and any violation can lead to dismissal from service.

There was a lot of exuberance and excitement on 15th August, 1947. My parents, myself, my sisters and my two uncles (Jaswant Rai and Balwant Singh) had gone with us and seen the hoisting of the tricolour at India Gate. My father had spent Rs 200 out of Rs 400 he had brought. His pocket with the remaining Rs 200 was picked at the time of witnessing of Independence Day celebrations. So we were penniless on 15th August, 1947. My mother's jewellery was sold to tide over the immediate financial needs.

In the meantime, news arrived of Hindu-Muslim riots and the migration of Hindus and Sikhs from the areas now forming Pakistan. In the prevailing violence, and massive killings of innocent Hindus and Sikhs in Pakistan and Muslims in some parts of India, the idea of returning to Khajurwala never occurred again. There was no news, about the rest of our relatives, including my grandfather. After a few months, we learnt that they had migrated from Pakistan and settled in a place called Jalalabad in Ferozepore District of Punjab. A large number of shelterless relatives descended on my uncle, Jaswant Rai in Jagadhri. His was more than a housefull. I saw floods of people, occupying every inch of available place, in Jagadhri. The word "refugee" was affixed for all those, who had migrated from Pakistan. I was one of the "refugees", along with my parents.

Towards the beginning of 1948, my father decided to move out of Jagadhri. So the planned to move to Jalalabad. First, we stayed in a village Kalyanpur, near Shahbad Markanda, with another Mahant family.We were, at the best, tolerated, as poor relations, who better be shunned. My father used to work in the fields as a labourer and cut the grass. I grazed the cattle of the land- lord, probably for some pittance of wages in the form of food. I was nine years old at that time. After some period of unwelcome stay, we moved to Kharar, (now near Chandigarh) with other relatives, like my uncle Mohan Lal. They were also refugees, like us. After a few months we moved from Kharar, to Abohar in Ferozepore District in 1950.

By that time, a massive drive, had been launched, to resettle the refugees. As a part of the resettlement, the lands and the houses of the Muslims, who had gone away, to Pakistan were allotted to the migrants from Pakistan. In this way, some land in Abohar was allotted to my father in lieu of the land (more than 1000 acres) left in Pakistan. My father also obtained a license for the dealership of arms and ammunition in Abohar. As people had a great sense of insecurity, due to partition, so a psychological climate was there in favour of possessing a licensed weapon. It was a thriving business. My father made good money through this business for sometime, alongwith farming.................

Settlement at Jalalabad

Some land was allotted to us in Jalalabad, at our request, in lieu of the land at Abohar. We moved there in 1951. It was connected to Ferozepur District Headquarters by train. One train would make a round of the 33 mile route, thrice a day and only one bus would connect the District Headquarter of Ferozepur with Tehsil Headquarters, Fazilka, via Jalalabad. In the early fifties, Jalalabad could boast of a middle school, for boys and a primary school for girls. An apology of a road, with a ramshackle bridge, connected the town, with the railway station, two kilometres away. The bridge or makeshift planks had been damaged due to heavy rains. The traveller had to take a tonga, from the town to the railway station. This tonga would halt near the broken culvert. Then one had to walk on a plank, with the luggage, slung over the shoulder or placed on head, to the other side. Another tonga would be hired, for the rest of the journey to the railway station.

This practice continued for about one decade despite repeated petitions to the District Administration. It took a long time, for the powers that be, to repair the damage. Unluckily the same story was repeated in the eighties when the seepage drainage bridge on the road from Jalalabad to Muktasar was damaged. It was not repaired, for about four years, cutting off Muktasar from Jalalabad. Before the partition, Jalalabad had a system of local electricity generation, which provided street lighting. It fell into disuse and was both damaged and looted at the time of migration of Muslim population, from there. Some vandals, pulled out the wires, leaving behind only street light poles Jalalabad had to wait till 1957, when it got electricity again, as a result of commissioning of Bhakra Hydel Project.

The superstitions, illiteracy and backwardness go together just like literacy and modernity. In the fifties and early sixties, the priests were consulted for curing common fever. Illiterate people really felt that they were under the spell of magic, at the time of sickness. Umpteen times my relatives would go to priests. They would request them to read some hymns or message on a glass of water. They believed that by drinking of such water, they could be cured of diseases. Whenever even a piece of cloth, was seen in the centre of the road, with something tied to it, the first presumption would be that it was a magic spell. It was believed, that it will bring disaster, to the person touching it. Even ordinary stones, kept in an odd shape would be sufficient to convert it into a place of worship of either good or evil.

Mahant by Birth

I find that wearing the robe of a holy man, and preaching something religious ,is one of the most paying professions.

One need not be either holy or religious himself before donning that robe. If I start doing it, I am bound to attract several followers.. I am qualified by birth, to do so, being a Mahant. I have never professionalized my being a Mahant. My father, grandfather or great grandfather never assumed the role of a preacher. I am confident of a good following even if I preach muck. I have relations, much less educated, than even a third standard student, who have been making, millions, by scrounging on their followers. Being Mahants, they go every year to their followers, stay with them for few days, enjoy their hospitality, and leave only after a handsome presentation, has been made to them. This is really begging in style.

In any case, I have not affixed, the word Mahant, to my name right from my school days. Very few people know, that by birth I am a Mahant. Neither my father nor grandfather had practised being a Mahant, except for wearing a saffron coloured turban. My grandfather in any case could not have been taken seriously as a Mahant or a holy man. My father did not do so, because of the happy-go-lucky attitude of my grandfather. I was not at all interested to be known as a Mahant, due to the malpractices associated with the Mahants in the 1920's, as evidenced by the Akali movements.

Several historical Gurudwaras were being run as personal fiefs by some Mahants. They were pocketing all the income from there, and using the same for their personal benefit instead of the community. This led to the Akali movement against such malpractices.

The then Government of India conceded to the demand of the Akalis and formulated and promulgated a Central Act for the management and running of Gurudwaras and their properties. This Act provided for the setting up of an elected Supreme Sikh Gurudwaras or Temple Management Committee. The control of historical Gurudwaras and other specified Gurudwaras was vested in the same. Elections were arranged at regular intervals and all Sikhs (and those believing in Sikhism) were eligible for voting and contesting elections.

Since Mahants were the cause of a Central Act, it naturally exposed them to ridicule the entire populace of Punjab. It was perhaps, due to this psychological reason, that I did not want to be known as being a Mahant. I have not used this prefix even once, though I am legitimately entitled to use it. Nevertheless, my father did contest elections to the Shiromani Gurudwara Prabhandak Committee (SGPC) in 1945-46 and was elected unanimously to the Supreme Body for the Management of the Gurudwaras. He was so religious minded that during his entire term, whatever TA and DA he drew for attending the official work of the SGPC, was donated back by him to the Golden Temple, Amritsar. This body has its headquarters in Amritsar. I occasionally wear saffron coloured turban, the colour of Mahants turban.

Radio : The Only Entertainment

Jalalabad could boast of only a single radio set in 1950. People would flock to its owner for listening to the music, news or other interesting programmes in the evening. In fact for quite a long time his postal address was only Mahant Harbhajan Singh Radio Wala'. This was enough for the letters to reach him.

In the fifties and early sixties, apart from the touring cinema talkies, the radio was the only entertainment in Jalalabad.

My favourite Radio programme, as of million others, was the programme of songs broadcast from Radio Ceylon and sponsored by a toothpaste company. It was easier to catch Radio Ceylon than any Indian Station. It was the most powerful Radio Station, in the region at that time. Indian radio, did not get out of the conservative influence, for a long time. It would broadcast only classical music, which was liked by a small minority of the older generation.

Very rarely, at the time, All India Radio (AIR) would broadcast film music. It did not go commercial, till quite sometime, when it found that all the money it should be making was made by a foreign station. It was said, that the then Minister for Information and Broadcasting was, an anti-film music man. He was fond of only Pakka Ragas (Classical music). Hence the artists singing ragas had a field day.

Ultimately, AIR introduced a second commercial channel Vividh Bharti. It depends heavily on film programmes, as most TV channels do at present. Even now, our country does not have a single powerful Radio Station, which can beam to all parts of the country. I did raise this point with a Director General of All India Radio. I complained to him that whenever I was in Jalalabad, which is just about 8 kms from Pakistan border in Punjab and about 300 kms from Delhi, I cannot even catch the English news broadcast there. But, he said that we have a 1000 Kws Radio Station in Nagpur which should beam to every part of the country. Perhaps, the high power station must be on paper. The position has not changed even in 1999. Even the Indian TV does not reach the nook and corner of border of India, as Pakistan TV does. Now, it appears from the Press Reports that something might be done to improve the situation, after the Kargil war.

My kind-hearted Father

In 1950's, the only public means of transport was tonga. There were only three cycles in Jalalabad. My father had one. Once in a while, I would be permitted to cycle to the school. There used to be at least five to six requests, everyday to my father, for the loan of the bicycle. He was too kind hearted a person to say "No". The result was, that he himself hardly, got to use it. Even when he cycled to the field, it was always, with somebody, at the rear seat, in the direction in which he was going.

When my father purchased a scooter in 1969, he made it a point that some needy person was given a lift, on the pillion seat. When he got his first Standard Herald Car in 1974, he saw to it, that it went full, wherever he went. Even after purchasing a Fiat and Maruti, in the successive years, he continued to use the car for the general public. In fact, several times, he was invited, for the marriage parties or engagement ceremonies, because of his car. It had become a joke, that my father was invited, for marriages, by the people going out of Jalalabad, not for his own sake, but for the free lift by his car. It was for the sake of the free use of his car. In fact, when he got the first colour TV and VCR in Jalalabad, people started asking for the same on the occasion of celebrations.

He never disappointed anybody, who approached him, for any assistance or help either financially or physically. He would accompany villagers, to government offices, to help them in their problems. He would spend his own money and take them in his car. As the Municipal President, he helped several sweepers, or poor employees, with money to tide over their personal problems, including the marriages of their children.

My kind-hearted father spread love and affection and goodwill wherever he went, till his death, in January, 1996. Despite the fact, he had a heart attack in 1982, he maintained an active pace of life. He was instrumental largely, in the starting of a Giani Gurbux Singh DAV college in Jalalabad.

During his life time, he donated more than two lakhs to the College. He used to visit one learned Giani (Swamiji), Giani Gurbux Singh, regularly and listen to his discourses for a number of years.Giani Gurbx Singh passed away in 1984. He left assets of more than Rupees eight lakh spread over in various places. His followers, including Hindus and Sikhs decided to set up a trust, with my late father Mahant Kartar Singh, as the Chairman of the Trust to perpetuate his memory.

Trust and College

My father felt that while Jalalabad had all the basic facilities, it did not have any college. People had to send their children 30 to 50 kilometre away for college education. He knew at first hand, that I had to go away to Ludhiana, 130 Kilometres away for my college education. The trust purchased six acres of land for the college. It then approached the President of the SGPC to accept the gift of the land, rupees six lakh in cash and start a Khalsa College there. It was felt that if the SGPC, were to start the college, it would be easier to run it. The reason was at that time the Akali Government was in power in Punjab. My father along with other members of the trust went and met the then President of the SGPC and made the offer. After many fruitless visits by my late father, the President of the SGPC rejected the request. His reason was that, already many academic institutions run by the Committee, were incurring heavy losses. It was not possible to burden the SGPC, with another, loss making educational institution.

After the rebuff, my father along with other members of the Trust landed in Delhi in October/November 1985. They had fixed an appointment with the then President of DAV Management Committee, late Prof. Ved Vyas. They asked me to accompany them. At that time I was on two years study leave. I told them, that though I was serving as a Deputy Inspector General of Police, yet I had neither office nor any other status. Hence I would not be of any substantial help to them. My father said that since I could converse in English. English being at premium, my presence would be advantageous to them. More with a view to respect my father's wishes than any other reason, I accompanied them for their meeting with Prof. Vaid Vyas, an academician and a soft hearted man. My father said that they had come with a request to start a DAV College in Jalalabad. The President said in chaste Punjabi that they were welcome. The DAV Management Committee, would be glad ,to start a college, in Jalalabad. But the trust would have to pay rupees eleven lakhs for Arts College, twelve lakhs for a Commerce College and fourteen lakhs for a Science College. My father said without a second thought, that the Giani Gurbux Singh Trust would, pay an amount of rupees fourteen lakhs for a Science College. At that time the trust had only about, rupees about six lakhs with it. I suggested that the formal foundation stone of the college should be laid on the 1st January, 1986 with the idea so that the college could start in the academic year of 1986-87. This was promptly agreed to by Prof. Vyas. The foundation stone of the college was laid on 1st January, 1986.

My father without any hesitation and against the medical advice moved from village to village and shop to shop along with other members of the Trust. He did collect the balance amount by public contribution. He had suffered a heart attack on March 17, 1982. The doctors had advised him not to exert himself. But for the service of the town and the student community, he ignored the advice at a grave health risk to himself. In fact, he started with his own contribution of Rs. 21000, though he had no personal advantage, as neither his children nor grandchildren were to study in that college.

Before the start of the college, the DAV Management Committee asked my father whether the Trust had any other pre-conditions. My father requested that since the lion's share of the finances was coming from the savings of the late Giani Ji, the college should be called Giani Gurbux Singh

College. The DAV Management Committee President went a step ahead. He said, that since 1986 marks the centenary of the DAV educational institutions, they would blaze a new tradition. They would name the college, Giani Gurbux Singh DAV Centenary College, Jalalabad. This is probably for the first time in the history of our country and that of DAV, that an educational institution, is named jointly after a Sikh and DAV. At the time of the formal functions on 1st January, there were the *Paaths* both from *Guru Granth Sahib* and *Geeta*.The college has grown from one room to a full fledged academic institution with more than 1150 students at present. It is recognised and affiliated to the Punjab University. My father continued, to be the Chairman of local Management Committee.He took active part in all its activities, till his death. I on a unanimous request, of the trust, succeeded him, both as Chairman of the Trust and the College Management Committee. This is the second educational institution he started in Jalalabad, the earlier one being a Girls High School, as a Municipal President in 1957-58.

Student Life

I studied up to 8th standard in Jalalabad and had to go for my education beyond 8th class to Ferozepore in 1953.There was no High School in Jalalabad, at that time.

I felt that I should learn Punjabi and accordingly joined Punjabi classes in the 4th standard in Government School, Abohar in 1950. I was eleven years old then and I did not know how to tie the turban. After a few days in the Punjabi class, the Punjabi teacher, a young Sikh, asked me whether I knew any *Paath* from the scriptures. I said I did not know and I would gladly learn the same. He got infuriated with me for not knowing the *Paath* and for not tying the turban properly. He slapped me in the class. This was the end of learning Punjabi as far as I was concerned. I promptly changed my language from Punjabi to Hindi. I felt that I had been unjustly humiliated by the Punjabi teacher. Till this day I have not formally learnt Punjabi as a language.

The imposition of even the most pleasant thing, can be revolting. This is what had happened to me. I continued studying Hindi till my graduation. Perhaps Punjabi as my mother tongue, would have been easier. It took quite a bit of time for me to forgive the Punjabi teacher for what he had done to me. I hold him, a fundamentalist, squarely responsible for my foregoing the knowledge of Punjabi. This was my own way of protesting as a child in which I have been the loser. Coercion is something, which never produces the desired results

In the middle school, at Jalalabad, most of the classes up to 8th standard were held in the open for want of class rooms. There were students and no or very few classrooms or even blackboard or even the gunny carpet for squatting on the floor. The position continues even now in most of the government schools in the country. There was only one playground for the whole school, with one physical education teacher, for over eight hundred students. The school itself was located at a distance of about two kilometres from the main town. We had to walk down.

After passing 8th standard in 1953, for further education, I went to Government High School Ferozepur. Out of a class of nearly 100, only the parents of six students, could afford education up to matriculation, for their children outside Jalalabad. I had no place to stay in Ferozpore, so I got admission in the school hostel. Staying in the school hostel itself was an education. I was exposed to various influences and different types of persons, away from the protective atmosphere of the home. One had to be on one's own. I had to wash my own utensils, clothes and make my bed. I had to protect myself from bullying by others. Even the mess servants would try to lord and lampoon me, as an ignorant villager. Since the villagers were looked at as bumpkins, the hostel mess staff would serve food very condescendingly, to all from the poor rural background.. It was the lack of money, which kept me, from seeing Hindi movies, to my fill, in the nearby Raja Talkies. Once in a while we would go and see the picture. I could afford only, the lowest class of ticket, costing five annas (the present thirty paisa). I do not remember, to have ever hired a rickshaw, in Ferozpore. Walking down two or three kilometres was routine. In hostel, we were totally ignorant that there could be anything like a bathroom, next to the bedroom. The back of the walls would be used as public urinals, by all of us. I somehow refused to fall in line.I would use the open ground or some bush for the same. After getting up in the morning, urinating is the first function of everybody. Each one would walk down to his favourite spot for the same. Some would use the walls, some the trunk of trees and some small bushes. Once in the cold winter, I had gone out in the morning and I thought that I was watering a bush. But unfortunately it turned out to be another classfellow. He was performing the same function in a sitting position. When he was sprinkled with some watery substance, he hurled choicest abuses on me. Perhaps rightly. This became a joke between myself and my unfortunate victim classmate, Hansraj, though it happened more than five decades ago.

College Education

I finished my school in 1955, with a bare first class, which I missed by 2%. My father was keen to send me to the best college, which at that time happened to be Government College Ludhiana. Its portals were closed to all those, who secured third Division. I took up F.Sc. (Medical), in the hope of becoming a doctor. I found it too much to dissect frogs and remember complicated and weird botanical names of every ordinary plant. Chemistry and Physics and molecules and atoms were equally confusing. After scrapping through 12th Standard, Medical, called Faculty of Science, or F.Sc., I changed courses midstream to join the Bachelor of Arts, with English, History and Political Science. My achilles heal has been the Mathematics. I was happy to say good bye to calcus, trignometry and algebra. Two of us, that is myself and Pundit Mahesh, my good friend,. had wanted to get admission to the same college. I got the admission, whereas he did not. Pundit after studying in Jullundur migrated to England. We had arrived in Ludhiana by train the previous night. We did not have any place to stay. My late father, had given us the address of a Dharam Shala in Bazar Sarafan, off Chaura Bazar. Mostly Sadhus, who lived on the charity of the people living close by and stray travellers were staying there. We were allowed to stay there. There was no bed or any bed sheet. We slept in the open on the floor, braving mosquitoes, for the night.

Next day we went to college and were interviewed for admission. I got the admission, but my friend, Pundit who later on migrated to the United Kingdom, could not. I was told that the fees was payable within the next two days. Otherwise, my admission stood cancelled. I went back to Jalalabad, collected the amount and came back. I applied and got a seat in the hostel of the college, hoping to qualify for admission to become a doctor. The big change, for me was the college education, being in English medium. The college teachers were very impatient to complete their courses. They had both condescending, and contemptuous, attitude to the boys like me, from unknown and backward villages. Lack of any connections, whatsoever in the government, just made them tolerate people of my background as a necessary evil.

Another winsome feature, was the co-education. It was something, to which we had never been exposed. However, co-education was only at the level of postgraduation and the number of girls was not more than 50 in a college of 1500 students. There was a separate girls hostel. It was a virtual prison for them. The only exposure of the girls to the boys was either in the dramatic society or debates, or musical competitions or annual day of the hostel. The college had an unwritten rule that in the plays, the boys and the girls had to maintain, a distance of atleast 18 inches between them.

The college had a swimming pool. To use it one had to pay a monthly membership fee of Rs. 5. It was a princely sum during those days. I had to pay it, out of my monthly allowance, of Rs. 125. I had to pay my mess bills, hostel charges, college fees, books, stationary and two visits by train to Jalalabad, every month. My parents were barely able to afford it. I had always liked swimming, so I availed of this facility. There used to be separate swimming hours for the girls. High fencing around the swimming pool ensured sufficient privacy for them. Girls were not only protected, but also wrapped and isolated. Mixed swimming, as is done, quite frequently now, was something unheard of, in those puritan times.

I got an opportunity, to function as an announcer in annual college sports. This boosted my confidence. Encouraged by the fact that my announcements had not been hooted, I decided to take part in debates and declamations in the college. I owe a debt of gratitude to a few friends like Keki Daruwala, S.S. Brar, who also joined IPS, a few years earlier, for their advice. They urged me to mug up my speeches and practice tham in an empty hall, imagining that I was speaking before the audience. My first few speeches, written by my well wishers, were too bombastic. They must have gone over the head of the audience, just as they went over mine. As perhaps, nobody understood them, I escaped humiliation and hooting. In spite of no public school background, I took part in all the debates and declamation contests in English. I had no option, but to memorize the entire speech. I continued my efforts and went on to represent my college in the prestigious contest at Indian Military Academy, Dehradun and in the University of Lucknow and Inter-University Youth Festival, in Mysore in 1959. I was adjudged, the top speaker of the Punjab University. It was only the persistence, which had paid off. My first visit to Mysore, made an excellent impression on me. When I appeared for the All India Services, Examination, I indicated Mysore State, as my first preference for service. But to be honest, I had expected it to be only a trial run and not selection in the first go. I had just done my B.A. and that too in third division. I had just appeared for M.A. (part I). Normally the candidates selected for these jobs were the ones who had spent years in studying. Government College Ludhiana, had a good tradition of contributing a substantial number of people to the All India and other services. All those who could get class one jobs, were looked upon with envy and awe. Several times, old students would come to the college in the Army/Police uniform to show that "they had arrived". I have a feeling that this was more of a show off than anything else, aimed at the girls in the college.

I stayed in the hostel for six years, and it made me self-reliant and confident. A few luxuries which are taken for granted these days by the students, were totally absent. There were no facility of fans in the hostel rooms. The boarders had either, to purchase their own fans or sweat it out. Rules were very strict for getting back to the hostel. Getting back to the hostel, after 8 p.m. in winter and 9 p.m. in the summer would entail a fine of four annas. In my last two years, I was the Assistant Prefect and then the Prefect of the New Hostel. One of my best friend, late Chaman Lal, always complained that I did not even excuse, his late coming. I imposed a fine on him also. The only privilege, which Prefect, or the Head Boy had was, that his room had a fan as well as an attached bathroom and a separate balcony. Traditionally the Prefect had always made it to the IAS/IPS. I passed my three years without the facility of fan. When I reached B.A., I mustered courage, to ask my father, to give me money for buying a fan as well as a cycle. I purchased a green coloured cycle, for Rs. 175. The cycle enabled me to move about in Ludhiana. It gave me a feeling of independence and mobility.

The parents of a classfellow, Aujla presented him a two wheeler scooter. He was the only resident, having a scooter. It was the centre of attraction . Most of the Professors even did not have a scooter. I had not even decided, about what I would do, after completing college education when I saw that several students were trying their luck in the All India Services Examination. Selected few, were the instant college heroes. They were almost VIP's not only in the eyes of the students, including the girls, but also the staff. Many such students behaved in a reserved manner and looked down upon the rest. Some bright students, who considered themselves as prospective All India Services Officers either the IAS or IPS, feigned superiority. They were serious looking and rationed their smiles even in humorous situations. In fact some of them were nicknamed, as IAS/IPS style seriousness. Unfortunately, for them, almost all such hoaxes, did not make it to any job worth mentioning. Some of them, were unexpectedly surprised when, as a total fresher almost just after B.A. I made it to the IPS in the first attempt. I can honestly say that if marks, in the college examinations were the only criteria, I would not have become more than a primary school teacher.

I took my entire stay in the college and the hostel only as great fun. The hostel mess did not provide for breakfast. For breakfast, we had to depend on the hostel canteen. Once in a while, I would enjoy eating an omelette at a cost of four annas. I could afford this, only once or twice a month. I had to balance my entire budget within Rs. 125. It remained my allowance for almost six years from 1955 to 1961, from my first year in the college to my M.A. I was not in a position to persuade my parents that the hostel cost had risen and the cost of a meal had gone up from six annas. Thirty Six paise to twelve annas (present seventy-five paise). They were not in a position to afford even Rs. 125 per month for my college education. There was a feeling, of being over charged, when the cost of lunch or dinner was raised from 36 paise to 50 paise. In retrospect, it was a luxury to have meat or paneer or cheese everyday, within that amount. The hostel mess, would serve one non-vegetarian and one vegetarian meal every day for Re 1/Rs 1.50 for Veg/Non-veg. One meal would invariably have cheese for the vegetarians and meat for the non-vegetarians. Tuesday would be observed as a vegetarian day. On Sundays, instead of meat, the non-vegetarian would get chicken at double the cost of a meal. The Mess Manager and the Prefect, by the courtesy of the contractor, were given bigger pieces. He was also given a second helping of the gravy. The mess staff would be deferential to him. In case of being late for dinner, meals would be kept for the boarders. There used to be only one radio in the common room for the entire hostel. It would be put on, and broadcast, with extra loud speakers. Mostly it would remain tuned, to Radio Ceylon for the Indian film music. The stay of guests, was not encouraged in the hostel. Women were not allowed in the hostel rooms. Amongst the boarders, there were certain professional rowdies. Their only interest was to bully and sleep. Some veterans had spent as many as six to seven years for a four-year B.A. course, with no inclination to cut short their stay. They would consume liquour and beat up others. They had formed groups of their own. In one such incident, may be the first of its kind either in 1957 or 1958 one student was stabbed to death, In another incident, one shot the other dead. It created a commotion, in the college but the gang leaders were hardly bothered. They continued their activities.

I noticed that every year several brilliant students would appear for the All India Services Examination and only some would make it. I had no plan to appear for any examination, but seeing a few friends making it to the top services, I decided to try my luck. I was particularly encouraged by the success of one of my close friend, Brar .He was not particularly hardworking. I felt that if he could be selected, I could almost comfortably walk into IPS, because of my strong determination and hard work. In the year 1960 I had just become eligible to appear for the IPS examination at the age of 20. After my examination of B.A. and M.A. Part-I. were completed, in August 1960, I was busy with the preparation for the competitive examination. At that time , the candidates for IPS had to appear, in only two optional papers, apart from the three compulsory papers of General English, English Essay and General Knowledge. I chose British History, as one of the optional subjects. I had studied it for my B.A. and English literature, as my second optional subject, which I was studying in M.A. I selected only about 15 possible questions, in each subject, and prepared myself thoroughly for those guess questions. For the compulsory subjects, I did not particularly prepare myself. The preparation consisted of doing thoroughly the questions and answers of the last five years. I finished my written IPS examinations in September 1960. I forgot about it. I speculated that if I passed, it would be a bonus. If I did not, it would be only a trial run. I did not expect to pass the written examination. It was because I compared myself, with others, who had appeared in the same examination. They claimed that they had put in as much as 18 to 20 hours a day in the studies. Their demeanour was almost forbidding, as compared to my 'take life, as it comes', approach. With hind sight I can say that you cannot study for months together, for eighteen to twenty hours daily. May be for one or two days you can do it. But surely it is not feasible for months together. I believe that consistent hard work and study for five to six hours, is more than sufficient to pass any competitive examination.

Interview Letter

I always believe that you must underrate yourself instead of bluffing. Your success is the proof of your competence. Obviously, I had done much better, in the IAS examination than what I was expecting. On one Sunday, that is on 12th or 13 December, 1960, I received a letter from my father informing me that "I would be glad to know that I have been called for interview for the Indian Police Service." The letter was in Urdu and had been sent by express delivery. It also said that the interview letter had been redirected to me by Registered Post. I received this letter in the forenoon just after I had washed my hair. Washing and drying of hair takes as much time in the case of Sikhs, as it does in the case of ladies. Since the hair dryers were not known at that time, we had to do hair washing on a sunny Sunday or on other holidays.

I could not believe, that I had passed the written IAS, examination, especially when nobody else had qualified from my college. I consulted a number of friends. They felt, that it might be a mistake, on the part of my father. However, one of my teachers Prof. J.R. Verma and the hostel warden said that I was quite capable. I had always underestimated myself. The receipt to the letter from the Union Public Service Commission on the 16th December, three days after the receipt of express letter from my father set all doubts at rest. I started hoping and also believing that I would be selected. Since my monthly allowance was fixed at Rs. 125, I did not have any suit or the money even to stitch a suit for the interview, or money for railway fare to Delhi. I approached a relation in Ludhiana and borrowed Rs. 150 for stitching a suit for the interview. For selection of the cloth, I took the advice of my class fellows Ajit Kumar, Chaman Lal and Darshan. It was from Darshan's shop Delhi Cloth House, I purchased brown colour woollen cloth. The stitching of a double breasted suit cost me Rs. 25/-. The balance was required for travelling expenses to Delhi. Undoubtedly it was an excessive amount for stitching. There was no option, as the suit was required, at two days notice. I had been one of the top speakers of my college and university. I was certain, that I would not be dumb, in the interview. I read a number of books on the art of successfully appearing before the interviews and consulted many. I was advised to be truthful. Those were the early years of India's Independence. A standard reply, in any interview, was that the individual concerned was seeking the job to serve the country. At which, most of the members of the interview board had replied, that the same could be done by being a clerk or junior officer and not necessarily a senior officer.

Impressive Interview and Selection

I looked upon the interview call, as another opportunity to visit Delhi.

On arrival at Delhi I stayed at Lajpat Nagar with my uncle Balwant Singh. At that time, he was working, as an Inspector, with the Intelligence Bureau. He advised me that before interview, I must go to the Gurudwara Bala Sahib, for the blessings of Guru Harikishan. The mortal remains of the eighth child Sikh Guru, were consigned to the flames there. He also said, that a very noble holy Sikh was living there. I should also seek his blessings. On such occasions, one does not want to take any chance. Each one of us, tries to appease and please as many gods and goddesses as possible. I was, and am no exception. I did go to Gurudwara and I was duly blessed by the holy man. My interview was held, on the first day of interviews for selecting the future civil servants of the 1960 batch. The then Chairman of Union Public Service Commission, V.S. Hejmadi was presiding over the interview board. In the waiting room, six prospective candidates were waiting to be summoned. Except for myself, the rest were coming for interview either for the second or third time. They were not sure, as to how they would fare this time. They told stories of the tough interviews. It was compulsory to pass in the interview. The minimum marks, for passing in the interview were 40%. I did not get scared by the stories of failure. I knew, I had still three more chances to try my luck. One of the members asked me as to why I wanted to join the IPS. My reply was that every young man, after the completion of his education, would like to have a good job. This service not only offered excellent prospects but also gave an opportunity to serve the country. I also said that I liked the IPS. Another member asked me as to why I liked the IPS. This was a tricky query. I replied that "Liking is something which cannot be explained in terms of the reason. When you look at a rose flower, you like it. You cannot say that you like it for its colour, or petals or smell. Liking is the result of a collective impression." The interview lasted about 15 minutes in which I felt that I had the upper edge. Finally, the Chairman asked "In case you are selected "Will you leave the IPS to join the IAS"? I said "No, I will stick to the IPS".

At the end of the interviews, all the candidates were to write as to what had transpired at the interview and what questions had been asked and what answers had been given. I wrote my impression in fifteen minutes and came out to be greeted by my relation, Amrik Singh. He asked as to how I had fared. My one word reply was "Selected" with oozing self-confidence. Next day I left for Ludhiana to continue my studies for completing the M.A. (Final) examinations which were due in May, 1961. At Ludhiana Railway Station, my class fellow and close friend, late Chaman Lal received me. He asked me about the interview. I replied. "I am selected."

For the next few days I basked in the expected glory of selection in the IPS in the college. I became casual towards my M.A. studies. Though I had boasted that I would be selected, I still had a lurking fear, of total let down in the event of non-selection. I did not want to be in the college, when the final results were declared. We were given two months preparatory holidays. I packed my bags and books and left for Jalalabad ostensibly to prepare myself for the examination of M.A. (Final). It was also to partly hide my ignominy in the event of my not making it to the IPS. My routine in Jalalabad was to study and keep myself physically fit.

2

Selection in IPS

One fine afternoon, in April, 1961, I got a telegram from my relation from Patiala, Ajit Singh, congratulating me on my selection in the IPS. Another telegram came from Chaman Lal congratulating me on appointment in the IPS. My father sent a special messenger to the District Headquarters, Ferozepore to get all the daily newspapers published from Delhi. And the news was confirmed.

I almost gave up studying for M.A. examination. My argument was that the purpose of studying was to get a good job. Since I had already been selected for a class one job, further appearing for M.A. examination was unnecessary. Here my father's advice was very sound and practical. He advised me that I should appear for the examination. If I pass, I get an M.A. degree and if not I still lose nothing.

In the meantime, a letter arrived from the UPSC, intimating that I was being considered for appointment, to the IPS and in the event of my selection, I will have to join the National Academy of Administration, Mussoorie at a very short notice. I wrote to the UPSC to hold my medical examination before 12th of May as my M.A. examinations were likely to start on the 15th of May, 1961. My request was accepted and I was informed by telegram to appear for the medical examination before the Special Medical Board at Amritsar on 10th May. I along with my father travelled by bus to Amritsar and was medically examined and declared fit. I returned to Jalalabad the next day and immediately left for Ludhiana to appear in the M.A. (Final) examination.

I finished my M.A. (Final) examinations on May 27th,

1961. Same evening, I left for Chandigarh, to spend a few days, with one of my closest friend, Ajit Kumar, now in the IAS.

On the 28th of May, a telegram was received from Chaman Lal saying that my order of appointment to the Indian Police Service had been received. The training would commence from 1st June, 1961. I should reach Mussoorie by 31st May. The same day, I left Chandigarh for Ludhiana paid all my mess bills, cleared my accounts in the Hostel. Immediately I left for Jalalabad to say "Bye, Bye" to my parents before proceeding to Mussoorie.

I reached Jalalabad on the evening of 29th of May. My parents very thoughtfully, had arranged the recitation of Holy Guru Granth Sahib. It started on 28th May, 1961 so that it could conclude on the day of my departure for Mussoorie. The Akhand Path was over by 10 A.M. on 30th May, 1961. The same day, I left at 3.30 p.m. by the train going to Ferozepore enroute to Mussoorie via Dehradun.

For the first time I travelled in First Class. On arrival at Dehradun, I spotted at the railway station a number of young-men belonging to various services on the way to Mussoorie, like myself. Four of us shared a taxi.

The training, at the National Academy of Administration, Mussoorie, was an opening of new vistas in Public Service. The young entrants in 1961, would occupy the top rungs of civil administration in the years to come. At first sight, the training did not give any impression of equipping us with the requisite qualities of public service. At that time, one point, which struck us all, was that good Public Administration, was nothing more than a sound common sense. The laws were nothing, except the codified common sense and ethics of the nation. We had a fine Director in the late A.N. Jha, who would mingle with us informally and clarify all our doubts.

Day to day running of the training programme was left to the two Deputy Directors, one incharge of the indoor studies, R.K. Trivedi, and the second for outdoor training, Brig. Sheriff. Whereas Trivedi was affable, the Deputy Director incharge of the outdoor training, would keep a tough exterior. The reason was obvious. Most of the probationers found outdoor activities, especially horse riding and P.T. too tough. By cultivating, the Deputy Director, incharge of outdoor, they had hoped to escape its rigours. Also the pleasant climate of Mussoorie, would tempt us, to lie in the bed, for far too long ignoring the outdoor syallabus of P.T. and horse riding. While some proxy was possible, in the case of P.T. where the instructor would leave the register, to our mercy to mark our attendance, in the case of horses, it was impossible to show ten horses having been ridden, with only two horse riders, present in the riding ground.

It was a cooperative and sincere batch. Wherever undetected, and feasible, we would generously answer the roll call for the others, by shouting "Present Sir". Whenever, the marking of the attendance, in the register was left to us, everybody would be present. The classroom and the class was so big, that one could comfortably finish, all personal correspondence, by occupying one of the back seats. The lecturers had to use, loud speakers to make themselves heard. Though the classes used to be a whole day affair at any given time at least 33% to 50% of the 1961 batch, could be found on the Mall in Mussoorie, or in the markets of Dehradun and a sprinkling in the Connaught Place of New Delhi. The snobbery of having studied in the public school, or having parents in the Civil Service, was very much alive and kicking in some of our colleagues.

The best part of the hot summer, from June 1961, onwards was spent, in the pleasant environs of Mussoorie. Once, all 270 of us belonging to all the services including the Indian Administrative Service, Indian Foreign Service, Indian Police Service, Audit and Account Service, Income Tax, Railways, Defence Account, Customs, Defence Ordinance, and Postal Service, were taken to Delhi on the 15th of August 1961. The highlight of the visit was a meeting with the then Prime Minister of India, Jawaharlal Nehru and the then President Dr. S. Radhakrishnan. It was a rare privilege to have come face to face and listen to the architects of India's freedom. We were overawed, just in the presence of Nehru.

Nehru exhorted us to build a new India and give a clean and efficient administration to the country. His mind was not with us. He seemed to be preoccupied with weightier matters. There was no visible security around him. It was easy to mix with him and shake hands. Meeting the P.M. and President was a formal occasion. Those were the days of Khadi. Each one of us, had to stitch a Khadi suit for the meeting. As it was only a one time use item, most of us used only the cheapest of Khadi. In the buttoned up Khadi suit we were looking more like waiters, of any top-class restaurant, than probationer civil servants. After calling on the dignitaries and attending the President's "At Home", some of us decided to visit Connaught Place. After finishing our tea, when four of us were getting down the stairs of a restaurant. Seeing four persons dressed up in the waiter's dress, coming down, a couple going" upstairs asked us "Is the top section closed?" We just smiled and went away. It was clear, that there was no difference, between the Khadi suit, we were wearing, and the universally recognisable dress of waiters. Nobody on seeing us would think us to be any one else but a bunch of young waiters and not trainee Civil Servants of India. Most of us used to detest horse riding. Some probationers could never mount the horses. This antipathy, was mutual, between the horses and the riders. Once a tall handsome, South Indian Officer, was taunted by the riding master, for his failure to mount the horse. In anger, he jumped over the horse, only to fall on the other side. His fall provoked laughter. He made another valiant effort to mount the horse. This time, instead of putting, his left foot in the stirrup, he put his right foot. He mounted the horse all right. But this time, he was facing the tail of the horse, instead of the neck. It provoked a giggle; he sighed and quickly said "What can I do? Your North Indian horses, have their necks on the wrong side."

Some of us decided to go for trekking from Mussoorie to Chakrata. It involved taking a bridle path of more than 30 miles. The party led by J.C. Pant, who later on rose to become Secretary in the Agriculture Ministry, had a very delightful stay in the night, enroute. Not having been able to find any place to stay, and no beds, the probationers entered a dark and dingy building for stay. Only in the morning they discovered that they had spent the whole night in a cowshed, when the stench of the cow-dung and noise, of the cows and calves woke them up. They had with them a member of the Royal family of Sikkim, Dasho Namgyal Wangchu, who also shared the cow shed. Another prank played by one of the probationers was spreading a rumour, that a ghost existed in Charleville, our residential block. This was based on the presence of lot of snow, outside the room. The rumour was rife for a week. The result was that all residential rooms in the Happy Valley (residential portion of the academy) were vacated post-haste.

As part of the training, IAS probationers were taken for Bharat Darshan. They were divided into two groups. One group was going to North India and the other to the South. Each was accompanied by a Professor from the Academy. One of the probationers, sent a telegram to the Director of the Academy, seeking instructions as to the disposal, of dead body of Professor Incharge, who had died. Prompt came the reply. "Cremate the body and bring the ashes". No ashes were brought. The Professor in the party returned alive to the Academy. The mischief-makers were traced out and suitably advised, not to play such jokes as it affected the life of the family of the concerned person.

The Dining Hall of the National Academy of Administration, could accommodate atleast 200 persons, at any given time for a meal. A colleague, who is unfortunately no more, had an eager desire to test his capacity for consuming omelettes. This stemmed from the fact, that during his college days, he could not afford to eat more than one omelette per week. But after joining the IAS, he went all out for the breakfast. On an average he consumed five and maximum of seven breakfasts of fried eggs, omelette, poached eggs, boiled eggs and half-fried eggs. The modus operandi was simple. First he would go to the farthest end away from the entrance. Second time he would come near the entrance, third time in the middle row and so on. In this way, keeping the seat changed, for each meal was his forte. This he continued till he found that heavy meals, had made him heavier. He gained ten pounds in two months.

The breakfast was the only edible meal in the Academy. The preparations of other meals left much room for improvement. One reason was that the paid mess staff, in spite of an elected mess committee, by the probationers, used to pilfer the foodstuff or under buy or overpay for the same. The vigilant eyes of the Mess Committee, led to the red-handed catching of the Mess Manager. It put an end to the scandal, at least temporarily. As the shopping plaza was atleast 4 km away from the Academy, the next popular stop, for us, was the Academy canteen. It sold the letterheads and other paraphernalia for declaring to the world that "we had arrived". We would write letters on the letterhead of the Academy, and prominently indicate the Service, to which we belonged. A part of the training, was the rock climbing course. The course was conducted using the rocky portion of the Academy. Tenzing, the climber of Everest, visited the Academy and addressed us. He was a hero to all of us without exception.

As the most eligible bachelors were available at one place, senior civil servants with their beautiful and eligible daughters and their mothers, desirous of civil servants as their sons-in-law, made a bee-line for Mussoorie. I understand that the position has not changed much even now. Many probationers enjoyed the hospitality of a number of groom seekers, without any final result. Most of the probationers, who volunteered to see the girls, were more keen to enjoy the hospitality at "Savoy", the top hotel of Musssoorie, than anything else. Probationers would, always associate with like-minded colleagues, irrespective of their services. Some would prefer, to gang up with fair sex in service. Some of them not only paired for the duration of the academy but also for life. Unfortunately we had a terrible scarcity of female species in the academy in 1961. There were only eight girls in the whole batch. Some male probationers would say, that there was nothing special to write home about the lady probationers. But the beauty lies in the eyes of the beholders (not holders): Some of the women probationers married their senior or junior service colleagues and led not necessarily a happy life.

Matrimonial Accomplishments at the Academy

In the later batches, most of the ladies became wiser and shrewder, determined to accomplish matrimony along with their training. This is evident, from the ever-increasing, number of marriages taking place in the Academy itself. I know one lady personally, who had decided to get married, with any willing batchmate in the Academy. She tried her best. But when she could not marry the person of her choice, she did the next best thing. She married another colleague who was in an equally good service and willing. Her reasoning was simple and practical. She was from a humble background. Her parents could never have arranged, a class one services match for her. It was made clear to her, by them when she came to join the academy. So she decided to improve her own matrimonial prospects. She succeeded in hooking a good match. I myself gave such an advice to the daughter of a friend. I told her that most of the service colleagues would have married for huge dowries and the best time to grab their grooms was in the cold climate of Mussoorie before they realised their worth in terms of the size of dowries. One of my class fellows who joined service (IAS) a few years later told me that the only reason for his marrying his present wife—his batchmate from another part of India was the cold weather of Mussoorie. Of course, they have been very happily married, despite the vast cultural gaps, difference in mother tongues, religions and even the colour of their skins.

The fact of early marriage in civil services for the girls is very important. Nearly two decades after having joined the service, I met a lady colleague, a few years junior, at a meeting in New Delhi. I had gone from Bangalore to represent the State Government at the meeting. She was a very charming girl and many boys of her batch had aspired for her. I very hesitatingly asked whether she had married. She said no. I told her that she had a large number of admirers. She could have married anybody of her choice. I asked her the reasons for not marrying. She said "she had missed the bus now being in her forties". I asked her for reasons. She beautifully analysed her and other girls' dilemma as under. "When we are in Academy, the boys are chasing us, because the numbers of girls there is very small. We do not pay any attention or encourage suitors or even think about marriage. When we come out of the Academy, the sphere of selection is considerably reduced. Most of the colleagues, marry girls much younger and more beautiful than they can find in Academy. Some marry for the sake of huge dowries. The boys in the civil services command a fantastic price in the marriage market. As most of us would have crossed 24 or 25 years of age, only the middle-aged civil servants are left for us. Our choice is further limited. The reason is most of the eligible bachelors in the civil services would have already been hooked. When you get senior scale or the Director's scale, the choice is even further limited and at a still senior level, nobody is practically available. And at sufficiently senior level, unless we encourage the boys or the prospective bridegrooms, nobody is going to come near us. So if,you miss the bus of marriage till the age of 35 or 40, you have almost missed it for good."I believe, the above is still the correct analysis which holds good for girls in civil services. Subsequent batches had also interesting episodes of young probationers chasing their lady colleagues. One batch, had a unique distinction of having a Majnu (the legendary lover of Punjab) who was reported to have proposed to every female probationer, without, much of success. He even went to the extent of proposing, to the visiting relation, of a probationer. Without knowing the background, he even proposed to a married lady probationer. In all fairness to him, he did not know at the time of proposing to the lady probationer that she was married. It is no secret, that married men probationers, do not feel very comfortable in revealing their marital status.

George Bernard Shaw, an Irish dramatist and one of the greatest critics of his age, had observed that the main objective of the female of the species was to hook a suitable match. She would perform all tricks, to gain her objective. In one case, a young lady probationer, under training would go on tour where her one-year senior colleague and an eligible bachelor used to stay. The persistent and frequent visit, beauty and friendly nature of the girl, and the extremely cold weather helped. They were married within less than a year. However, some flings during the Academy blossomed into beautiful and durable marriages. But it has not been so, in all cases as a large number of romances at Mussoorie withered. Many couples of Mussoorie days, who were almost inseparable, found different life companions. The element of monetary gains in marriage of the boys has played havoc with the dowry scale, in some states and communities. In some cases, members of the All India Services have got dowries exceeding five million rupees. A very senior IPS officer who has retired as Director General of Police of a Central Police Organisation had to eat a humble pie, when the prospective bridegroom demanded Rs. 25 Lakhs for marrying his daughter. The officer being honest, to the core, called off the marriage and married his daughter in a less greedy family, without much fanfare. In one case, a South Indian probationer who had been allotted a North Indian cadre wanted his dowry in the form of change of his cadre to his home state. He made this condition for all those who approached him. Ultimately his cadre was changed but to another state near his home state. He, however, ditched everybody and married again for monetary consideration. He told all parties, that since the condition put by him was not fulfilled by anybody, he was marrying his choice. Nice way to deal with the seekers of civil servants as bridegrooms.

Another young lady, in a subsequent batch, had a number of batch mates vying for marrying her. But, neither this beautiful damsel approved any person, nor her parents selected anybody for her. The young-men proposing to her were not of the right caste. The parents and the girl wanted only a Garhwali Brahmin as a bridegroom. The result is that this young lady is still a maiden, now in her early forties, without any sign of her becoming a bride. A young probationer belonging to an All India Service was missing his home and home state very much. He had been allotted to a South Indian Cadre. He asked me as to what he should do to get his cadre changed to his home state. I advised him in jest that the best way to get the cadre changed is to marry some girl in the cadre, to which he wanted to go. He promptly purchased the civil list, scanned his fancied cadre/ cadres, tick marked the young eligible girls. His efforts did succeed. It is a different story, that the lady used to taunt him saying, that he married the cadre and not her. Due to the constant bickering and taunting, the marriage ended in a divorce. Even as a matter of economic necessity, it is in the interest of the probationers and civil servants to marry each other. Such marriages have by and large worked out satisfactorily. There have been only a few cases of mutual incompatibility leading to friction and rarely to divorce. It is a very small percentage. By a common consensus, and after discussion with a number of colleagues, I have come to the conclusion, that generally, women make very tough and hard taskmasters, much tougher than men. At least, those, who have worked with me, have excelled beyond my expectations.

Women officers are very tough, with their women subordinates. The common refrain amongst the lady officers is that, they would like to avoid working under women officers. They complain that women officers, adopt a schoolmaster approach towards them, which is not fair.

In the case of probationers at the Academy it is not only the boys who run after the girls. Sometimes it is vice versa. I am aware of a case where a boy from a North Indian State was allotted to a cadre thousands of miles away from his home state. One day in a far-flung, sub-division, he got a call from a fellow probationer to his surprise. The caller straight away asked him "How about coming home?" He was a little non-plussed. He asked "How". The reply was "Marry me and get your cadre changed." This was both a bait and a dowry offering, of course, the boy did not fall for this and he is happily married and now in the Central Government. So must be the lady, I presume. In another case, a probationer had two love affairs going on at the same time. One was at home, with her childhood flame, and the second with a fellow probationer at the Academy. Ultimately, she did not marry, either of them. In one case, the Chief Secretary of a State managed to get himself invited to deliver a lecture to the trainees. His only objective was to find a suitable match for his young daughter. He cornered a gentle probationer, who was allotted to his State cadre and asked him to find a suitable match belonging to his caste and sub-caste for his marriageable daughter. The poor probationer went around to almost anybody who appeared to be even almost close to the caste required by the Chief Secretary but he failed in his mission. For his failure, in not complying with the wishes of his Chief Secretary, he earned the displeasure. He had to suffer for not succeeding in the mission assigned to him.

Allotment of Cadres and other Shippets from the Academy

Horse riding used to be a compulsory subject for All India Service Probationers. It used to be a horrifying experience to many and especially to some girls. In one particular year the daughter of a very important civil servant joined the service. This young lady would rather die than come near the horse. The rules regarding making horse riding compulsory were amended suitably. The reason given was not specific, but public interest. The Academy life had its lighter moments with some of us having fun at our own costs. The probationers from different services and different parts of the country were allotted rooms together to promote national integration. In my case, my roommate was S. Sathyam from the IAS who was from Tamil Nadu. Later on, I was allocated the South Indian cadre of Karnataka and my roommate Sathyam was allotted the North Indian State of Madhya Pradesh. In one case a fair IAS probationer from North India had to share room with an extremely dark complexion official from a different service. This officer had a massive build. The North Indian who was short statured would say that whenever he and his roommate left the room together, the people around them were bound to comment that a cow and buffalo were moving together. On another occasion, one of the probationers belonging to an All India Service observed that "all of us were a bunch of mediocres". To this a smart lady probationer replied "Mr! speak only, for yourself." Once during a formal dinner, one of the probationers put half of the butter plate in his soup. A senior officer of the faculty looked smilingly and said humorously "Mr!, Butter is not the main dish here."

The Academy had its share of bullies. Once a tall probationer after washing his hands in the wash basin could not find a clean towel. In the meantime another young and skinny probationer came to wash his hands. When he was half way through, the tall probationer patted his back and affectionately slapped him. In the course of showing affection, he wiped his hands clean with a grin. There was nothing the other could do. One of the probationers was in the habit of carrying tales against others to the Director. The Director got fed up with this backbiter and scolded him. "Mr! this is not a school where you backbite each other. If I find you doing it again, I will have you thrown out." The matter did not end here. The persons complained against came to know about this. The next day when it was biting cold and there was snow all around, the backbiting probationer was stripped naked and thrown on the ice. This marked the end of his career as a backbiter. Some of the guest lecturers used to come well prepared, but others just tried to pass the time, allotted in small talks. The best part of the classes in Mussoorie was, during the informal interaction with the staff and amongst ourselves. While we were at Mussoorie, the IAS probationers got their cadre allotment. It brought its own quota of joys and tears. In one case, a South Indian probationer started crying uncontrollably when he was allotted a Northeastern State. I asked him the reason for this dramatic situation created by him. He said that in the State of allotment, he will be either drowned in the river Brahmputra (there used to be heavy floods in the river), or a snake will bite him to death, or he will be killed by a Naga (at that time there was the problem of insurgency in Nagaland). Alas! he was killed in the battle against insurgency about two decades later, but not by Nagas. Another probationer from an Eastern State who was given a North Indian State remained depressed for a long time and till retirement, he was not reconciled to this allotment.

In Mussoorie, we had the first taste of the government red tape. We were informed, not to expect any salary, at least for the first two to three months. Before the present system of separation of accounts from the audit came into existence, no salary could be drawn, except on the authorisation of the Accountant General. In the case of people located in Mussoorie, it was the AG UP, at Allahabad, who had to authorise us, to draw our salary from the local treasury. In this connection I am reminded of a joke, which I must share with you. Once somebody asked a question "What is an Accountant General?" A wag replied immediately, "He is an Accountant who draws the salary of a General.

Fortunately or unfortunately, we had been advised, prior to joining the Academy about the likelihood, of not getting our salary for the first few months. So in the bargain our parents/families had to support us for a few months more. We were required to stitch the buttoned up black coat for formal dinners. There used to be at least, two formal dinners every week. The idea was to perhaps drill some formality into us, as we would be out in the field soon, heading our respective charges. Our starting salary was Rs. 350 only. Plus we were given an allowance of Rs. 40 taking the gross emoluments to Rs. 390. Our mess bill alone used to be in the region of Rs. 325. Still, we had to pay income tax. I felt, that this was the unkindest cut of all. May be, the deduction was of Rs. 25 or 30, at the present time I cannot exactly remember. It made us realise that the probationers of the Indian Revenue Service were living off us. Fortunately they were as resentful about paying the income tax as we were, when the cashier deducted income tax. We felt that it would be worthwhile to cultivate the probationers of Indian Income Tax Service, as they could guide us, as to how to pay less, to the government legitimately, without violating any laws. This has stood me in good stead till now. On my own, I cannot even fill the income tax return. So I have always to depend upon a colleague to scrutinise whether my income tax return is correct. How simple and easier it would be if the salary could be income tax free?

Leaving Mussoorie

The end of the foundational course, brought us to the close, of a wonderful chapter in our lives and services. We left Mussoorie with a happy heart and a big bundle of photographs of the green memories there. Only later on, we realized the blissful existence led by us there. With the dispersal of all services from Mussoorie except the IAS, the Academy wore a deserted look. As IPS probationers had to go to National Police Academy, Mount Abu. we moved from Mussoorie, to Mt.Abu with a brief break at our respective places. It was a very short break and some of us were never to visit Mussoorie again. Only about 45 of us were in the IPS and arrival at Mount Abu was almost a climb down. I was a little fortunate in visiting Mussorie, in 1968, when my wife, Surinder, three years, after the marriage had joined the Indian Information Service there. The next visit was only in 1995/1996 as Director General, Indo-Tibetan Border Police to the ITBP Academy located in Mussoorie. However the humorous part of the combined stay continued in Mount Abu also. One of the probationers while introducing himself would always say that "I am so and so, 5th rank." Everybody got furious with him in throwing about his rank. We did a lot of research to beat him at his own game. We found that he had succeeded in the fourth attempt. So the next time when he tried to show off his higher entrance rank, a colleague chipped in, immediately saying "4th attempt." When my turn came to introduce myself, I jokingly with a mischievous smile replied, "Joginder Singh, first attempt at the age of twenty." This put an end to such brazen show-off attempts and ranks

3

Police Academy Memorable days at Mount Abu

Our routine at Mount Abu was evenly balanced between the outdoor and indoor classes. In the mess, the room had to be shared between two of us. My roommate was R.C. Jha, whom I have always affectionately called "Bhagwan Ramchander" as his full name is Ramchander Jha and this affection has continued. It was further cemented, by both of us being together in the Central Reserve Police from 1987/88 onwards till 1993. Later on I succeeded him as Director General, ITBP on his retirement on 31st January, 1995. As we had to share the bathroom it was a fairly cooperative existence. It was a dry type bathroom. The dry commodes, had to be cleaned by the scavengers. As two of us were sharing the room as well as the bathroom, two commodes were provided for two of us. We scrupulously used our respective commodes. First thing in the morning, after the ablutions, was the walk and run to parade ground, as a Section. The entire batch had been divided into Sections starting with A, B, C, D and E, Sections. Each one of us was given responsibility to work as a Section leader. This privilege consisted in marching the entire section together from the Rajputana Mess so that we could reach the ground in time. The Section leader would march outside and give the commands such as 'quick march', 'double march', 'chest in and chin out', etc. We would find fault with some of the colleagues just to tease them. This would be reciprocated when the turn of others would come to be section leaders.

Sathyam, my roommate from IAS, told me the interesting

episode of his matrimony. When he was getting engaged, the bride's side asked for his photograph. Now he did not want to delay the matters, and with an undue alacrity, he sent the only photograph he had. It was the joint photograph of Sathyam and myself. The photograph reached the bride's side. The bride's (Saroja's) brother came to the house in Madras with a Sikh friend of his. He was shown the joint photograph of us. The Sikh boy looked at my photograph and said, "Quite handsome fellow. Go ahead." He was corrected and the bride-to-be said "Listen, I am marrying the other fellow, the South Indian and not the Sikh." Saroja confirmed it

After the first half an hour of the P.T. exercises, we were required, to change into uniform, at the parade ground itself. The room bearers, brought the uniforms. Within fifteen minutes, we would change for the drill period. The drillmaster, always tried to play, Hitler on the ground. He would hurl, all kinds of invectives, for any small mistakes. Once on the ground, he shouted at a probationer saying "don't grin like a monkey." On hearing this unexpected statement of the drillmaster, the victim Pullana, stepped out of the line, saluted him and told him that he had no business to use that type of language. He further put in, his written complaint to the higher ups. Pullana though looked timid showed real guts. This put his bullying, to a stop for some time. The Commandant and Deputy Commandant had pulled him. He was an Inspector working on adhoc promotion as DSP. His repatriation would have meant his reversion.

Rivalry between D.M. and S.P.

We had two Commandants at the Academy during our tenure. The first one was late B. Banerjee, an introvert. The second one was S.C. Mishra, an extrovert and we could put all our doubts to him for clarification. One topic, which came up with sickening regularity, was the relations between the Collector and the Superintendent of Police. Endless debates on the superiority and inferiority, of the two, continued. Unfortunately, nobody put the things in the proper perspective that each of the district functionary—whether it was the Collector or the Superintendent of Police or the Sessions Judge or the District Surgeon—had a specific role to play. This endless debate of equality or inequality continues both in the IAS and IPS Academies even now. Nobody emphasises, even now that despite the best rules and regulations, no relationship can work, unless there is a will to work as a team. Even now, there is no change in the position. It is time that the emphasis was laid on the co-operative and combined working, rather than on position laid down by the archaic laws framed by the British. In this debate between the police and the Executive Magistracy, it is the public, which is the victim. This is a subject on which a treatise could be written, favouring either side, depending on whose cause you want to support. I personally have not felt any difficulty or problem in working as a team. The best of my friends have been the Deputy Commissioners of the Districts where I have served. Instead of telling the IPS officers under training that you have joined one of the best and most honourable profession and the service, we were advised by the prophets of gloom to the contrary. I have never believed dooms day prophets. The only difficult item, for me, in the outdoor in Mount Abu was the climbing rope. Otherwise, the outdoor training proceeded reasonably smoothly. Horse riding was still a fearsome item for some probationers, who would try to select the tamest of the horses. One probationer resigned and went away on the ground that he was not in a position to perform all the outdoor items satisfactorily. The authorities tried to persuade him to stay, and do as much as he could. In fact, the Deputy Commandant of the National Police Academy E.L. Stracey advised him: "Whatever you can do, do? Whatever you can't, you can't?" But all his persuation failed. This young probationer resigned and went back to his teaching job, from where he had been selected for the IPS.

Any type of physical training programme, should inculcate, an interest for life. Then only it can be called a success. Moreover, it should take into consideration, the kind of facilities which would be available later on, so that the interest generated in sports and games would last a life time, consistent with the job requirements of the IPS officers.

Faculty and Trainees

In the faculty, except three officials—the Commandant, Deputy Commandant and the Assistant Commandant—all other Gazetted Officers were of the rank of the Deputy

Superintendent of Police. They were equivalent in rank to all the probationers. Out of respect and also with a view to curry favours, most of the probationers would, address them as "Sir." Only the Non-Gazetted Officers, (NGOs) that is the Inspectors and below (95% of the staff) were junior to us. They were expected to salute us, off the parade ground. when in uniform. The position was that, on the ground we were subject to the Commands of the Non-Gazetted Instructors. But outside the parade ground they had to recognise the higher ranks of the trainees and salute them.

The Intelligence Bureau (IB) also used to send its Sub-Inspector's for training to Mount Abu in the 60's. As they were NGOs, there was no interaction, between the IPS probationers and the Sub-Inspectors of the IB. They were also expected to behave and show respect to the IPS probationers, on the same footing as the Non-Gazetted Academy Staff. We were categorically told neither to mix with the NGOs nor to enjoy their hospitality. The barrier was not a healthy feature between the officers of the same age group and almost similar education. It looked very artificial and snobbish.

Its importance did not dawn till a couple of years after we assumed the charge as District Police Chiefs. The reason was that the Sub-Inspectors as the Officers-in-Charge of the Police Station headed the Police Stations. If once the IPS officers fall, into the trap, of accepting the hospitality, of the Sub-Inspector's who are much lower paid comparatively to the IPS officers, they would slide, to further malpractices and accepting the gifts from the corrupt subordinates. No Sub-Inspector could afford to look after, the District Chief and his retinue from his salary. So necessarily, he would have to force the business community and other moneyed powerful persons, to pay, during the inspection or the visit of the senior officers. Since it was drilled into us, not to accept the hospitality of the subordinate staff, as we could not repay, the same or extend the same in return, this solid advice, has stood the test of time.

Moreover, in a uniformed and a hierarchical organisation, such mixing is bound to send wrong signals. The signals could be, in the form that a particular officer, is the favourite of somebody. With his blessings and support the subordinate can get away with anything. Naturally this will breed indiscipline of the worst kind, and can at times ruin the organisation. As it is, many sins are committed in the names of the senior officers without their having any inkling of the same. The training in Mt. Abu, Police Academy, was tough, both intellectually and physically. We had to learn many new subjects, like Forensic Science and Forensic Medicine, Map Reading, Motor Vehicles, Basic Accounting and the Indian Laws. Law, for those, who did not have any legal background was a tough proposition. We had to acquire the proficiency of a law graduate in less than eleven months, whereas a law degree takes, three years.

After a tough one year in Mt. Abu, we passed out on 22nd October, 1962, the day China attacked India. Our next destination was our respective cadres for further training and posting as regular Police officers. The group had to be broken up into the number of persons going to the allotted State. In my case, it was Mysore, alongwith Vasanth and Father Colaco. I did not realise, that I may not meet any of my batchmates, for the next few years, and some after two decades and some never. I had my District training in Mysore District. Mostly, I was left to my own. Nobody really had any time for an ASP under training. I was finally posted as a regular Sub Divisonal Police officer in Bijapur at Indi in December, 1963.

Trapping a Police Officer

Checking of the motor vehicles, personally was one of the duties of the Assistant Superintendent of Police. We were required to write down the number of vehicles checked in the monthly diary to be sent to the District Superintendent of Police and the Range Deputy Inspector General of Police. Very conscientiously I would check all the vehicles. I checked one truck, at Zalki crossing on Bijapur-Sholapur, highway. I told the driver, to move on as his papers, were in order.

I casually sauntered to the rear of the vehicle. The driver was giving a piece of paper with something wrapped in it to a Head Constable of the checking party. I caught hold of it and opened it. It contained a note of Rupees Five. I was very wild with the driver. I asked him as to why he had given this bribe. He said that was given for the meal expenses of the

Head Constable and others. I scolded him that his conduct would give the impression that the ASP (Assistant Superintendent of Police) would check the vehicles in the front and his subordinates would collect the "Mammul" (the illegal payment) probably with his connivance, at the rear. Rupees Five may appear, a very small sum today. But in 1964, it was almost equal to the Daily Allowance of Rs.5.50 drawn by the gazetted officers. It was enough to cover the cost of one dozen eggs, chicken and half a kilo of rice.

I immediately ordered the Sub-Inspector of Police, Chadchan to get two independent witnesses and make a Panchnama (seizure memo) of what had happened as well as seize the illegal gratification. It was done. The other drivers told me, that this was a common occurrence. No vehicle is allowed to go away without some payment. They also uttered, that it was for the first time, in their lives, they had seen a police officer trapped by another senior police officer. Otherwise the normal impression, given to the drivers on the highway was, that the amount collected was also shared by the higher ups. That is why I said that "many sins are committed in the names of the senior officers without their being aware of the same." A departmental enquiry was ordered against the Head Constable for accepting the bribe. In the meantime, I had been promoted as Superintendent of Police, Bidar District. I came back to Bijapur District, to appear as a witness, in the departmental enquiry, after one and a half years. The Superintendent of Police, Bijapur District who had conducted the enquiry, told me that except for myself all other witnesses had turned hostile. They denied the occurrence of the incident itself.

I myself questioned the witnesses later on, after the formal departmental inquiry was over. They replied that honest officers, were rare to come by. They were transferable. The IPS officers were not a permanent fixture of the district, whereas the constables and head-constables were. It was more important for them, to keep them happy and satisfied. That is why nobody had complained about their corruption. They appreciated my efforts. They also reminded me, that after my transfer, whatever fear the subordinates had, had disappeared. Moreover, as District Police Chief of another district, I could not be of any use or help to them. It was for this reason that they were reluctant to testify the facts and had said that the incident never happened. It was perhaps, to prevent such misuse of the names, of the officer, that we were told not to enjoy the hospitality of the subordinate staff.

The guidelines during the training at Mount Abu for mixing with NGOs have been implemented only partially. On social occasions almost all of us have participated whenever requested as a matter of routine to boost their morale and show solidarity with the force. Quite often Sub-Inspectors of the IB have tried to pass out as IPS probationers of the same batch. During my posting in the Commerce Ministry, I had gone to Europe in 1983. When returning to Delhi from London by an Air India flight, a gentleman occupying an adjoining seat was staring at me, very uncomfortably, very closely. As he was an Indian, I asked him what was his occupation. He said he was a businessman and returning after successful negotiations of a big export order. Then he asked about my profession. I said that I was an IPS officer working as Director in the Ministry of Commerce. He suddenly warmed up and said that he was also an ex. IPS officer who had resigned his job to take up the business of garment export. I asked him his batch in the IPS. He said, 1961. I said it must be some other batch. He insisted that he belonged to the 1961 batch. When be persisted that his batch was only 1961, I told him that I myself belonged to 1961 batch and I had not seen him at all. Since his wife was sitting with him and he did not want to look small, so I did not press him for further details. Later on, on straining my memory I recollected that the concerned gentleman was a directly recruited Sub-Inspector, of the CBI. He had come with his Superintendent of Police to see me in Udyog Bhavan few years ago. For the rest of the journey he only had a weak smile for me, as if pleading that I should not broach this topic anymore. I silently and discreetly accepted his request.

Republic Day and Crowd Control

During our training in Mount Abu, we were taken for a brief visit to Delhi to see the arrangements for crowd control on the occasion of Republic Day, 1962. The meter gauge train, was the only means of coming to Delhi . We were lodged in the Kingsway Camp, Police Officers Mess. It was for the first time, that we were wearing the uniform, outside the Police Training Academy. We were quite conscious of this and very excited. I felt that all eyes would be rivetted on me as the new police hero. Unfortunately, I was in for deflation. Nobody looked at me or my other forty-four colleagues. Even the constables of Delhi Police did not look at us. Apart from the usual courtesy calls, on the high dignitaries, we were required to be present at Rajpath, India Gate at 3 a.m. on the morning of 26th January, 1962. We woke up at 2 a.m. and moved in the transport to help the Delhi Police for crowd control. We took our positions at 3 a.m. in various enclosures. It was a long weary wait for the function, which was to start, at 10 a.m. and go on till 1 p.m. The first visitor to arrive at the enclosure was at 8 a.m. where we were on duty. The Delhi Police was firm but courteous in its duty, notwithstanding the ranks. Some senior army officials threatened many subordinate officials. Some of them wanted more persons, to be taken inside the VIP enclosures, than what the invitation card indiciated. This led to the unpleasant task of the policemen to say 'no'. Poor constables and others, manning the gates suffered humiliations.

The return journey from Delhi to Abu Road was by the same meter gauge train, which had brought us to Delhi. We arrived at Delhi Station well before time, to board the train. By the same train, a newly wedded Christian couple were travelling. The bride was saying 'bye bye' to her relatives assembled at the platform. As is customary, she was kissing, her relatives, just before boarding the train. One of the probationers, now a retired Director General of Police, well known for his pranks also stood in the line, in the hope that he might also get a kiss. The bride did come to him. She passed him, with a look of disgust and anger. The first three months, of physical activities were tough for us. Most IPS trainees had come straight from the academic world or from jobs which did not require, any physical exertion. Later on we got used to the rigorous schedule of the training. As the Training Institute for the IPS officers was located at a place, inconvenient for train or air connections, the guest lecturers were hard to come by. The permanent faculty, took most of the classes . I believe even now the same situation prevails in the CRP Training Academy, which is functioning in the place vacated by the National Police Academy, on its shifting to Hyderabad. As the IAS examinations used to be held in September/October, some IPS probationers did try their luck for the same. More than half a dozen of them left IPS for IAS/Central Services as a result of 1962 examinations. Ahmedabad was the nearest centre for taking the IAS exams and if nothing else, it was a welcome change from the dreary climate of Mount Abu. Those who sought to appear for the IAS examination were dropped from the passing out parade, which was the star item of the National Police Academy. It was only once a year, and perfection was sought to be achieved in the smart slow marching and quick marching. Slow marching requires a lot of effort for months together, much more than the quick marching.

The unfortunate happening of India-China war in October, 1962 marked the passing out parade. Though the incident happened far away from Mount Abu, we all felt the tremors. We were ready to plunge into the war for the country. All kinds of rumours were floated that all the IPS probationers were being sent to the North East straight away. The fervour of patriotism, was so strong in our hearts, that somehow we felt, that even bare handed we would be able to defeat the enemy.

Training Schedule in Mount Abu

There was hardly any time for fun and enjoyment in Mt. Abu as the training schedule kept us busy from 6 a.m. to 10 p.m. As the outdoor life would tire us, we would tend to doze off after lunch for a few minutes and also in the evening after the games. This was apart from the dozing off in the class, if the seat position permitted. So much so, that due to over tiredness, in the evening, I once slept through at a formal dinner and got up only at about 10 p.m. I sneaked into the gathering, just when the sweet dish, was being served to pretend that I had been there all through. The only outing, sometimes in the free time, was to Nakki Lake. Occasional boating was also possible there in the half dry lake of Mt. Abu. But this was the only place in which some tourists could be seen. Especially during the summer season, people would visit Mt. Abu from Gujarat. Mount Abu, being the only hill station, for Rajasthan and Gujarat States. Once a rumour was spread, that a mermaid, was seen in the lake. It led to a big tourist draw. Most of us, tried to locate the mermaid. It tuned out to be another wishy -washy story. The passing out parade saw the end of collective existence, as a batch. We have never met as a full batch again. We were given a break and told to join our respective states. During the joining time, I went back to Jalalabad to see my parents. In Jalalabad, the government had just stationed a Punjab Armed Police Battalion. Pritam Singh Bhinder, IPS now retired, who had just got married, commanded it. I called on him and introduced myself. He was happy to find some company in Jalalabad for a few days atleast. We exchanged notes on the training and life at Mount Abu. My connection with Jalalabad and Punjab was over with my proceeding to my adopted State, in the South. It was called Mysore at that time. The journey from Jalalabad to Ferozepur to Delhi was a familiar beat. Having stayed in Delhi for an overnight journey, I boarded the Madras-bound Grand Trunk Express from Delhi for a three-day train journey. One advantage of the foundational courses was that I had colleagues in various services. I had written to my batchmates, late Dardi and Sampath Kumar, in the IAS to meet me at railway station and make arrangements for my stay in Bangalore. The two of them allotted to the IAS cadre of Mysore, received me at Bangalore railway station. Their presence was confidence boostings, in a new place, where I did not know anybody personally. They took me to the Sudershan Guest House, next to the Vidhan Soudha. With around me, there was no question of homesickness, or thought of my home, 3000 kms from Bangalore.

4

Begining of the Career

The staff posted at the Police Training College was not the best. Most of them had only a passing interest in the job. Some of them used to express openly that their posting, to the Training Institute, was against their wishes. It was a punishment posting. Even the Principal, who was of the rank of the Superintendent of Police, was most keen to get out. He tried his best and succeeded in becoming the Superintendent of Police of Mysore District The incoming officer, who came from the same district, equally felt slighted. He was talking all the time of the unjust treatment, given to him. We were the captive audience and had no option to express sympathy. In this process, the biggest sufferer was training of the force. It is expected, that the head of the training institution, should visit the classroom or parade once in a while, or sit through a guest lecture, or take classes. None of it was done. The Principal, instead of checking the standard of the parade, would come half an hour late, take the ceremonial salute and then go away. Sometimes he would keep the parade waiting for as long as one hour. This was not the ideal way to train any rank in the Police.

Posting at Mysore

Going as a visitor, to any particular place, is one thing. Being posted is absolutely different. After the training period at the Police Training College was over, my other batchmates, Vasanth Kumar and Colaso left for their District Training. I was posted as Assistant Superintendent of Police (under Training) in Mysore itself. On my request, the range DIG of Mysore, Late Quadir Ali, IPS, allotted me a house in the Police colony. It was an unpopular, haunted house. It was the last house in the colony inhabited by the constables and other non-Gazetted officers. I had no vessels for getting my food cooked. I wanted to have my North Indian Chapatis and vegetable or chicken prepared. I had still to get used to South Indian food. I did not know the local language, Kannada. I took the help of Colaso to act as my interpreter, for making purchases in Mysore. As rice is the staple food in the South, there was hardly a cook, who could make Chapatis. The Chapatis made in my home resembled the world map. About making the *Dal* or vegetable, the cook asked me as to how did you make the same. I said that you put some oil or Ghee in a pot. After this put vegetable, water, salt and pepper, keep it on the fire. The food will be ready in half an hour. He followed the instructions to the letter and spirit. So I and my guests Mr. and Mrs. TP Issar, had the pleasure of eating the ladies finger (*Bhindis*) in flowing water for the first time in our lives !

The training for the IPS officers, in the district, included working, in all police ranks practically, from that of a Constable to Inspector, for one week to one month. Mysore was and is the second, largest city, after Bangalore. The training involved a lot of touring and personal movements. The District Superintendent of Police had his own Jeep/ Station Wagon. During his own training and posting, he was not given, any vehicle by his District Superintendent of Police. So he insisted that, like him, I should also go on a cycle. Perhaps it was a good way, of breaking down, any sense of pride, or ego, of belonging to IPS.

My first one-month, consisted of attachment, with a rural police station. One week each, was spent working actually as a constable, headconstable, station writer and sub-Inspector incharge of the police station. Language was the main problem for me. I still had to learn Kannada. As English was also used at the Police Station level, I could manage. A few Muslim constables knew Urdu. This made communication easier. Hindi use, was confined only, to a few north Indians, posted in Mysore.

Once my District Superintendent of Police, G.V. Rao, (IPS, 1949) took me on a tour, during his inspection, of a Police Station. It was to expose me to the police department. It was to be training, through seeing him function. He took me in his personal car. I shared meals prepared by his cook. My parents had drilled the sense of being honest and fair into me. Especially the tales of corruption, in the police force, made me very cautious. I offered to share half the cost of petrol and the cost of meals with him. He explained that the old IPS tradition was, to make the ASP's stay with the Superintendent of Police, as a member of his family. It was a part of my training.

South Indian with Chief Minister

The meals in Mysore in the 60's were consumed, squatting on the ground. Myself and the Superintendent of Police were generally in uniform. One of the unwritten code, of wearing the uniform, is that never allow it, to be crumpled, by sitting or taking a position, which will spoil the crease. This is more so, when any VIP, like the Prime Minister or Chief Minister is touring your area. Once, during the visit of Chief Minister, Mr. Nijlingappa I was accompanying the S.P. for the VIP duty. I had been introduced to the Chief Minister. Nijlingappa, exuded love and affection. When the lunch time came, the Chief Minister sat with the local MLA and public men for the meal.

Not finding me, (as it was not possible to miss the only turbaned Sikh, in the IPS cadre of the State at that time) at lunch, the Chief Minister sent his Private Secretary to invite me to join him. I showed reluctance to go, primarily because the squatting would spoil the uniform. The Private Secretary said "Sir, probably you don't like our meals and don't want to eat with us." I smiled and said that I had already eaten the meals in the jeep with the S.P. As he insisted, I joined them, for another meal. I was asked to sit, next to the Chief Minister. I was served a South Indian meal on a plantain leaf. I managed to finish, whatever was put on my plantain leaf, without giving any indication of my not being used to the same. The Chief Minister appreciated the same. He said, that it was my first step, towards integrating with the people of Karnataka. Now I relish South Indian food much more than any North Indian preparation. This is what national integration is all about.

My boss, the then District Superintendent of Police, also advised that all meals should be taken at regular and fixed time. He also said, that the maintenance of good health, should be the first primary duty of everybody. From that day I have rarely deviated from the timings of my meals.

Liquor

I developed a kind of revulsion for liquor in 1956 when we had gone as students from Government College Ludhiana to Jammu and Kashmir. We decided, to trek to Amarnath Caves, from Pahalgam. It used to take almost three nights, to go and come back. On the second night, I was feeling very cold and shivering. The Professor incharge gave me some brandy. It was such a powerful brandy, may be one of the illicit brands, that it burned my insides. I went out in the night, and ate snow to quench my inside heat. Only then could I sleep for a few hours. This was my first and last encounter with liquor. It is not withstanding the fact, that my late father consumed liquor. My late grandfather was a confirmed hard drink addict. I neither drink, nor offer drinks with my hospitality at my home, right from day one till now. Despite prohibition, almost everybody in the high society, I met socially, was fond of liquor. But I did manage, to hold on, to my conviction. The lure of free liquor did not hold any temptation for me. People do not insist on drinking, unless you are inclined.

Expenses of the Police Stations

Another practical anomaly, which struck me, was the unrealistic yardstick. laid down, for meeting the various expenses, of the Police Stations. For instance, each Police Station, was given a contingency amount of Rs. 4 per month for stationery. As per law, the copies of the statements, recorded by the Police, against an accused person, have to be furnished to him, to defend himself. In every case, whether the statements of ten or hundred persons are recorded, the copies of the same are to be furnished to the accused. One allegation frequently made, against the Police, was that they would insist on the complainants to bring sufficient stationery.

While there can be no defence, of any malpractice or harassment to the public, the fact remains, that any starvation of funds, for legitimate purposes will or can lead to malpractices. Another unique and impractical rule, which came to my notice, was that for the prisoners, kept in the police lock-up. Only about Rs.1.75 was authorised, per day to cover the cost of their breakfast, lunch and dinner. This was the position in 1960's. The fact remains, that if the prisoners were not fed, by their relations or friends, they would soon be living on water and air. Another reason to, their being away, from committing any excesses or illegal acts, was fear of the quality and quantity of food in police stations. Perhaps, the quality and quantity of meals, served within the legal scale, would be a greater deterrent than any imprisonment.

Electricity was a rarity. The police stations were sanctioned eight annas (fifty paise) per month for kerosene, for meeting the expenses of thirty days, for lighting and working in the night. The contingent financial power of the District Superintendent of Police was Rs. 25. In this amount one could purchase only one chair. The sanctioned staff of the police station for all duties including the court duty, village beat, service of summons and execution of warrants, was between ten to fifteen persons including the constables, head constable, assistant sub inspector and sub inspector or officer incharge of the police station, for a rural police station. The strength of urban police station could go up to twenty. There had to be a sentry round the clock which took away at least three to four men, and a Station writer who would maintain all the Station records. In 1960's the policemen were neither getting any holiday nor any compensation. But today the situation has slightly changed.

In fact, when I became the Superintendent of Police, Bidar District, I proposed to the Inspector General of Police in the Annual Police Officers' Conference, in 1966, that we should either give weekly holiday to the policemen or give them some monetary compensation. Everybody laughed at me. When I pressed my point, I was told to do it in my own District, without any extra expenditure and without diluting any police duties. I was at least fifteen years, ahead of time, when the proposal was accepted, to provide the holidays or give, one month's extra salary to policemen, for their work on holidays. The lack of funds has been the bane of any desire for improvement. Many sound proposals have crashed because the Government does not want to spend on police. Another problem was the lack of chairs and benches for staff and public use. For any annual inspection, or visit of senior officers, it was the accepted thing, to borrow furniture from the rich people on returnable basis after the visit was over. In fact all the Police Commissions set up between 1860 and 1902-03 onwards have recommended several improvements. Their implementation would have raised the cost of policing the country. The maintenance of peace and tranquillity, is fundamental to all development. If there are disturbed conditions, no development is possible. The least, that has to be assured, is that the minimum needs, of the department be met. It is only in this way, that we can prevent people from being harassed and compelled to bring petty items, like stationery, for the working of the police station. Another feature, which struck me, was the abysmal poverty, in which the lowest of the lowly policemen, were living. Some of them were suffering tuberculosis, primarily due to malnutrition. With very large families to support, for lack of family planning advice in the 1960's, these were the common stories of the police in Mysore. Except in big cities, Police Housing was almost non-existent. The lower Police subordinates were living in slums. That kind of existence brutalises even the finest specimen of humanity.

It was to take a decade and the vision of the late I.G.P. S.N. Hosali, to put Mysore Police Housing on a sound footing. He started a drive to acquire land and modernise the police with vehicles and better communication. The result is that in most of the Districts of Karnataka (formerly known as Mysore), housing facility is available to well over 60 per cent of the staff. In some areas, it has exceeded 80 per cent. As a result of his drive I myself was able to raise the percentage of Police Housing in Bidar District from 5 per cent to 50 per cent in three years from June 1965 to March 1968 as the District Police Chief.

Theft in House

In Mysore, I had acquired the reputation of being a tough, honest and strict officer, by constantly checking the police staff on night rounds, beat patrolling and investigation of cases. In fact with a view to discourage me, a theft was committed in my house. When I returned home, at about 2 a.m. on one night, in May 1963, I noticed the lock of my house broken and my articles scattered. Probably the thieves could not find, anything worthwhile to steal. There were a few cooking vessels, four chairs and a table and some old wearing apparels. The only valuable thing, which I had cherished and lost in the theft, was a photograph album containing the photographs, in National Academy of Administration, Mussoorie and National Police Academy at Mount Abu. Amongst the photographs stolen, were the photographs with the first Prime Minister of India, Jawaharlal Nehru, and the then President of India, Dr. S. Radhakrishnan addressing us in August, 1961. May be I had returned earlier than expected and so the thieves did not find enough time to totally clean the house. I duly registered a case in the concerned police station. It remains undetected till date. After my training, I was posted to Bijapur District, incharge of Indi Sub Division.

Residence in a Mill Godown

On arrival at Indi, I noticed that it was a totally backward area with no residence for the Assistant Superintendent of Police. I was keen to rent out some place where I could stay for a few days, when not on tour. Finding a place to stay, was a problem. At that time Indi did not have electricity or water supply. I noticed some electric lights in the evening. On enquirings I was told these lights. belonged to an oil mill. So I thought of finding a house near the mill so that I could draw a line for my personal use. But no house was available. However, I found an abandoned godown with a row of three verandhas one in front of the other near the mill.

I enquired and was able to rent out the same from the mill. The landlord a mill owner, Chandershekhar, charged me a rent of Rs 20 per month, along with an electricity connection to my "Residence". But there was no water supply. The water had to be stored in pitchers. There was no flush and the concept of attached latrine, in or near the residential portion was totally alien. One had to use the fields as open-air latrines. Next morning, I went to the nearby fields to answer the call of nature. I noticed a person was following me. I ignored him, feeling that he himself might be in search of a lonely spot, like me for the same mission. But when I found him too near me, I scolded him as to why he was following me. He replied very politely that he was a "Walikar". He was carrying a water pot for me. I told him to buzz off, as it was a personal function, where no public participation was required.

During the course of the day I asked the Sub-Inspector as to what is a Walikar. I was told, that the British Government had made a grant of land to some village functionaries. Walikar was one such village official whose ancestors were the beneficiaries. So in return, he was expected to be an odd job man, for life to the senior most Police official of the Sub Division. This kind of bonded slavery had continued in an informal way even after the Independence. I frankly told my Sub-Inspector, "I did not need anybody to look after me." From my side, the Walikar was a free man. In this way I disbanded an old British tradition, which was another name for getting free service.

Criminality in Mysore

Indi Sub Division was larger, than many present Districts, in some States. From one end to another, its length was about 180 kilometres. Murders were very frequent. Mostly the cause was "woman", and many times "a woman nothing to write home about." During the year 1964, out of 365 days, I was on duty for 361 days. Out of 361 days on duty, I was on tour for 341 days supervising the investigation of grave crimes. As compared to the turbulent North, it is generally believed that a State like Karnataka (Mysore) would have no crime. But it is a myth. The occurrence of a serious crime, in One State, is of academic interest to the other. The distances, in a large country like India, can at the best, give a hazy and incomplete picture of the happening elsewhere. It is the only local newspapers, which can give an idea of local occurrences. In Bijapur District in the 1960's, large number of serious crimes were reported. The crimes, involved the elimination of the families or contract killing. The caste war had stepped up the crime. It was because, the "Haves" were not willing to share the "Goodies" with the "Have Nots". At that time in my Indi Sub Division, it was quite common, to have mistresses. It was a matter of prestige. Large number of murders, were detected with the help of mistresses and ex-mistresses.

Extramarital Relations in Crime

First thing to look in any murder, was the marital life

and extramarital relations of the deceased. In 90 per cent murder cases, this was the only clue. While camping at Hippargi police station in 1964, I received the news, that a dead body had been discovered in the village pond. Since I was staying nearby, I decided to visit the scene myself. According to the Karnataka policing pattern, three to four police stations were put under an Inspector of police. It was the Inspector, who would supervise the working of the police stations under his charge. He would have to, investigate all the grave crimes, including murders, dacoities and other serious cases himself. After reaching the village, I went to see the place where the dead body was found. It was a slushy pond. In the hot afternoon, the young boys, grazing the cattle, decided to clean it, so that they could find some drinking water. Even slushy water was difficult to come by, both for human and animal consumption, in the hot climate of Bijapur. After they had removed some slush, they found a human arm. They got scared and ran to the Police Patel of the village (This system of Police Patel was again a British Institution for involving the villagers in policing the rural areas).

We got the slushy pond cleaned and found a highly decomposed body there. It was in a high state of decomposition. It was impossible to shift it, to the nearest medical dispensary, for fear of its disintegration. The medical officer, had to be summoned there, for conducting the post mortem examination. He gave his opinion that death was due to asphyxia, and drowning injuries to the abdomen. The doctor opined that the deceased was first stabbed, when still alive. Later on, he was thrown into the slushy pond, where the body sank under its own weight. The villagers were unable to identify the dead body. Everybody pleaded total ignorance of the crime as well as the deceased.

However, after some probing and prodding, we were able to find that one Shivanna was missing, from the village for the last two months. Then inquiries started into his background. One of the villages recalled, that the clothes on the dead body, resembled the clothes of Shivanna. Another person said, that height and the physical structure appeared to be of the size of Shivanna. The inquiries in the neighbourhood villages up to 10 kms did not indicate any other missing person. So we concluded, on the testimony of the villagers, that the deceased, must be Shivanna.

Further inquiries revealed that Shivanna was having an extramarital affair with the wife of another person of the same village. The lady, Gauramma, at the same time was carrying on with another person apart from Shivanna. Neither was aware, of the affair of the other, with the same woman. When they came to know of it, they had a fight, in the field near the slushy pond, in the presence of their "lady love". Each wanted the other to give up this lady. In this fight which ensued, Shivanna was badly injured. A sickle, used normally for reaping the harvest, was the murder weapon. He was thrown into pond while still alive but too injured to help himself.

The woman related this entire story in interrogation. But as the whole case was based on her extra judicial confession, not being admissible before a police officer, it ended in acquittal of the accused. I insisted on the Investigating Officer, Inspector, Hiremath, to go deep and find out as to why the husband of the lady had not objected to the activities of his wife. The Inspector was not keen to do so. But on my orders, he found another aspect of the case. The husband of the lady, was fully aware of the going on. But as he himself, was carrying on with the wife of one of the lovers of his wife, so he kept quiet.

Robbery at Tamdaddi

One of the serious cases of theft/robbery, which occurred in my area, was at a village Tamdaddi in the limits of Police Talikota. In this theft, the robbers removed the safe itself from the house. The inmates of the house claimed, that they did not hear or see anybody, committing the theft and carting away the iron safe containing over a lakh of rupees. But later on when we solved the case, one of the robbers said that they spent about four hours, in trying to open the safe, in the house itself. Since their efforts did not succeed, they brought a bullock cart and took it away. They were helped by one of the members of the family, on the condition of a share of the plunder. As the householders were keen to cover up the member of their family, they did not tell the truth. The entire loot in the unopened iron safe was dug up from a nearby field after one year at the instance of the robbers.

In most of the cases the people did know of the modus operandi. But they did not want to depose, for fear of being involved with the police and the courts of law. In fact, the reluctance of the people to appear as the National Police Commission (1977-81) has beautifully explained by a witness, to the Police Commission headed by Dharam Vira, as under; "The biggest single hurdle, which inhibits the citizen from coming forward to help the police, is the deplorable conditions prevailing in the courts of law. The lot of witnesses appearing on behalf of State against a criminal is certainly pitiable. More often than not, the case, in which he is to appear, is adjourned on one pretext or the other. This is invariably done, at the end of the day, after keeping the witness, waiting for the whole day. While fixing the next date, the convenience of all concerned, except the witness, is kept in view. If the witness fails to turn up on the next date, coercive steps are taken against him. If he appears on the adjourned date, the chances are, that the case will be adjourned again.

"When ultimately the evidence is recorded, the witness is browbeaten by an over-zealous defence counsel or declared hostile or unreliable by the prosecution. After undergoing this agonsing experience, the witness is not compensated, for the loss of the earning of the day. Even the out of pocket expenses incurred by him are seldom reimbursed. The most difficult problem, faced by a witness, in our courts is a complete lack, of any amenity or facility, to make the long wait bearable. What to talk of drinking water and urinals, etc., in most of the courts, there is no place where a man can sit, unless he forgets all about his dignity and squats on the floor of the verandah or under a tree. The sight of people, sitting under the blazing sun, or in torrential rain, is also not so uncommon, as it may seem to be. Chairs or benches for the convenience of the witnesses, are nowhere available.

It is small wonder, then that disinterested persons, fight shy of extending a helping hand, to police and only those persons agree, to come to its aid, who have an axe to grind. A man going to the railway station, or a bus stand, to catch a train or to board a bus, has to spend an hour or so there. Yet he demands and gets, basic amenities like drinking water and a shady place to sit under. But a man, who has to wait for 5 or 6 hours, in a court of law, is not provided with any of these facilities. The plight of witness is further aggravated, by the fact, that he is required to prick, up his ears, so as not to miss, his name being called, in a most unceremonious manner, by the court usher. The accused suffers for some crime committed by him, or for some acts of Commission or omission. But a witness suffers for no fault of his own. All his troubles arise, because he is unfortunate enough, to be on the spot when the crime is being committed and at the same time "foolish" enough to remain there till the arrival of the police.

It is for these reasons, that people do not take the victim of a road accident, to hospital or come to the help of a lady, whose purse or gold chain is being snatched in front of their eyes. If some person offers help, in such cases he is to appear as a witness, in a court and has to suffer not only indignities and inconveniences but also has to spend time and money for doing so. Sometime the witnesses incur the wrath of hardened criminals and are deprived of their life or limbs."

Murder in the Presence of Passengers

In the full view, of a crowd of passengers, and in broad daylight a murder was committed, at a small railway station. I personally visited the place of offence, within half an hour, as it was in my area. I questioned some passengers and the railway staff. Everybody denied having seen any offence being committed. They said that they were busy with their own affairs. It is no wonder, that criminals get away with the dastardly crimes. Because nobody feels interested to take up the responsibility to protect the overall interest of the society. Of course, we traced the accused through the background of the deceased. Here the motive of the murder was that the deceased had deserted his wife for a better looking mistress (sister in law). He had not heeded the warnings of the accused, that if he continued with his nefarious activities, he would be killed, and his head presented to the village goddess. The accused voluntarily surrendered to the police accepting his guilt. He was finally acquitted as he retracted his confession in the trial court. Nobody was willing to testify against him.

Open Air Latrines : Public Nuisance

In most villages even now, there are no attached water closets or latrines even in the houses of the well-to-do. The concept of the attached bathrooms, with WCs, is basically an American concept. Indi did not boast any signs of modern civilisation except a metalled road connecting the Sub-Divisional Headquarters with the District town of Bijapur. It had no water supply, electricity or even a touring cinema theatre. All the populace including men, women and children had to make a beeline to the fields nearby in the morning to answer the call of nature. The lazy ones would not take the trouble of going to the distant fields. They would use the metalled roadside to ease themselves irrespective of the traffic on the road. It hurt the sensibilities of the people as well as womenfolks. Several respectable people of the town requested me, to put an end, to this public nuisance. Now if the laws are to be enforced strictly, you can arrest any respectable law-abiding citizens for some minor infringement or the other. A careful study of the newly passed and enforced Mysore Police Act showed that committing public nuisance was a punishable offence.

On a persistent public demand, I directed the local officer incharge of the police station to take necessary action. Ending public nuisance is the incumbent duty of the police. Other duties, include, the destruction of stray dogs and take necessary action for the confinement of the persons of unsound mind. So next morning as some of the people started using the metalled road as the open air latrines, they were hauled up extra along with their pots (lotas) and taken to the police station. They were duly produced before the magistrate at 2 p.m. and fined Rs 5 each on the admission of their guilt. This public nuisance ended quickly like this. It was not the fine which mattered but the very humiliation of being produced in the court along with their lotas without breakfast and lunch, till 2 p.m., which had the desired effect.

Transfer of the Boss

My boss P.G. Harlankar was transferred from Bijapur to Bellary District. In his place Abraham Verghese, IPS of 1955 batch, was posted. I did not know him. I was not sure about his attitude to subordinates and also to myself. But the new boss turned out to be as nice as his predecessor. I continued enjoying his hospitality, advice and guidance in my work.

Verghese had a very good sense of humour. He would find gentle humour in every situation.

He had the unique distinction of having got arrested a close relation of the then Chief Minister of Karnataka, under the Prohibition Act. Instead of shifting him, the government sent him for an advanced course for six months to Mount Abu, IPS Police Academy. Thus, he was posted out gracefully. Verghese felt, that the Departmental Head at that time, that is the Inspector General of Police, had not stood by him. Instead he was given a caution for a trivial matter of delay of a report in one case diary. He felt that the least that could have been done was a pat on the back by the Police Chief. May be the Inspector General could have told him privately that "Well done". With a hind sight the chief could not have gone against the displeasure of the Chief Minister.

After retirement and after having seen many Chiefs, I can say with confidence that the tribes of the Chiefs supporting their subordinate at the cost of their jobs is almost extinct. Now the first instinct in any body's mind is to save his own skin and further one's own cause. Verghese introduced me to the great English writer P.G. Woodehouse, which kept my sense of humour alive. P.G. Woodehouse is a delightful writer. It is a treat to read him again and again.

One of the duties of the Sub Divisional Police Officer is to supervise the grave crime, on the spot. He also has to go through the case diaries and comment on all the crimes. The requirements of the law is, that the investigation of the cases be done on a day to day basis. The case diaries, which are a record of investigations done, should be written on the spot. But in practice, case diaries are written only when the case shows some progress. There were complaints also that the cases are registered only after their detection. To put an end to any malpractices, I started signing on all the registers during my surprise visits to the police stations. One allegation frequently made, was that several persons were illegally detained in the lock-up, to extort money. So my first work on reaching the police station was to proceed straight to the lock-up, check whether a proper record of the persons detained in police custody was available or not. It took only a few surprise visits and three suspensions from service of police officers to put an end to such malpractices.

I am of the firm view that it is only acquiescence to such practices by the seniors, which leads to public harassment, encourages illegal activities and corruption. I openly say in official meetings, that I would not go out of the way to harass anybody. But anybody going against the laws and indulging in malpractices, would not be spared. This had the desired effect as only after a few months, my officials realised that I meant every word, I had said.

Promotion as Dt. Police Chief

After serving more than a year and four months as SDPO, I proceeded on earned leave to Jalalabad in May, 1965, to meet my parents. After availing of leave, I left for Bijapur on 7th of June, 1965. On the way, I dropped into the Ministry of Home Affairs at New Delh. Shanti was working as Under Secretary in the North Block. I was informed that some IPS officers had been promoted in Karnataka, to the rank of the Superintendent of Police. On going through a Bangalore based newspaper, I learnt that I had been promoted and posted as Superintendent of Police, Bidar district. Normally it is difficult to believe newspaper reports. But newspapers, do publish important government notifications. I took it as correct news and sent a telegram to my parents about my promotion and posting. As I had already reached Delhi, I did not wish to go back to my native place, Jalalabad. After few days I received a letter from them, informing about their happiness on my promotion. I was the first member of the family, first person from Jalalabad and perhaps first one from Ferozepure District, who had been selected for the Indian Police Service. Now in the same series, I was promoted as Superintendent of Police of a District. The promotion was to be effective from 23rd June, 1965. I reached Bijapur and rejoined duties as ASP for a few days. I did not wish to idle away on extended leave to wait for 23rd June.I arrived at Bidar on 22nd June 1965 by train. The name of the railway station of Bidar was "Mohammadebad Bidar", I was welcomed by the DSP Bidar, Chinnaswamy with a Police Band and taken to the Circuit House in Bidar known as "Habshikot". It was only an ego boosting exercise.

First Day as S.P.

It was customary, to call all the District Police Officers at the time of either retirement or transfer of the District Superintendent of Police. I met all of them with my predecessor Srinivasan. Most of the Police Officers were double my age. They had put in at least two decades of service. Almost all of them had risen from the ranks of Constables. I was only 25 years of age at the time of my assuming charge of District Superintendent of Police. I could see, in the eyes of most of the subordinates, a gleam, indicating that I was almost a child. I would only be a Plaster of Paris in their hands, to be guided or moulded as per their wishes. While addressing them, I made it very clear on the first day that I would not tolerate the following :

(1) There should be no diluting the intensity or gravity of the crime. It was a universal complaint, that police officials do not register, all the complaints made to them. If at all they register, they make the robbery or dacoity as a case of simple theft. A case of hurt with serious weapons, is generally entered in the Station House Diary, as a simple hurt and a non-cognisable case.

(2) I emphasised that we were there to serve the public and harsh behaviour was totally unacceptable.

(3) I underlined the fact, that the performance of a police officer, would be judged by percentage of detection, of property offences and grave crimes, and not on the basis of salutes or arrangements done. I highlighted that during my visits and inspections, one day would be devoted to meeting the local officials, heading other departments. The second day, would be devoted to meeting the local leaders and headmen of all the villages.

I also added , that I would like to meet each member of the police force during my visits, except those on leave or on duty. It was not a difficult task as the total strength of the District Police including the Armed Police was just 550. I put it very clearly, that me were to go by the law of the land, and not by the individual whims. Just when I was addressing the conference, I casually opened a registered letter. It contained a complaint, that though a dacoity had occurred, in the limits of Basavkalyan police station, the officer-in-charge of the police station, had not registered the case, despite various visits and requests. I immediately questioned the Circle police Inspector, Humnabad Circle, Sangappa Shetty under whom the police station fell. He pleaded total ignorance of any occurrence at Matala. So I said that day after tomorrow, that is 25th June, 1965, I would personally visit Matala. I wanted to spend one day more in the District Headquarters and familiarise myself, with the immediate problems, facing the district. I felt that almost all officials, attending the meeting, did not take my views seriously. They all felt that new brooms sweep clean for sometime. Then they fall into old ruts and routines. I noticed, that the policemen of Bidar, were not only slack in their duties, but also had slack turn out and bearing. So I told the town DSP that I would be attending the parade and P.T. every morning with the men at the City Armed Reserve. He should also attend the P.T. and parade with the Civil Police at the town police station premises. Most of them had not attended the parade. Their uniform needed alteration. Obviously, they were not using the uniforms regularly. I was requested, to give them one week so that they could be fully prepared. I did not want to appear to be obstinate so, I said "yes".

On the 25th of June as promised, I left in my "Willy" Station Wagon for the village visit. area. On the way I visited roadside police stations of Bagdal, Mannaelkheli and Humnabad. I reached village Matala at 3 p.m. I questioned the complainant, named Reddy. He said, that a dacoity was committed, in his house a month back. He ran away from the back door to the policemen, who were camping, in the village. Instead of taking any action, the policemen on duty including the Head constable, told him to go to the police station at Basavkalyan, for lodging his complaint. After hearing this reply of head constable, he went to Basavkalyan police station, which is 15 kms away from his village. The Sub Inspector who was the officer incharge of the police station, told him that he was busy and was going for court duty. He (the complainant) was told to come, after two days, for registration of the case. He again approached him after two days. Still the officer incharge did not register the case on one ground or the other. I verified the facts from the Police outpost staff. They admitted that such an offence had taken place. I went back to the Basavkalyan police station, and got a case registered and ordered the suspension of the

Officer in charge of the police station as well as all the staff of the Police outpost. The disciplinary proceedings, against all the guilty policemen continued for over two years. Unfortunately, all the witnesses, even the complainant, turned hostile and denied having gone to the police station to lodge a complaint. I was asked to be the Inquiry Officer by the Government. Since all the public witnesses had backed out, there was no option but to hold the accused officers not guilty. After the complainant had deposed in the formal inquiry, I summoned him privately. I asked him, as to why, he had told a lie, in the regular inquiry, when during my visit to the village, he had a different tale of woe and harassment by the police. He felt very ashamed but his reasoning was that the accused officers fell at his feet with their families and begged him to save them and their jobs. They also brought religious leaders of his caste, who made him take a vow that he would not harm the policemen. He also said, that I as an S.P had taken, very strict action against the careless staff. Since I could be transferred any time and he would have to live with the same policemen in the District. In this case he was right because lower subordinate policemen upto the rank of sub-inspector are not posted out of the district. He said that almost all the corrupt policemen, were making offerings, to the deities praying for my early transfer. They were, also trying to hook in, the local politicians in this venture. In my summing up an Inquiry Report and recommendations to the Disciplinary Authority, I wrote : "The Superintendent of Police is personally convinced, about the occurrence, of such an offence, as seen from the records of the Police Station and various other reports, but the personal belief of the Superintendent of Police, is no substitute for the evidence. As no evidence, is forthcoming and as all witnesses have turned hostile, I recommend their exoneration." I sent this report as Inquiry Officer, to myself as Disciplinary Authority. In my final orders, I had no option but to exonerate all of them. I also treated their entire period of suspension as duty, as per the rules.

Chronic Absenteeism

One of the common weaknesses of human beings, is to avoid all the obstacles and choose the path of least work and maximum rest. In Bidar, a very common malady was, habitual absenteeism, and unauthorised extension of repeated warnings and admonitions, had no effect on them. Their trick would be to wait, for the change in their seniors, They again would repeat, the same lapses, with impunity. I got prepared a list of such officials. So whenever such worthies failed to turn up, on the ground of ill health, they were ordered to appear before the District Civil Surgeon, for a thorough medical examination. The doctors would admit them in the hospital and strictly confine them to their beds. For hard-core absentees, doctor's strict instructions were not to leave the bed at any cost. They were to answer the calls of the nature, on the bed itself. It is obviously, a severe punishment for a healthy person. In case of those who were the highest category malingerers, the bitterest of medicines, mostly vitamins and quinine for malaria, were administered. In still other cases, harmless injections, including the painful milk injections, were administered. Such a "patient" had to be woken up, every six hours, given a prick and fed on very lean food meant for seriously sick patients. Thanks to the District Civil Surgeon, who devised the new ways to deal with the problem, the absenteeism disappeared. Whenever a policeman was asked to appear for medical examination and treatment in the District Hospital, he preferred to be fit. Policemen preferred to perform their duty, rather than be admitted and given the painful injections and the bitterest medicines. So what persuasion and cajoling could not do, the District Surgeon did for the District Police. This had a healthy effect on the discipline in Bidar Police. I always requested the Chief Medical Officer, that those genuinely sick, should be looked after well and given the best of treatment. I put the chronic absentees, on my personal staff, so that they had no occasion or chance to be rude or late for their duty. Almost all of them, were victim of bad reputation and campaign, of damning, by their own colleques.

One Man Set-up

One of the best sources of genuine and fake news and views is your personal staff. As S.P. I had only one stenographer by name Sangivikar. He would keep me fully informed of whatever good or bad was going on in the district.

There used to be a District Special Branch to keep the S.P. apprised of the political, economic and general situations in the district. But my P.A. had more information than the entire District Special Branch.

The District Special Branch, would gather news, from the local newspapers and produce, some kind of a report, on the political, economic and crime situation in the district. I doubt whether any higher ups ever read it. It used to mostly an inane affair. Most of the times, I would not feel like sending it forward. Once I said, that why not we say that we have, nothing significant to report this month. But I was advised, by my colleague Superintendents of Police, to never say that I had nothing special to report. It will only go to show, that I was not working. So, however insignificant or colourless, the required reports must be sent in time. This has been the practice in the Government and continues even now. This truth has been repeatedly brought home to me again and again. It only proves that let the sleeping dogs sleep and never stir a hornet's nest, etc. If you want to have a peaceful existence. For instance, as IGP, CRP, a report was required to be sent by me to the Director General of the CRP, about the foreign exchange, spent on foreign tours every month. But the fact was, that nobody had a chance, to go abroad, from the CRP. So much against the advice of everybody in my office, I took up this matter with my Director General . I said that nobody can go abroad without the permission of the Head of the Department/Govt. Calling for such a return from nearly 100 officers was not only a waste of time and stationery, but also absurd. The Chief saw the absurdity of the return and had it discontinued. He ordered that if any such information was required it should be available in his office. It should not be called from the lower formations.

It is a very unfortunate tendency, in all higher offices, including those even headed by me, to call for fresh information, every time it is needed, instead of ferreting out the same from the records in the office. So whenever I was posted to any office, my first direction was that for the first two months I would sign and see every single communication, going out sent or received, by my office. This practice kept me fully posted, with whatever was going on, and what changes could be or should be brought about, to improve the efficiency. My staff officers never appreciated the same. It took away their authority, to raise endless objections to anything, which might come from a subordinate formation. Another of my dictum has been that it is the field formation, which is the reason for the existence of the higher formation. The field must be given the full support without any reservation. To implement it, my orders have been that my office shall not say "no" to any proposal received, without my approval. Nothing will be rejected till I am convinced that a "No" is the proper answer. But for saying "yes" no prior consultation or orders are necessary from me. Prior consultation and orders, however, are must for saying "No".

In Bidar, I found the police stations with broken furniture. There were not even enough benches or chairs for the public to use. When I enquired as to why not even four chairs were there in each police station, I was informed that this was due to the lack of sanctions. When I checked up the position in my office. I was told that my contingent power for purchase of such items was only Rs. 25. In this amount, only one chair could be purchased. I stretched the interpretation, to saying one chair, per police station, per time of sanction. Thus, in the jargon of finance, I split the sanctions. Every month I sanctioned one chair, per police station. In six months, all the police stations had four to six chairs each. It cut out the dependence, on the other offices and public for the furniture, during the visit of senior officers. The position with the kerosene supply was not different. Only three out of fifteen police stations, in Bidar had electricity. The rest had to manage with lanterns and petromaxes. It took me again about six months to equip the police stations with kerosene lamps, petromaxes, torches and torch cells for night patrolling. The official amount sanctioned for purchase of kerosene of rupees five per month, was too low to suffice even one week's expenses. This is one aspect, in which I could not succeed in improving because it was not only beyond my financial competence, but also of the State Inspector General of Police. However, when I found that even my office had run out of the stationery supply, I wrote a letter on the following lines to the late S.N. Hosali, I.G.P.

"Dear Sir"

I have repeatedly brought to your notice about the lack

of funds for stationery and other office expenses. The stationery in this office has been exhausted and this letter is the last letter, on the last paper of the stationery of this office. After this letter, it will not be possible for us to send any more communication from this office, till we receive the stationery or the sanction for the same."

This had the dramatic effect of waking up the Chief's Office and promptly according us the sanction for purchase of office stationery. This bold step made me very unpopular, in the eye of the officers, of the Head Office. They were always keen and on the lookout, to find any lapse on my part. But I did not give them any chance. To prevent similar happenings under my charges, I have prescribed a monthly D.O. in every organisation, I have worked. In this D.O. apart from other difficulties, the officers working under me, were required to indicate pending matters in my office, in the office of their immediate superior officer and also in the Head Office or the Government. During my visits and inspections, I made it a point to mention, about the difficulties and pending matters, in my inspection notes. This enabled me to get a total view of the pending cases, and problems faced by the field offices.

"Yes Boss"

Despite all these efforts, lower rung officials, were loath to show anything pending with their immediate superiors. They felt that if anything is shown pending with higher ups, it would be construed, as a complaint, against them. In an hierarchical service and organisation, no junior officer wants to annoy, his seniors, for fear of being harmed. People tend to be petty and take offences at trivialities. I am personally aware of a case of a senior police officer harming the interest of his junior simply because he had not called on him. Both of them belonged to the IPS, with only two years service difference between them. When he met the senior officer, a Director, of a Central Police organisation, at a social gathering and expressed a wish that he wanted to formally call on him, he was brushed aside. He was in the empanelling committee of the IG's and above. He curtly told him, that he would be taught a lesson, which he would remember for life, as he was in a critical zone of promotion. And the senior officer kept his word in under assessing him, so that he does not get promoted. The harm was undone in a review when the prejudiced officer had retired. So for this reason nobody wants to offend the seniors. Such instances can be mulüplied from all services under the government in every department. The result is that there is a premium on sycophancy and saying "Yes Sir" to everything that a senior says. Sycophancy, has crossed limits. In some cases every word uttered, by a senior, is taken to be a pearl of wisdom. There is a great harm and danger in telling the truth, especially if it is not to the liking of the superiors. In several cases, officials play safe, anticipate the wishes and act accordingly. There are other cases, where subordinates approach seniors for guidance, as to what kind of note be put up or orders passed. Over centralisation is the bane from which all of us suffer in greater or lesser degrees. When we are seniors we want to centralise everything. When we are juniors, we are in favour of decentralisation.

Hyderabadi Hospitality and its Impacts

Bidar District was a part of old Hyderabad State. Traditionally lavish hospitality was its hallmark. I felt the effects of rich and oily food, in three to six months. There were no videos and no televisions in Bidar in 1966. The only source of entertainment was the solitary cinema theatre there. A friend once took my photographs and had slides made of the same. I saw my slides on a projector. Instead of seeing a handsome Joginder, I saw a huge bloated giant. The giant, weighing 200 pounds was none except myself. My normal weight of 162 pounds had become 200 pounds courtesy Hyderabadi food. It was mentally unacceptable to me. I did not want to face the fat giant again. I immediately went on a crash diet. My friend Doctor gave me three dozen tins inscribed as "Metrical". It was an American preparation of metered calories. During the day nothing was to be consumed, except one tin of Metrecal, in water. It contained 800 calories of food in the powdered form. In about 55 days, I brought down my weight to an acceptable figure of 165 pounds. But I had forgotten one important lesson. It is not the weight reduction, which is important, but the weight maintenance. Weight can be kept under check, by a two pronged strategy of dieting and exercise. I was continuing with the second but had relapsed into the same old eating habits. Before I realised the damage I had done to myself, I had reached against 187 pounds. This ding dong battle with the weight has been a constant feature of my life. The free lunches at the Government cost and heavy socialisation, take their toll, in the form, of disfiguring of ourselves, with pounds and pounds of fat.

The level and standard, of Hyderabadi hospitality, can be judged by the fact that for breakfast alone at the time of an Inter-District conference on crime, the then S.P. Mehmood Bin Mohammad, provided as many as six non-vegetarian dishes. The items included liver, keema, two different preparations of mutton and two different forms of chicken at the delightful site of Nizam Sagar in Medak district of Andhra Pradesh. The free lunches, competition at various parties for providing more dishes, heavy socialiation, with richer and large variety of dishes are in fashion even now. In a climate like this, it required a lot of efforts and restraints not to over eat. As the number of District Officers was very small, so in every party one would meet the District Magistrate, the Executive Engineer and the District Civil Surgeon. As the judiciary had been separated from the executive, the District Sessions Judge, would avoid attending any party.

5

Entering Family Life

End of Bachelorhood

I had told my parents that I would not get married, till I got promoted as Superintendent of Police. My reasoning was that as an Assistant Superintendent of Police, I had to lead a nomadic life. The nature of the job, was such, that one was not sure, as to where one would spend, the next day or the night. So when I got promoted, my father broached the subject of marriage. I conveyed my yes. An advertisement was inserted, in the *The Tribune*, the only Punjab English newspaper, inviting proposals for marriage. 470 offers were received. Some offered very tempting dowries, others flaunted high connections at the political and official level. Some girls in reply to the advertisement were almost pictured as the twin sister or even better than the "Helen of Troy." In one case the person replying to the advertisement, offered to bring the girl, to the district where the boy was serving to avoid any inconvenience to the boy. After a rigorous elimination, based on education, family background, age and height, the total selection for correspondence was reduced only to five. The beauty of newspaper advertisements on the matrimonial is, that the party inserting the advertisement and inviting proposals need not give its address or its contact point. The anonymity is a great facing saving device. Finally the correspondence, with only one family was started. It fell through on the grounds that the girl would like to work after the marriage. Somehow when one is heading a District, one feels that one's wife should not be working under anybody. So nothing came out of the first matrimonial advertisement. The parents of a few snooty girls of my own class and other classes from my college, had also responded. Some of them were good and I could have married. But they were so conceited in the college, that there was no point in taking a chance. Second time again an advertisement, in the newspapers brought a much more overwhelming response, including from the father of the girl which I had selected earlier. But this time they relented, and said that if the boy does not want the girl to work, they would not insist on any preconditions. My parents fixed up with the various parties, a meeting between me and the prospective brides in Chandigarh, on 14th of December, 1965. I flew from Hyderabad to Delhi and journeyed by train to reach Chandigarh on an extremely cold morning. I was told to contact my father at a given telephone number, 4287.

When I reached early in the morning, I had nowhere to go even for changing my clothes. I tried to get a room in a Hotel in 22 Sector in Chandigarh but was refused. I was told that the hotel was full and a room would be available only after 12 p.m. I met the same fate in another Hotel Mount View. Having no contact point, with my father, except the one he had indicated, I was at loss, to establish a contact. I remembered that my classfellow, Ajit Kumar was in Chandigarh. I promptly went to his house and was happy to see him there. He had already joined IAS in 1964 batch and had come to Chandigarh to see his parents. When I telephoned the contact telephone, I was told that there was no Mahant Kartar Singh there.

I did not tell Ajit, the exact purpose of my visit though he guessed it correctly. In the absence of anything to do, we started roaming around in Sector 17 market. Ajit gave a name to the aimless roaming as "Dame Gazing". There I met my father providentially. He asked as to where I was since the morning. I told him that the number he had given, had given a negative response. So hurriedly, he telephoned and fixed up our calling on the girl's parents and meeting the girl at 5 p.m. He also fixed meeting with other parties at 7 p.m. We reached house number 20-B,4-A at the appointed time, We met the girl's father and her brothers. We were served tea. The girl also came gracefully and offered me a cup of tea. After a few minutes, my father privately asked my opinion. I took less than five minutes to make up my mind. I said it is alright. I will marry this girl. I told my father that the remaining visits to see other girls be called off. Let them be lucky, to select better partners, than what they would have found in me. I had found my mate and I had no intention of searching better or richer girls. The father of the girl asked me whether we had any demands. I said "none". I also said that since some of my colleagues from Karnataka were likely to be in Delhi and would attend my marriage, let the marriage be on 19th January, 1966. This date was not fixed in consultation with any priest or astrologer, but intentionally for the convenience of my friends who wanted to attend the wedding ceremony.

This is how I met and selected my wife Surinder Kaur.

Bridegroom Left Behind

In order to complete the responsibility of the marriages in the family, my father planned wedding of my younger sister Manjit with Sardar Balbir Singh of Sirsa on 14/15th January. My marriage was fixed for the 19th of January, 1966. My other sister Sarala had already been married off to Sardar Trilok Singh of Saharanpur in 1963. Though I was the eldest of the children, my marriage was the last. The war with Pakistan had just ended in September/October, 1965. So the celebrations were kept on a very low key. Chandigarh was just coming up and the members of my marriage party were more keen to see the new city, than my marriage. A bus and a car was hired. Bus to carry the marriage party. The car was for the bridegroom and his best man. In my case, my best man was Sardar Trilok Singh, my brother-in-law. The most irritating thing about the marriage ceremony was, that I was asked to bow and touch the feet, of persons, I had never seen in life. There was almost a glut of them. I just kept my cool. The limit was crossed when my parents tried to overcrowd, the car to oblige all and sundry.

Glut of Uncles and Aunts

On the occasion of wedding, it is the bridegroom and the bride who are the major attraction for the day. But in my case, all the importance was given to the uncles and aunts. They insisted on travelling, in the old car hired for the occasion. On the 18th of January, 1966 the marriage party left Jalalabad at 8 a.m. We had planned to reach Chandigarh by 5 p.m. I was in a foul mood and cheesed off with an overloaded car full of uncles and aunties. There was hardly any place for me and my best man. Somebody at Ferozepur, got a brain wave of buying flowers, for decorating the car. It was a different matter, that the garlands and flowers would either dry up or fall off from the car in the further journey of 180 kms. The bus and the car were parked at Ferozepur bus stand. The car, after off loading me, was taken to the city to get flowers. One of the members of the party said, that since the car travels faster, the bus should move to Chandigarh, ahead. The logic was that car in any case would catch up with the bus. The motive was to get an hour, or so more for sight seeing, at Chandigarh. So the bus left, leaving me and my best man to come in the car. Since we had some time, we started getting our shoes polished. The car, hired for the marriage, saw from a distance, that the bus was not there and moved on. The occupants had concluded, that the bridegroom had already gone, in the bus. So they asked the driver to proceed to Chandigarh. We saw the car a distance, driving away, leaving the star of the marriage, that is myself behind and stranded.

I tried to hire a taxi or any other vehicle, which would take me to Chandigarh by the reception time at 7 p.m. No transport was available. The bus to Chandigarh was scheduled to leave only at 1 p.m., which would have reached Chandigarh by 10 p.m. So I went to the nearest telegraph office and sent a telegram to my father-in-law from my father's side. The telegram said that "Regret that due to unavoidable reasons the marriage party will arrive late."

Finding no vehicle, for my transportation to Chandigarh, I did the next best thing. I called on the Senior Superintendent of Police, Ferozepur District and explained my problem to him. In some States like Punjab/Haryana/UP the Head of the District Police is called the Senior Superintendent of Police whereas in some States, he is just called the Superintendent of Police, as it was in my case in Bidar. Even his efforts, to hire a private vehicle did not succeed. He asked his Additional Superintendent of Police, Pritam Singh Hura (1962 IPS, Punjab) to drop me at Moga. In Moga, there was a better chance of hiring a vehicle. In the meantime the bus drove on merrily for four hours. None of the passengers , felt the absence of the person, for whose marriage they had been invited. Their eagerness, to see Chandigarh was so strong, that they had no other thoughts in the world except to reach Chandigarh as soon as possible. When the car caught up with the bus, my father realized that the bridegroom was neither in the car nor in the bus. After making this discovery they started their return journey, to Ferozepur to trace me. They had turned back from Ludhiana. In the meantime, my hired vehicle from Moga, caught up with them. I had lost my calm, especially when they tried to find fault with me. I told all the members of the party that they could get off from the marriage party. I did not need any of them, for the treatment they had given to me on my wedding day. I threw out all the passengers from the car and told them they could get back to their houses as far as I was concerned. I drove off in the car to Chandigarh with my best man. The car took me to my destination at 9 p.m. In the bargain the entire reception party had been ruined. The marriage party reached, only after 10 p.m. The bride's side was intrigued at the delay and the telegram received by them. They interpreted it, as a ruse to either extract dowry, or to cancel the wedding. Nobody believed the truth, that I had been left behind by the avid fans of Chandigarh, who in their anxiety, to reach earlier had caused this terrible mix-up. My wife after 33 years of married life considers that 18th January is the day of fight between us. Only 19th is the wedding anniversary when we were actually married. The Sikh weddings are a relatively simple affair and the actual ceremony takes about 17 minutes. My father-in-law, late Sardar Tirath Singh, had very thoughtfully, told the priest solemnizing the marriage, to cut out the frills and lectures and confine himself to the actual ceremony. The wedding was over in twenty minutes, after the breakfast, at 11 a.m. we left Chandigarh for Jalalabad by about 2 p.m. On the way at Kharar, we heard the news of the election of Indira Gandhi as the Prime Minister to succeed Lal Bahadur Shastri. I some how felt that my life was linked with Mrs Indira Gandhi, as both of us entered a new phase in our life on 19th January. This time I made sure that no unwanted free loaders were allowed to travel in the car . Apart from myself and my wife, my mother was the only other occupant of the car. We reached Jalalabad at about 10 p.m. Nearly eight hours of journey enabled us to chat and understand each other. There was no traditional welcome for the bride, as the marriage party reached late in the night at Jalalabad. In fact the next day's *The Tribune* carried a humorous story on my marriage. It made light, of the eagerness, of the marriage party, to see Chandigarh, rather than see the bridegroom married. It said, that in the end as all stories end happily, this also ended happily, with the bridegroom making off, with his bride, with at least the solemnization of the marriage, in time.

What transpires, between the wife and husband, on the first night after marriage, remains a secret for life shared by the couple. Next day, as it happens in all small places, with everybody related to everybody, through some relationship or the other, there was a crowd of women, to see the "bride". I still do not understand why after the marriage, the approval of neighbours and other's is sought or solicited as to how do they like the bride or the "bridegroom". Most of them approved of the selection, but some were critical of lack of my dowry. To this, I countered, by saying that we ourselves had made it clear, that we had no demands.

It is traditional for the bride to visit her parents, with the bridegroom, after the wedding. We went to Chandigarh, after two day's stay at Jalalabad. I had met my in laws, very briefly, first at the time of engagement and later on at the wedding. We did not go anywhere specifically for honeymoon. As my leave was ending so in the second week of February, we left for Bidar via Delhi and Secundrabad. The journey from Delhi was bungled. Despite the reservation, having been done 20 days, in advance, we did not find our names, even on the waiting list. Somehow we got two first class seats and travelled. At Secundrabad we were met by a friend and travelled by road to Bidar by my Standard Herald car. Herald car was the only car available with almost no waiting period in the 60's. Any other car had a premium equal to its price. The only other cars available in the market were Fiat and Ambassador. Those cars, were in love with the mechanics. Almost, from the showroom, these cars had to go almost on weekly basis for touching, repairs and maintenance.

Buying a Car

After my promotion as a Superintendent of Police, I had applied for allotment of a Standard Herald Car. I was told that it would be a wild goose chase to expect any other car from the Government Quota. A few months before my marriage, I got the allotment order. The authorised dealers, M/S Unicorn Limited, Bangalore, wrote to me that my car was ready. I had to pay Rs 14216/-, as the price. It was to be paid at the time of delivery. I was asked to collect the car, within one month. I did not have that much money. So I applied and got a government loan of Rs 10500. I had sold my motor cycle and with a few hundreds rupees savings, was able to manage Rs. 14216/-. The cost of the petrol was only 50 paise a litre. As Bidar was quite far off from Bangalore, I had not been able to call on the Inspector General of Police after my promotion. When I broached the subject with my immediate superior, the Deputy Inspector General of Police, Belgaum, I got the impression that he would not permit me to go Bangalore. I was looking for some excuse to go to Bangalore on official duty.

In the meantime, a Cipher message was received. Cipher is a code and it has to be deciphered. We were asked to act on it quickly. Since at no time I, had been trained in Ciphers, I promptly informed, the State Special Branch Superintendent of Police, P.S Chellapa, that I did not know anything about deciphering secret messages. I suggested for my training, in Bangalore. I also told him that I would like to combine it with caliing on and meeting all other senior Police Officers as well as collect my car.

In the meantime, I asked the neighbouring SP, the details of the message in simple English . The message was something like this, "A yellow coloured small plane has been sighted in the State and possibly it might be an enemy plane. If sighted in your jurisdiction, it may be detained." It was a strange and an impossible order. The District Police, has no means to detain a flying plane. Secondly we were not told whether we could open fire with bolt action muskets or a few. 303 Rifles in the District. I doubt it whether any rifle shot fired from the ground can disable a plan or force it to land. I sent a message back, seeking instructions as to how the District Police should detain a flying plane and whether we could open fire with the muskets we had. No reply was received. Regarding Bangalore visit, I promptly got a message from the Chief's Office asking me to come to Bangalore for training. As I had an indication of the mind of my DIG, who did not want me to go to Bangalore, so I devised my own method of dealing with the situation. I had the permission of the Chief to visit the Capital. I was also aware of the likely hostility of my immediate boss, the DIG. I booked my seat by air from Hyderabad to Bangalore. On the day fixed for departure, I sent the following message to the Deputy Inspector General of Police, Belgaum, my range DIG, "Permission received from the Chief office to visit Bangalore. Leaving today, will come back after three days after confidential work." I had ordered that the message be transmitted after I had been airborne. Due to the technicalities of the classification of tour messages being low priority, the DIG got the message after I had reached Bangalore. DIG's violent reaction, came in a crash message, after I had reached Bangalore. He said that I should return back immediately. I had my training of two day's cut to one day. I stayed for one day in Bangalore. Fortunately the company delivered the car, the same day. So I drove back in my car. It was really an ego problem of the DIG and nothing more. Here the overall boss gave, one set of orders. His junior, the DIG tried to prove, that he was the real boss, countermanding the orders of the IG. On my TA Bill for the journey to Bangalore, a number of queries were made by the DIG's office. He did not pass it for three months. I told the DIG, face to face, during his visit to my District, that if he had any objection, to my visit to Bangalore, he should have taken it up, with IG, rather than delay countersigning my Travelling Allowance Bill. When this had no effect for more than two months, I wrote him a letter, asking for his permission to send a representation to the IG for his not passing my TA Bill for the journey.

He quitely passed it with cuts. I was entitled to the road mileage for journey by road from Bangalore to Humnabad. I was sanctioned Travelling Allowance only as if I had travelled by train. This was less than one third the amount to which I was entitled to. Normally when you travel between two places not connected by train, you are eligible for TA at the rates fixed by the State Government. But for the above visit to Bangalore, a new set of rules was applied in my case, to teach me a lesson. There was no network of Railway's in the entire Bidar District except from Bidar to Hyderabad and vice versa. The train would take you first to Zahirabad a distance of about 17 kms and then to Hyderabad. Zahirabad itself was in Andhra Pradesh.

The road network in Bidar District was primitive and non existent. For visiting, at least three-fourth of the district, one had to first go to Zahirabad in Andhra Pradesh. Then only one could proceed to the areas, leading to Humnabad and to other parts of Karnataka. For going to Bangalore, one had to travel either via Zahirabad or via Hyderabad in Andhra Pradesh. So to settle score with me, my TA Bill even for journey by road areas in Bidar, which had no rail connection was regulated as under; First 17 kms would be allowed as if journey was by train and for the rest road mileage would be sanctioned. I protested that it was totally against the spirit of the rules. When two places are not connected by railway, it cannot be the intention, that you would not get mileage by road. Even when, a part of the distance, is connected by train, you cannot be given for that journey, the railway fare and for the rest road mileage. The whole journey is to be treated as a journey by road. Or alternatively the charges for transportation of the car for the portion covered by the Railways should be sanctioned. It took more than two years, of paper battle, before this obvious point, was conceded and the TA Bills passed.

When I reached Zahirabad, with my wife for the first time, after our marriage, I told her the story of the TA Bills. She found it hard to believe, the lack of obvious common sense. She perhaps felt, that I had made it up, to add some humour, spice and colour to otherwise three hours of journey from Hyderabad to Bidar. We reached Bidar by about 10 p.m. The SP's Bungalow, was spread over in an area of ten acres. Next morning when she got up, she found it too large for a family of two. To keep herself busy, she took over the running of the household. She discovered that before marriage, my monthly consumption of Dalda Vanaspati was 10 kgs and monthly purchase of onions was 35 kgs. She asked me as to what I was doing with those items, apart from a large quantity of mutton, chicken, pulses and vegetables. I myself was surprised at those revelations. I told her frankly that I had no idea, as to how much of each item was required, for the running of the house of a single person. I had never bothered to check. I would only pay for the articles whenever the servants told me that the money given was finished. My role was confined, to the payment of the bills and keeping the receipts carefully. In retrospect, I feel those quantities explained my bloated and plump figure.

I was quite happy with my wife, She had no company and nothing to keep her busy. Even the social life was limited. My salary as the Superintendent of Police was Rs 740 per month. Out of this car loan, provident fund and income tax had to be paid. My net salary in my hands after deduction was Rs 464. She carefully monitored all the expenses. After one month, she brought down, the monthly expenses to Rs 250. My wife suggested that we must purchase a fridge. It will provide cold water and ice. The left over food from one meal to another, could be preserved. At that time no District Officer including the Deputy Commissioner had a refrigerator. I myself did not know what a refrigerator was. I was sceptical, whether the refrigerator could perform, all functions, claimed by my wife. On enquiry we found that the cheapest model would cost about Rs 1200 We wanted something still cheaper.

Bidar's Air Force Station

The Government of India decided, that an Air Force Station, for training purposes should be established in Bidar. Bidar already, had a large runway. This order brought a large number of Air Force Officers to Bidar. The Defence Services including the Air Force, have an established system of having Officers Mess. Air Force authorities decided to make me an Honorary Member of their Mess. The officers, including the Station Commander, Group Captain Suri, were a friendly lot. When we mentioned that we wanted to purchase a fridge they readily agreed to procure one for us from their canteen which was at least Rs. 150 cheaper than the market. So with our saving, effected over a period of 5 months, we purchased a small fridge. It was unpacked from the crate, with loving care and affection, before installation. We ourselves would handle it. Even the domestic help, was forbidden to touch it. It is required of the senior police officers, including the S.P.'s and ASP's to personally perform night rounds and check of police patrolling. This is the only way to prevent crime. Such checking is also expected, to include the checking of various guards including the Jail and Sub Treasury Guards. I used to be meticulous in these duties.

Within two days of my return, after my marriage, I resumed the night patrolling. It was primarily, to dispel any impression that I had slackened after marriage.

My night patrolling started with District Headquarters of Bidar at 11 p.m. and went on till 4 a.m. I visited different police stations, as far as 75 kms. from Bidar Town. This sent the required signal, to the entire force, that acquiring a wife did not mean in anyway the neglect of duties. My wife did have a humanising influence on me. She would generally not approve of any harsh treatment or punishment disproportionate to the lapse. Not that I agreed with her, but at least she made me aware of the other's point of view. She said that, my losing temper spoiled, the peace at home and made her scared. Her observation made me more circumspect. Not that I stopped punishing people for their lapses. Perhaps I started telling her less and less. Many times her advice was not only timely, but also excellent. I made it a rule that it was unfair, to burden her, with my official problems. So I decided to solve all my official matters myself. There was no "petticoat government" running my charge.

6

Policing, the Police

One of the major problems faced by the Police Chiefs is the policing of the Police. A lifetime of dealing with the seamy side of life, makes police officials develop a cynical outlook on life. In police, the same is reflected in the form of either minimising, or burking the crime, or in harshest treatment to the poorest of the poor. I had made it clear that in the Independent India we were there to serve the people and not vice versa. It was brought to my notice that in a case of serious incident, where the victim died in the District hospital Bidar, the officer in-charge had not even registered a case. He had not even made any entry in the Police records of Khatakhincholi police station. I came to know of the happening only, when the District Civil Surgeon,sent a report to the police. I immediately ordered an inquiry. It was proved beyond doubt, that deliberate burking of the crime, had been done possibly, for some monetary consideration. After following the proper procedure, I dismissed the guilty policeman. He went in appeal against my decision to the range Deputy Inspector General based in Belgaum. We had been getting circulars and orders, from the same officer, that as District Chiefs, we must be very strict, in maintaining discipline and burking must be dealt with nothing short of dismissals. The same officer set aside my order of dismissing him from service. I rang him up, and told him that it was a totally wrong action on his part and would convey wrong signals to the force. The only change he did was that instead of reinstating him in service in Bidar District, he posted him to a neighbouring District. I was still dissatisfied. I did something unheard of at least in the annals of police in India.

I went in appeal against the DIG's decision. I wrote a personal Demi Official letter to the Inspector General of Police that in this case there has been a miscarriage of justice by the DIG, who had shown uncalled for and unwarranted leniency, to a person whom I had already shown sufficient leniency, I had merely dismissed him and not prosecuted him under the Indian Penal Code for burking and suppressing of the offence. This really shook up both the DIG's and IG's office because no policeman had ever done such a thing, at least in Karnataka. The DIG had a poor reputation integrity wise and was amenable both to monetary and political influence. I had done this in my fifth year of service. It only shows that when you are young "you rush in where angels fear to tread." Probably I had no worries and no vested interest and I felt that the worse that can happen is my transfer to any other place.

Flames of Communal Riots

Elections were to be held in the country in 1967. More than 450 olling booths were set up in Bidar District. The instructions, for the election were, that there should be at least one constable per polling booth. With a total force of about 500 including the sick and trainees, it was a Herculean task, to man the polling booths. With the total deployment done, I was left with a reserve force of seven men, which included my own guard and driver. For the first time, Jan Sangh, the predecessor party of the BJP had decided to contest elections from Bidar to the State Assembly. The Congress candidate was a sitting MLA and also a Deputy Minister, in the State Government, Maqsood Ali Khan and his Jan Sangh rival was Chanderkant Shindol. On the election day, a dispute arose between the supporters of the two rival candidates. The representative of the Jan Sangh claimed that bogus voters were coming, to cast vote for the Congress candidate. The supporters of Congress candidate alleged that Jan Sangh supporters, had removed the Burkas, to verify the genuineness of the Muslim lady voters, so that no man by putting on a Burka does the proxy voting. First it started with the stone throwing. Arson followed when a few shops and houses were set on fire. I saw the mobs of the two communities, surging towards each other menacingly. I myself along with my driver, and guard, started lobbing tear gas shells, into the unruly crowd. There was no sign of the violence and arson abating. I went to the nearest telephone and sent the following message to the IG "rioting, looting and arson in Bidar. Request rush reinforcements". I was also aware that by the time any force came from Bangalore, which was 480 kilometres away, the whole town would have been burnt. I also telephoned the Station Commander of the Indian Air Force, to rush to our help, with all the force he had, otherwise he would not see anything of Bidar town as I was battling the mob with just a seven men reserve force.

Fortunately, the Air Force came in a big way with their armaments, and vehicles and they started patrolling the city. At our request, they also sent up their trainer aircraft's to sensitive areas. This enabled us, to assess with pinpoint accuracy, the trouble spots and the trouble makers. We were able to bring the situation, under control without any loss of life or even firing. Notwithstanding the trouble, the city had a polling of 65 per cent. In the meantime a message came that the IG wanted me to speak to him immediately. The option for me was to leave the trouble spot for making a phone call or ignore it. I did not ignore it but told the wireless operator to send a message back that a hostile crowd had surrounded me and as soon as I could get out, I would speak to him. There were no ways of easy communication. There was no such thing as straight trunk dialling (STD). You had to book a call and wait near the telephone for at least one or two hours. I did it after four hours, after bringing the situation under control. He was quite happy with what I had done in that critical situation. The Deputy Commissioner, late, N.K. Prabhakar Rao, IAS of 1956 batch, was a valuable colleague. He was a type, who would fight with you, any battle shoulder to shoulder. His presence in another part of the town, brought a similar situation under control. Sometimes, the Policemen complain that when the trouble arises, the Executive Magistrates make themselves scarce. But here the Deputy Commissioner, was in the forefront, of the battle with me. Under the law it is only the District Magistrate who can summon the armed forces or paramilitary to the aid of the civil authorities. Here I had summoned the Air Force and they had responded in the national interests. The Deputy Commissioner-cum-District Magistrate signed the requisition, as if he had summoned them, to keep the record straight. He did not create any fuss.

The incident had generated a lot of bitterness and distrust between the two communities. I convened a meeting of the two candidates and the prominent citizens in my office, along with the District Magistrate. Instead of a peaceful discussion the members of the two communities started blaming each other for communal riots. I kept on listening for sometime. I intervened to say that any more disturbances and recriminations, would compel me to arrest all those spoiling the atmosphere, including the candidates, contesting elections, without any fear or favour. I urged them, to ensure peace, in their respective areas, failing which I will have to take some very unpleasant and tough measures. Nobody had heard such a plain talk. Since the District Magistrate was in my office sitting with me, everybody presumed that it was a joint decision. This had a salutary effect. I suggested that the shops must open next day and the business, should go on, as usual. For any serious rioting or incident, it is essential that the senior officers including DIGs and if possible the IGs should visit the place. Bidar was more than 300 kms. from the range of Headquarters. The only way to travel to Bidar was by road. When the DIG got the message of trouble, he rang me up on the first day. Since I was busy with quelling the riot, I could not speak to him. Next day when my meeting with the citizens, was going on a call came from the DIG. He started berating me that I had not dealt with the situation tactfully. The real cause was the uncomfortable road journey on pock marked and potholed road, for two days, to reach Bidar. When I found that without realising the gravity of the situation, he was going on and on with his lecture, I just said: "I cannot hear you. He said that he could hear me clearly. I kept on telling him that I could not hear him and would call him up later on." I did not want to appear to be rude to the DIG in the public meeting. I put down the phone and told my personal staff that if any call comes from the DIG when I am in a public meeting, they could tell him that I had gone for the city rounds and would call him later on. The DIG was bitter, on my not receiving the call, when he came to Bidar two days later on. I explained to him that I was busy in public meeting when he was pulling me up. I had no other option, but to cut the call, as he was in no mood to listen my version. After going around and seeing how I had tackled the critical situation, he paid me rich compliments with a copy of the letter to the I.G.

Mass Rape at Bhimalkheda

During one of the meetings with the press, it was brought to my notice that a mass rape had been committed at a village called Bhimalkheda in Mannaelkheli police station. The Police had refused to register a case. Perhaps, it was on the ground that the rape victims were from the family of a big bully and a known rapist. Perhaps there was an element of fear coupled with glee, that a sort of poetic justice, had been meted out, to the family of one, who himself had been guilty, of similar offences on the village womenfolk of the other community. The offence, had been committed more than two weeks ago, on a dozen women belonging to the minority community. The victims included the old and the young, married and unmarried. When I made enquiries, I found that no case had been registered. At least the district records did not show the occurrence of any such offence. I sent an officer from the district headquarters, for an inquiry. I followed it up, with my personal visit to the village. Preliminary enquiries showed, that such an offence, had taken place. Almost all the young people, of the village belonging to the majority community had taken part in the rape. It was done in a spirit of reprisal. A few days before this well-planned crime, the entire youth of the majority community, had taken an oath, on a flame to teach a lesson, to the rowdy.

The preliminary enquiries, also revealed, that no complaint, had been made to the police station. I was personally not inclined to believe the same. But since the aggrieved women themselves, said that they had not complained, I had no option but to accept their version. A case of rape and criminal trespass was registered. All of those, who had perpetrated, the crime, were nabbed. The women were sent for vaginal medical examination, which is essential to prove the charge of rape. As most of the victim women were married, the medical opinion was not helpful. The Doctor reported that no opinion could be given as they were used, to frequent sexual intercourse. In the case of two young married girls, the medical evidence showed ruptured hymen.

The only evidence, against the accused numbering 25 was the statement, of the victims. Despite weak evidence, the case did succeed in the Sessions Court. The case was based on the circumstantial evidence. The accused were convicted and sentenced to five years of rigorous imprisonment. However, they were acquitted by the High Court in an appeal. But as they had spent a lot of time in jail, first in police custody, then in judicial custody and later on as prisoners, this had a good effect on the law and order climate in the district. The local press blew up the case, as my personal success, for having taken up the challenge and proved that the District Police Chief was totally impartial in his dealing with all the communities.

Expectations of the People

Since I was freely accessible to the people, the result was that I was more busy than anybody else in the district in trying to redress the grievances of the people. I had two DSP's to assist me, one at Bidar and the other at Bhalki. Both of them were the old types of police officers, who resented doing even their duties. I advised and cautioned them. They were very good in giving me VIP treatment during my visits. I made it plain, that what I was interested in was the actual police work and prevention of crime. In the case of one of the Dy. SP, I received reports, about his doubtful integrity. I called and told him about the complaints. He denied the same. I warned him that I would ignore everything. But henceforth, he should ensure that all property crimes, were detected, especially the grave crimes of robbery and dacoity. That would be the condition, for my not taking, any action against him. I watched him for three months. I noticed that instead of any improvement in the situation, the crime position had deteriorated. Not only, was he not, visiting the scene of crimes and the affected areas, but he was also keeping the investigating officers, tied down to mobilising political support for his retention in the area. I called for his explanation, for non-performance from the period he was working under me. He refused to give any explanation. He told another officer, that he had a lot of political clout. Nobody could touch him whether he worked or not. It took me a week of hard work to prepare a report Under Rule 56-J, of the Mysore Civil Service Rule for his compulsory retirement. The report along with, the supporting documents was sent by me, to the IG under a D.O. in which I said that pending his compulsory retirement, another officer may be posted in his place. I also said, that if no other officer was available for posting, then it would be better to keep the post vacant. I would hold additional charge. I said that it was essential to meet the rising expectations of the people at least half way. It would not be possible to do so till the officers orient themselves to work better and in the right spirit. My efforts to make the officer work had not yielded the desired results. It appeared that no action was taken on my letter. But I was proved wrong, when within 45 days of my report, the government compulsorily retired the officer and pensioned him off. Knowing that my DIG would make money from this officer, for diluting my report, I kept him out of the picture. He only came to know, about my report when the DSP had been sent home. DIG was unhappy with me.

On my request two directly appointed IPS officers of 1965 batch, L.N. Revannasiddaiah and late Yeshwant Gol were posted as ASP's at Bidar and Bhalki respectively. Both of them were very sincere, honest to the core and very hard working. They never grudged doing duty beyond the prescribed office hours. I told them that we were a team to produce results, in the form of better service to the people. I also related my own experiences, of ASP's days. I told them that they would be free to discuss any and every subject with me both on official and personal matters. I also said that they would be my guests during their visits to the District Headquarters. But they should not, conceal anything from me, about the policing and crime situation. They proved to be an asset, in changing the total perception and image of the police in Bidar District. Another help came in the form of posting of Viswanathan, IPS(1966), for training in the district with me. He was very enthusiastic about his job and proved equally tough in dealing with all situations.

Appreciation of Good Performance

Bidar was a small district. A news item appeared that a number of foreign nationals, were overstaying in the State. I asked the District Special Branch, to put up a list of the foreign nationals, who had come to Bidar on a visit from Pakistan. The foreigners under the law are required to register themselves with the District Police. I also asked them to put up their date of departure from India. I was shocked to find that most entries were only one sided. Hundreds of those who had come had not gone back. Some of them had even married and settled down in the district. I told my officers, to launch a drive, to trace overstaying Pak nationals. They must be sent back, to the country, from where they came.

As a result of the drive launched by me—perhaps the only district at that time in the State of Mysore—I was able to deport a large number of foreigners out of India. The Government conveyed its appreciation of the work done by me as under:

No. GAD 83 SPS 67

Mysore Government Secretariat,
Vidhana Soudha,
Dated, Bangalore, 10th July, 67

From
The Chief
Secretary to the Government of Mysore
Bangalore.

To

Shri Joginder Singh,
Superintendent of Police,
Bidar.

Sir,

Sub: Appreciation of good work done

The Inspector General of Police has brought to the notice of Government that you have been responsible for launching a drive to trace Pak Nationals who had evaded leaving India after the expiry of their permits and that you have made untiring and praiseworthy efforts in tracing Pak Nationals. I am directed in this connection, to convey to you the appreciation of Government for the excellent work carried out by you, in spite of serious handicaps of difficulties met with in handling such work.

Yours faithfully,
Sd/-
(K. Narayanaswamy)

Transfer to Bijapur

The people of Bidar irrespective of party affiliations, and religion gave me unstinted support for making it trouble free and crime free. After about two years of stay, I was transferred to Bijapur District as Superintendent of Police. I was thrilled to be posted to the District, where I had served as an ASP. Moreover, I considered it an honour to be posted to the largest District in the state; at least three times the size of Bidar District. But the posting was cancelled a few days later. I felt unhappy, but I kept quiet. I did not know the background, of either the posting, or the subsequent cancellation. After few days an important politician came to see me. When he was talking to me, I said that strange were the ways of the Government. "One day they issue an order and a few day's later they cancel the same." I said that I was disappointed that I was not allowed to go to Bijapur District. He said very hesitatingly that he along with all the MLA's and MP's of the District was responsible for the cancellation of my transfer. I said that I had not made any request to anybody for stay in Bidar. My seniors and colleagues would misunderstand, that I had sent a deputation to get my transfer cancelled. He said that it was for the first time, when all the politicians of all parties, in the District had agreed unanimously that S.P. Joginder Singh should not be allowed to be transferred to any other District. He also said that for the first time people of all the communities were getting full protection. The police had stopped being repressive, which had been going on since the Nizam's time when Bidar was a part of the old Hyderabad State before Independence. So, for this very selfish reason, they had approached the then Chief Minister, S. Nijalingappa, in the overall interest of the District. He apologised for taking this step but, at the same time said, that as long as I was in Karnataka or Mysore State, they would like me to serve for the maximum period in Bidar. Since I had no vested interest in any place in Mysore State, I took it as a compliment, that the people through their leaders had appreciated the work done by me.

7

Training the Police

Policemen's Traning

A new Mysore Act had come into existence, in 1963. No police official was familiar with its provisions. The constabulary was ill trained. Some of them had no training at all. Even now, the police system is such that senior officers are sent for training. The constable, who is at the cutting edge level of policing, in the country, gets trained only once in life for periods ranging from six months to one year. This is only at the time of his recruitment. Afterwards for his entire career spanning over 30 years, he is not sent for any training. He is not exposed, to any changes, which take place in the policing. This is the position regarding the civil police. The Gore Committee set for the purposes of reviewing the police training in the country had the following observations to make, in 1973:

"The role of the Indian Police has changed after independence. The country has since witnessed considerable political, social and economic changes aimed at the establishment of a welfare state. This process of change is likely to continue. A clear understanding of the deeper currents of this process is required by policemen of all ranks not merely in the context of their law and order role but also in the context of other functions entrusted to them. Various steps have been initiated, from time to time, to infuse the police, with awareness of sympathy with and responsiveness, to the aims and objectives of the changes that are taking place in the society, in the course of discharge of their statutory responsibilities. But the impressions persist, in sections of the public mind, that the police, especially at their levels of contact with the people, are either not aware, of their changed role, or have not moulded their attitude as a public service, as required by the changed conditions. This calls for immense tasks, of imaginative, training of new entrants along with the retraining of the existing personnel."

Earlier U.K. Government had appointed a Committee under the Chairmanship of Lord Desborough in 1919 tc have a look at post-war situation. The Post-war Committee of U.K. Government (1949) observed in its fourth reports:

"As a result of their enquiry, the Desborough Committee were satisfied, that a policeman, has responsibilities and obligations, which are peculiar to his calling and distinguish him, from other public servants and municipal employees." They considered the Police "entitled thereby to special consideration with regard to their rates of pay and pensions."

"A candidate for the police, must not only reach certain standards, of physical developments, but must have a constitution which is sound in every way. The duties the police have to perform are varied and exacting; they are increasing and will probably, still increase, in variety and complexity, and a man cannot make a good policeman, unless his general intelligence, memory and power of observation are distinctly above average.

"His character should be unblemished; he should be humane and courteous and generally he should possess, a combination of moral and mental and physical qualities, not ordinarily required in other employment's. Further, when he becomes a constable, he is entrusted, with powers which gravely affect, the liberty of the subject, and he must at all times, be ready, to act with tact and discretion and on his own initiative and responsibility in all sorts of contingencies. The burden of individual discretion and responsibility, placed upon a Constable, is much greater than that of any other public servant of subordinate rank.

"The Police also stands, in a special relationship to the community. Each constable on appointment, becomes one of the duly constituted guardians, of law and order, for and on behalf of the citizens as a whole. He undertakes special responsibilities, in regard, to the prevention and detection of crime, and while he does not relieve the citizen, from all responsibilities, for the protection of his own property, and for bringing offenders to justice, he claims to be and is, the principal agent in the prevention and detection of crime of all kinds and generally holds a position of trust which it is important he should be able to maintain.

"We consider it essential, that the sense of obligation, to the public should be preserved in the police, and the reason we dwell, on these considerations at some length, is that they are fundamental to the views, we have formed as to the status of the police and the pay they should receive.

"A number of police witnesses have urged that in various ways a Constable is subject to social disabilities by reasons of his employment. Moreover, he must at all time, both on and off duty, maintain a standard of personal conduct befitting his position and this does impose on him certain restrictions, which do not exist in the ordinary employment's and hardly apply in the same degree, even in the case of other public servants. He is liable to be called for duty, at any time in an emergency, and in order that he may be available for unexpected calls, he may be restricted in his choice of residence. The special temptations, to which a constable, is exposed are obvious and as any lapse must be severely dealt with. It is only just, that his remuneration should be such, as will not add to his temptations, the difficulties and anxieties incidential to inadequate pay. The policeman's calling, also exposes him to special dangers. He may at any time have occasion to arrest an armed criminal and he may occasionally have to take part in suppressing violent disorder."

"The policeman is also put to certain special expenses by reason of his employment, for example, he not only requires good and substantial food, but the cost of his housekeeping, is increased by the irregularity of the hours, at which he has to take his meals.

"We entirely agree with these observations. The policeman's responsibilities are essentially unchanged, but they are now exercised in a wider field. Legislation since 1919 had added to his duties and increased their complexity. More recently, the wartime shortages and the resultant rationing and control have created a whole range of offences, which frequently offend less against the conscience than against the law and have led to an increase in crime.

"The organisation and technique of modern criminals, their use of cars and their increased tendency to carry firearms, have all added to the difficulties and dangers attached, to preventing crimes and capturing criminals. Moreover, the police have had to deal, with a much wider cross-section of the public since motor traffic regulations. The liquor licensing laws, rationing and control have brought increased chances of wrongdoing to even the well intentioned and the well to do.

"Since 1919 there has been a notable spread of educational facilities and they are to be extended in near future. A police service, which has to deal with a better-educated public, must itself be properly equipped for its task....

"So far the spread of knowledge has not lightened the policeman's task; in fact, it had added to his responsibilities.... We are convinced that police responsibilities are more exacting, now than they were when the Desborough Committee reported in 1919 and are not likely to become less; and we have had this in the forefront of our minds in all our enquiries into police emoluments".

So far as India is concerned, in the post-independence era, the law and order situations arising out of conflicts, linguistic, communal, agricultural and labour problems have, completely kept the police tied in handling such problems, which are not the result of any police making. On the one hand, the police are expected, to strive for closer relations, with the public and on the other; as the guardians of law and order they are to deal with the agitation's which are more often than not violent in nature. Challenges to authority are bound to be there in pluralistic society, and agitations and disturbances in a democratic set-up further increase these.

The Police Committee on training (1973) observed: Additionally there is the problem of the right use of authority by the parties, which are in power.

"There have been instances where Governments have been accused of using police machinery for political ends. There are also instances of the individual politicians interfering with the administration and the work of the police. As may be expected, in a society in transition, the norms which should govern the relationship between the party in power, the individual politician and the police have still to be developed."

Compulsory Refresher Course for Constables

The Police Committee on Training observed : "thus, by and large, the only training that Constables receive throughout their service is the basic training on recruitment. A vast majority of them, mark time as Constables, without any hope of promotion and they perform their duties in a mechanical way. The lack of any further training, coupled with, any lack of promotional opportunities, seriously affects their efficiency and has an adverse effect on the image of the police. We consider a refresher course for the Constables essential to maintain their professional efficiency and to ensure that they maintain the attitudes desirable in police officers. A Refresher Course, of four weeks duration, should be compulsory, for Constables at intervals of seven years. The human relations content, of this training programme will have to be substantial, with emphasis, on development of correct attitude and the preventive and social aspect of the police work. To be purposeful and effective this training should be imparted in the police training school. The refresher course should also be utilised to identify constables of a promising type for being encouraged to work their way up."

Syllabus Suggested for Refresher Courses

It was felt that it would be desirable, if all the constables could attend the course. But since their number wouid be very large, the course should be restricted to those constables, who are capable of deriving the most benefit from it. Constables who have completed 25 years of service of 50 years of age, those who have a persistently unsatisfactory record of service and Constables who have done a promotional course, or have been approved for promotion need not be sent for refresher training. (Source : page 60 of the Report of the Committee on Police Training, 1973). The syllabus for the refresher course of training of constables could include the following subjects as suggested by the Training Committee:

1. Fundamental Rights and Directive Principles of State

Policy.

2. Political, social and economic changes in India, since Independence and their implications for the Police.
3. Major social problems—upliftment of weaker sections of society.
4. National integration.
5. Current affairs.
6. Understanding human behaviour.
7. Police behaviour towards the public.
8. Principles of Police conduct—selected cases to emphasise the importance of courtesy, impartiality and integrity.
9. Prevention and detection of crime with particular reference to beat, patrol, surveillance and collection of intelligence.
10. Investigation—elementary knowledge of scientific aids to investigation—preservation of the scene of offence and police portraits.
11. Maintenance of order with particular reference to student and labour problems, political agitation's and communal disturbances.
12. Role of Police in social defence—juvenile delinquency.
13. Application of science and technology to police work.
14. Revision of important provisions of I.P.C. and Cr.P.C. cognizable offences relating to obstructions or deterring public servant from duty and powers of arrest.
15. New legislation.

There are a large number of constables whose academic qualifications are meagre. Many of them are even illiterate or semi-literate. Since it is otherwise also desirable to raise the educational standards of police, opportunities should be provided to constables for self-education.

As regular classes may not be feasible for the constabulary whose duty hours are irregular, because emergencies requiring the deplcyment of men in large numbers are frequent, the solution lies in encouraging and evening classes for improving their educational qualifications, to the extent this can be done without detriment to their duties. Constabulary could be encouraged to join the correspondence courses. It will also be desirable to sanction suitable allowances for the constables who pass the high school and other higher examinations in the form of advance increments and this will provide necessary motivation to the man for self-development.

The post of the Head-Constables and Assistant Sub-Inspectors are generally filled by promotion, which means, that Constabulary level is the feeder category for the promotion to the above ranks. There are some States like Punjab, Haryana, and Himachal Pradesh where these posts are filled both on promotion basis as well as direct recruitment.

Syllabus Suggested by Committee

The Committee on Police Training felt that all Head-Constables and Assistant Sub Inspectors, who have put in seven years service, in their respective ranks, should be required to undergo, at intervals of seven years, a refresher course of eight weeks duration, focussing on scientific methods of crime detection. It should include an attachment to the State Forensic Laboratory for a week. Their knowledge of law and procedure, with regard to investigation, should be refreshed and they should be acquainted with new laws and court rulings and the preventive and social defence aspects of the police work. Police-citizen relations should form a part of the course. (Report of the Committee on the Police Training, 1973, p. 61). The following eight-week course syllabus was suggested for the refresher course of the Head Constables and Assistant Sub Inspectors of Civil Police:

1. Fundamental rights and directive principles of state policy.
2. Political, social and economic changes in India since independence and their implications for the police.
3. Major social problems—upliftment of weaker sections of society.
4. National integration.
5. Current affairs.

6. Understanding human behaviour—individual group and crowd.
7. Police behaviour towards the public.
8. Principles of police conduct—selected cases to emphasize the importance of courtesy, impartiality and integrity.
9. Modern concepts in criminology.
10. Criminogenic factors related to psychology, sociology, economy and politics.
11. Defiance, individual defiance—juvenile delinquency.
    (a) White-collar crime
    (b) Collective defiance—organised crime/defiance of authority.
    (c) Vice (gambling, alcoholism, prostitution and drug addiction).
12. Penology, punishment—prisons, correction and reformation-probation, parole and corrective institutions, recidivism.
13. Police as a part of the criminal justice system-inter-organisational co-ordination and co-operation.
14. Prevention of crime especially/special types of crime likes dacoity and burglary, collection of criminal intelligence.
15. Crime investigation, preparation of F.I.R., procedure and methods of investigation, preparation of case diaries.
16. Revisions of Criminal Procedure Code and Indian Evidence Act (relevant sections only), Constitution of India.
17. New legislation and rulings by the Courts.
18. Scientific aids to investigation and detection of crime.
19. Application of science and technology to police work.

During the course of this refresher course, there should be attachment to the State Forensic Laboratory for a period of one week. It is essential to put the Constabulary through a Training Course as suggested above to make the police responsive to the needs of the changing India. The National Police Commission (1977) in its first report had observed:

"It is thus seen, that the constable of the present day, has moved far, from the predominantly mechanical role, assigned to him by the 1902 Commission and has now to interact with the public in larger number in a variety of situations where he has to apply his mind, exercise his judgement, use his powers of persuasion and appeal and enforce law with public understanding and co-operation. It is the Constabulary, who form the cutting edge of police administration and face the public most, during their visits to Police Stations and movements on road.... It is the Constable's behaviour and response, which create the first and foremost impact, on the public mind.

The staff, who functions at the police station level, largely determines the police image in the country. The constabulary constitutes a large majority of this staff and forms the foundation and base for the entire police structure. Any attempt at a meaningful police reform has necessarily to start at their level only, since no restructuring of the system will be practicable or enduring unless the mass base of the system is rendered healthy and efficient."

The Commission had also observed: "With enormous changes in police tasks, both quantitative and qualitative...the police system cannot afford, to continue the same policy, regarding its constabulary, who form about 90% of the strength of the police force in sheer number, and whose quality of performance really determines the overall impact of the police system on the public.

The growing compulsion and pressure of police work will continue to make a large number of police personnel, at the level of Head Constables and Constables, interact face to face with the public in a variety of situations. Head Constables and Constables can no longer afford to train and function as mere automations, recruited, trained and developed mostly to perform duties of a mechanical character."

Basic to the training is the fair selection so that the best candidates are selected for the trying and tough police jobs. The Police Committee on Training observed:

"The nature of the Police role, administrating competent, politically neutral and imbued with the spirit of seller's service in a democracy requires that the members should be selected impartially. A police officer enjoys vast wide discretion. Recruitment procedures, should, therefore, be so devised that they are free from political, personal or corruptive influences.

The need for objectivity in selection cannot be overemphasised."

Much before, any committee was set up, to improve the performance of the civil police, I decided to start a training programme only for Constables and Head Constables of the Civil Police. I was told that I had powers to grant Daily Allowance only for ten days and beyond that it would have to be referred to the higher officers. My brief experience, as the District Superintendent of Police had taught me that, if you want to do anything, do it within your powers. The moment you refer the decision to the superiors or senior formation, either your original proposal gets totally changed beyond recognition, or largely amputated which is often not found acceptable or worth recognition. So I have made it a principle that I should not trouble higher-ups for something which is in my powers. This has stood the test of time and I am glad to record, that whatever has been done, within my own power and initiative, has evoked a positive response.

So I had a syllabus prepared which included the New Mysore Police Act, a portion of Indian Penal Code, Indian Evidence Act, Criminal Procedure Code and Minor Acts, P.T. and Parade for a course which was to run for ten days only. I said that each of the police stations would depute two Constables or one Head Constable and one Constable for the training and two courses would be run every month. In this way, I had calculated that I would be able to train 60 policemen every month. In a period of 10 months, the entire police force would be put through the ten-day programme. I also suggested and it was agreed to by every participant, that every police official should have his own copy of Mysore Police Act. So, apart from the training, the entire police was equipped with the instrument of their trade, that is the Mysore Police Act.

Unused Graveyard Becomes Training Ground

The training of the policemen at the District level had a general effect of toning up, in making them more responsive, to the public needs and their problems. As the training/ parade ground was a small one, I noticed an abandoned and unused graveyard by its side. It had not been used for any burial for the last fifty years. So I decided that the dead had rested sufficiently long. They had been buried very deep.

They would have no objections, to the levelling of the ground for police training. In a period of six months, we had removed all traces of a graveyard from the area. The abandoned graveyard, was a part of the Police parade ground. In this way we had prepared the biggest parade ground in the entire State. There were some rumblings about the levelling of the graveyard. Some people tried to give a communal colour to the whole issue. I explained to the press, that it was a Police area. No disrespect had been shown to any community. Since my credentials had already been established as a totally impartial and a non-communal officer, even the murmur died down.

As the policemen had done this job as a fatigue duty, they were suitably rewarded for this work. Probably nobody remembers today, that the biggest Police parade ground was less than one-third of its present size till 1967, with a graveyard around it.

Mischief in Dispatch

Receipt and issue section in any office is considered the lowest of the postings. It is a general belief that those who are not considered fit for doing any proper job are posted there. Unless orders/ communications are dispatched in time, the prompt issue of the orders or working hard on holidays or till late in night is nullified by delayed dispatch. As Superintendent of Police, Bidar District, I had given an out of turn promotion to a Constable as a Head Constable for his apprehending a desperado at a considerable personal danger to himself. After about a month, I visited Hulsoor Police Station and found him in the guard as a Constable. I asked him as to why he was still working as a constable, when a month back, I had promoted him. He replied that he had not received any order. I felt very upset and had a thorough enquiry made into the delay of despatch orders. During the informal inquiries, it was brought to my notice, that the dispatch clerk had sent message to the promoted Constable to come and see him. The Constable took leave and met him. The despatch clerk demanded Rs 200, just for, sending his promotion order, by post. The Constable had refused on the ground, that he did not have that much amount. It was equal to his, one months salary. Cut up with this refusal, the despatch clerk had just not despatched his promotion orders for over a month.

I ordered the holding of disciplinary proceedings against the dishonest clerk for lack of devotion to duty and deliberate negligence. I dismissed him from the service. I was reminded of this incident three years later on. At that time, I was working as Chief Security Officer, to the Government of India in 1969-71. One of my former colleagues in the Indian Police Service, Pran Khanna had resigned from service and joined the Private Sector. I invited him over, for a meal to my place. I started discussing with him his life in the Private Sector. He was quite happy and was making a lot of money. He was earning in one month, what I earned, in the whole year. What a big difference! But he had a bitter complaint, against the Government Offices, in general. He had to have a lot of permissions and licenses for his business. He said, that he had to bribe several people and for some category of people, like those in the despatch section, he had made it a practice, to pay a monthly goodwill amount, so that his letters were either handed over to him personally, or despatched with the quickest of speeds. I reminded him, that as an ex. policeman, he owed it to the country to rid it off the corrupt and undesirable elements. He was very forthright and blunt while replying that he was in the business, like other businessmen, to make money and not cleansing the society.

Slaves of Phone

Alexander Graham Bell (1847-1922) invented telephone to bring people together from distances. But his great invention has sometimes made us its slaves. Some people stick to it like glue. A late batchmate of mine Pratap Singh Dardi, when he was in IAS, long before he got his marching orders from the service, came to Bidar District. He was the State Director of Treasuries. He had come to inspect the working of the District Treasury. The Deputy Commissioner, Prabhakar Rao was a good man. But telephone was his weakness. May be there were very few District Officers, corresponding to his status and may be there was no other entertainment. He had substituted telephone for all those activities. A call from him, or to him, would not last less than half an hour. If you were lucky, it could take twenty minutes.

As District Officers, we transacted a lot of official business, on the telephone. Once I was getting ready to go to Nanak Jhira Gurudwara. (It is said that Guru Nanak Dev, the first Sikh Guru, had visited Bidar at the invitation of a Muslim saint. He had stayed with him, at his place.) There was a terrible scarcity of water in Bidar. The people were finding it too difficult to find brides for their sons, as the womenfolk had to trudge miles, to fetch drinking water. When this difficulty was brought to the notice of Guru Nanak, he by his wooden sandal struck the ground, and created an ever-flowing source of potable drinking water. The fountain of the water is still there. It is called Nanak Jhira. A Gurudwara has been built there, to commemorate the visit of the Guru to Bidar. It is about 120 kms. from Nanded in Maharashtra. The 10th Sikh Guru, Govind Singh, had passed away, there, after being stabbed, treacherously by the agents of the Mughals. One of the five beloved ones or Punj Piyaras, willing to sacrifice himself, at the behest of Guru Govind Singh also hailed from Bidar. Receiving a telephone call from our common friend, late Prabhakar Rao, at this time was most unwelcome. So after making polite conversation for about five minutes, said, please speak to Dardi. So Dardi spoke to him for sometime. From the other side it was only a monologue. The Deputy Commissioner, at the other end was narrating a story of setting up of a sugar factory in Bidar. Dardi also wanted to come with me, to the Gurudwara. He had no interest in what Rao was telling him. He called my servant, Hollappa and told him to hold the telephone and keep on listening to what the person on the other side was saying. He also told him to say "Hoon Hoon" periodically. So the servant kept on listening to the one sided monologue in English. My guest Mr. Dardi went inside, tied on his turban, put on his suit and came back. He took the phone from my servant and told Rao, at the other end, that he had done, a great job despite difficulties. He told him, that he would see him in the evening at the dinner as he had to go to Gurudwara. So for half an hour, the Deputy Commissioner, had carried on, conversation, practically with himself, as the servant did not understand a word. He had not realised that the person for whose benefit he was telling the story had handed over the telephone receiver to a servant. The servant was only responding with a periodic "Hoon", "Hoon", at Dardi's prodding. I kept this as secret for about four years. Then, I told Rao, the disastrous effects of long telephonic conversations. But still it had no effect.

Colourful Differences between the Languages

The Superintendent of Police is required, under the rules to inspect all the police stations, in his District once a year. Earlier as a bachelor, I used to go on tours, all alone. After marriage, my wife was my constant companion, on tours as well as for walks. As every State has its mannerisms, in Mysore the women are called "Ammas" which, in my mother tongue (Punjabi) means an old woman or a grandmother. My wife got used to it, after an initial hesitation. I was reminded, of the differences between the languages, during my visit to Indonesia in 1976. I wanted tea. In many countries tea means only the tea brew and not tea with milk and sugar as we drink in India. When I asked for tea Solo, with milk and sugar, nobody could understand it. Ultimately I was successful in tracing an Indonesian, who could understand what kind of tea I wanted. He said that I should ask for Tea with "Susu", the equivalent of milk in Indonesian language. I did ask for the tea with Sugar and "Susu" and I got what I really wanted. But "Susu" in Punjabi and also in Hindi means urine. It is an often -used word, for a baby's urine. During the official tours, the biggest battles, used to be with the mosquitoes. The mosquitoes, would be on the lookout, to gain an entry into the mosquito nets. Their strategy and numbers were infinite. Without mosquito nets, it was impossible to sleep. Most of the mosquito nets kept in the Government tourists bungalows were either torn or damaged. We would take our own mosquito nets along with the bedding on tours. This was the only way to dodge the mosquitoes.

Boiled water was another item, to be necessarily carried, on tours. The water was brackish and in some places contained guinea worms. It is a kind of worm, which gets into the body, and comes out from the ankle after travelling the whole length of the body. This was more common and prevalent in my previous posting as an Assistant Superintendent of Police, Indi, in Bijapur District. The whole district of Bidar, had water works, supplying water only in five places including four Tehsils and the District Headquarters. The rest of the District had to be on its own and manage, whatever, water it could have locally.

8

Serving in Punjab

ADC to the Governor

Towards the end of 1967, late, Dr D.C. Pavate, the Vice-Chancellor of Dharwar University was appointed as the Governor of Punjab. During my earned leave in December, 1967, I visited the Chandigarh Raj Bhawan to call on him. The Governor had earlier expressed a wish, that I should be appointed, as his ADC. The advantage to the Governor, would be my knowledge, of two states Punjab and Karnataka, as well as familiarity, with languages of my native state and the state of my adoption. He asked me again whether I would be willing to join him in Chandigarh. I said it would be an honour to do so. He took up the matter with the Governments of Punjab and Karnataka and my services were loaned to the Government of Punjab. I joined him on 2nd April, 1968 after relinquishing charge in Bidar.

In Bidar my wife was feeling lonely, as I was busy with my job. One day, when we were sitting outside in the lawn, in 1967 January, she said that she had one ambition in her life, which had not been fulfilled. I enquired as to what it was. She replied that she had always wanted to appear for the Allied Services, Examination. Her last chance was only in September/October, 1967. She had done her, M.Sc. in Zoology. Somehow I had a belief that only the Arts people, especially MAs' in English, which I had done, could be selected for the IAS examinations. I said "Try your luck." She sent in her forms. She worked very hard and qualified in the written examination, much to my surprise. She was interviewed for the IAS and missed IAS by 3 marks. Candidates securing less marks, than her in the total, had made it to the IAS in 1966 examination. But from 1967, 25 per cent seats had been reserved for the demobilised ex-servicemen. They had to appear only in three, against normally eight papers, for general candidates. She was disappointed, as her name did not figure in the IAS list. Some of my friends, who had tried their luck for the IAS earlier did not succeed. However, through the category of demobilised ex-servicemen, they made it to the IAS.

My wife found her name very high in the Central Services List. She secured 27th position out of more than 405 candidates selected as a result of the same examination. In fact she was higher in the All India Merit of the Central Services than her brother Berinder Singh. Berinder had earlier joined the IPS through 1966 examination. In the 1967 examination, he got a much lower position, compared to his elder sister and my wife. He preferred to choose the Indian Revenue Service as against the Indian Information Service chosen by Surinder..

Clash Between the Governor and CM

Unlike the District Chief who has a distinct work of his own and a clear-cut sphere of duty, the duties of the Raj Bhawan staff are mostly ceremonial. As ADC, my job was, mostly hanging around the Governor, and keeping his appointments. There was no file work. The files of the State Government, were routed through, the Secretary to the Governor. The ADC had generally, to make himself pleasant and acceptable to the Governor. In my case, I had to act as an interpreter also, from Punjabi for convenience of the Governor. The Governor knew neither Punjabi nor Hindi, while most of the Ministers of the Punjab Government did not know any language, other than Punjabi. When I joined the Governor of Punjab, Sardar Lachman Singh Gill headed the State Government. Gill had defected from the Shiromani Akail Dal Government, headed by late Sardar Gurnam Singh. He formed a minority Government with the Congress Party, extending support from outside. One of the populist steps taken by the State Government was to make Punjabi the official language with effect from 13th April 1968. It had the dual effect of legitimising the use of Punjabi......the only language known to the Ministers of the late Lachman Singh Gill Ministry and Gill himself, and giving an upper hand to the Ministers who could officially ask all matters to be put up to them in Punjabi. It was felt, that this measure would win them popular support.

Chief Minister, Lachman Singh Gill had a robust common sense. Having been a PWD contractor, he realised the importance, of link roads for the villages. It was he, who started the programme, of linking all the villages with the big Mandis (market towns). But he had another side to his personality , which was not to the liking of many. He would streamroll his views and orders. It was during his Ministry, that one former Deputy Minister of the Government of Punjab was found guilty of beating college students. The Deputy Minister, beat them with a hockey stick, because they had heckled him, during his speech. The Minister was axed. Few weeks afterwards the CM wanted to reinstate the Deputy Minister. In June, 1968, a message was received that a swearing should be arranged. As the message was from the office of the Chief Minister, I went upstairs to the residential portion of the Governor, to inform him of the request of the C.M. The unique feature of the Lachman Singh Gill Ministry, was that it was the Ministry of defectors only. When I told the Governor that necessary arrangements had been made, he said : "Please request the Chief Minister to come and see me first." The arrangements for the swearing in at the Raj Bhawan were simple. A public address system would be installed in a tent and tea and biscuits would be provided. The austerity drive had been taken up very seriously in the Raj Bhawan. All the expenses were kept to the minimum. I requested the Chief Minister to come and meet the Governor about the swearing in. He asked me whether he should come all alone or bring the prospective Minister with him. I said that it would be better if he came all alone. Nonetheless, the Chief Minister had sent a new car for, "the would be Deputy Minister. The Chief Minister came and met the Governor. As both (Governor and Chief Minister) did not know any common languages, so, I had to act as an interpreter. Arguments went on some thing like this. The Chief Minister said that it was his right to make anybody a Minister in the Government. The Governor said that it may be so, but he was not going to swear in the gentleman concerned as a Deputy Minister. The Chief Minister pleaded with the Governor calling him "Dady", as the full name of the Governor was Dada Sahib

Chintamani Pavate. This also had no softening effect on the Governor. Then the Chief Minister threatened to have the Governor transferred, using his clout with the then Home Minister Y.B. Chavan. The Governor said that he was not after any office and would perform, what he considered his constitutional duty. He also said that he had not canvassed for the job of the Governor. In fact it was the then Chief Minister of Karnataka, who had persuaded him to accept the job. The Chief Minister of Punjab then used a bullying tactic. He said that he had consulted "Chavan Sahib" who had said that a Governor was nothing more than a rubber stamp. He had to stamp and sign wherever the Chief Minister wanted him to sign and stamp. The Governor said that he may be a rubber stamp, but in this case, he was not going to budge an inch, for stamping where Chief Minister, wanted him to stamp.

Changing tune once again, the Chief Minister also told the Governor that he needed the support of each MLA, especially because his defector colleagues had joined him only in the hope of becoming Ministers. The Governor said that he knew his position very well, but as a Constitutional authority he was expected to be true to his oath. He would be going against his oath, if he swore an unfit person, to be a Minister. The Chief Minister said that if the Governor did not accept his request, he would have no option but ask his industrialist friends from Ludhiana to look after, and compensate sufficiently, the candidate for Dy. Ministership. This threatening and cajoling went on for about two hours without either side yielding. But the Governor stuck to his guns and the Chief Minister had to back out.

Victory of the Chief Minister

Chief Minister Gill was cut up with the Governor. On one occasion, he pulled up the Secretary to the Governor, right before the Governor. The Governor's aide was hauled up, for all the unnecessary delays and the queries made by the Raj Bhawan on the proposals sent by the Government, for the formal approval of the Governor. The Chief Minister told the Secretary to the Governor, that there were several Secretaries before him, with the Governor, but none had created any problems, as he had done. The Governor just smiled and said nothing. Once on a "At Home" in connection with the Independence day, 1968, the Chief Minister openly and brazenly told the Governor that the standard of hospitality of the Raj Bhawan had fallen. Even on important occasions "simple items" like fish and chips were missing. The Governor pointed out that since his sumptuary allowance was fixed by an Act of Parliament, he could not exceed the budget allocated for the same. The Chief Minister said that the State Government would be happy to arrange all functions through the State hospitality Department. The Governor declined saying that it would be going against the spirit of the Act of Parliament. Once Chief Minister Lachman Singh Gill created history, by getting appointed a State Civil Service Officer, as a member of the State Public Commission. There is nothing wrong with any appointment of a State Civil Service Officer! The appointment was more resented. by the Secretary to the Governor. The Secretary felt that all such jobs were almost informally reserved for retired IAS officers. There was a long que, of the retired IAS officers, to the Secretary to the Governor, for the jobs in State Public Commission. He tried to persuade the Governor to reject the proposal, but without success. The Chief Minister went a step further when he proposed the appointment of the same officer as a Chairman of the State Public Service Commission, on a salary equivalent to that of the Chief Secretary. Here also the Secretary tried his best, to get the proposal spiked by the Governor, but to no avail. The Chief Minister met the Governor personally and got the proposal cleared. The stalling efforts did not end here. Obstacles were put through the Accountant General. A letter was got issued, that the officer who had been appointed as a Chairman of the State Public Service Commission, could not draw salary equivalent to that of the Chief Secretary. At best he could get Rs 200 as special pay over and above his own last drawn pay. No pay slip was issued to the Chairman of the State Public Service Commission. The State Cabinet passed a resolution, saying that the salary and allowance to the members and the Chairman of the State Public Service Commission would be payable by an Executive order of the Government and not on the authority of the Accountant General. Thus, the attempts of the Secretary, to overrule the Chief Minister, through the smoke-screen of the Governor did not succeed. The Governor did record a note of disapproval to the proposals, on the pressure of the Secretary. But he approved the proposal. The entire trouble arises because of vested interests of services to guard their turf.

ADC Touring with the Governor

A Governor gets importance during his tour more out of courtesy and deference than for any other reasons. Only for such functions, where people are unable to get the Chief Minister or other Ministers, the Governor is the last refuge. In fact days would pass, without anybody coming to meet the Governor. During the periods when a popularly elected Government is ruling, the role of the Governor is only ceremonial . The only regular visitors at that time are the Vice-chancellors of the Universities in the State, as Governor is their Chancellor. Being an academician, Pavate felt more at home with the people from the Universities, than with politicians. While passing through a place, the Governor would suddenly ask its name,-the population, and the main profession of the people there. It was difficult to remember, the details of the places in the State. But at the same time, the Governor did not expect, his ADC, to be a dumb creature. So I memorised the complete details of all the important towns, like, population, history, state of industrialisation and educational level. I did this to enable me to answer any query the Governor may make during the journey by car. This continued for a long time. Many times the name and details of a place were given by me as the details of the other. There was no chance of the Governor either verifying or even remembering what he had asked. It is said that at one occasion, during the British rule, one visitor was introduced to the Governor of Punjab as Mr Brown. The visitor tried to correct the ADC by saying that he was not Brown, but John. The ADC took him to the side and said "Mr. John you have been introduced to His Excellency the Governor as Brown and Brown, you shall be, as long as you are in the Government House." I suggested to the Governor, for asking the Deputy Commissioners and the District Superintendents of Police or Senior Superintendents of Police, over for a meal, during his visits to the Districts. This was a welcome innovation and was appreciated by the District Officers. The Governor got first hand information of what was happening in the State. During his visits to Delhi, the Governor used to invite himself to stay in Delhi The format of the communication sent to the President used to be something like this when the Governor had to visit Delhi:

"Dear Rashtrapatiji"

I propose to visit Delhi from ....to.... If there be no objection I propose to stay in Rashtrapati Bhawan."

Once or twice, I expressed my reservation on the format, saying that it tantamounted to almost inviting yourself to stay at Rashtrapati Bhawan. As the letters used to be put up by a Major, called the Military Secretary, I did not press for any change. The Major was a matriculate only. No better draft could be expected from him.

The practice of staying at Rashtrapati Bhawan continued for some months. One day suddenly the Governor said that "During our visits to Delhi, we will stay in the State Government Guest House at Kapurthala House." May be and perhaps rightly the Governor felt that he would feel more at home in the guest house of the State Government. In the Rashtrapati Bhawan, everything went with a military precision, and not necessarily, as desired by a visiting Governor. The Governor also mentioned that in the State Government Guest House, he could entertain visitors and other guests, at any time he liked and also have the food of his own choice. At Rashtrapati Bhawan, he had to go by whatever menu was there for the day. The Raj Bhawan, in Chandigarh, was both his office and residence.

Governor Pavate, was always cheerful and smiling. But he did not like too many policemen or security arrangements, around him. The Raj Bhawan continued to be heavily over-staffed. For instance there used to be one category of employees who used to be called "Masalchis". Their job was to prepare Masalas or condiments for the vegetables to be cooked in the Raj Bhawan. Another category of employees was assigned the responsibility of cleaning the glasses of windows and doors of Raj Bhawan. Still another category was responsible for shining brass in the Raj Bhawan. The work was compartmentalised in Raj Bhawan. For instance the Assistant Khidmatgar, could bring the food for service, only upto the entrance of the Dining Hall. The Khidmatgar would serve from the entrance door near to the dining table. Only the Head Khidmatgar had the privilege of serving the Governor.

Frills of the Raj Bhavan

I suggested to the Governor that at least half the staff of Raj Bhavan could be cut out without impairing on the efficiency. The Governor did not respond to the suggestion. After a few days, I again reminded him. He felt that it was the duty of the Government to provide employment. He would not cut any jobs in the Raj Bhavan. The Raj Bhavan functioned as almost a Guest House but only for the VIP's. The Governor would meet them, generally on one meal, either at breakfast or at lunch. Though over staffed to a great extent, it was a well run establishment, costing a fraction, of what the Kings, in the past spent on themselves. Its accounts were subjected to the audit. The Governor of Punjab had an Estate named "Dane's Folly" in Simla. It was the summer retreat of the Governor. It was acquired, by one Mr. Dane, during the British rule. The Estate had a few fruit trees. The amount realized from the sale of the fruits was credited to the Government treasury. The family of one of the former Governor (now deceased) of Punjab, treated the fruit trees, as their personal property. They pocketed the proceeds of the sale of fruits. The audit rightly objected to it, but the amount had to be written off as the concerned "His Excellency" had passed away long ago. In another case, the family of an ex-Governor, while leaving the Raj Bhawan, had packed a few costly items, like chandelliers, carpets, and silver. These could not be retrieved despite the best efforts. When all these instances were brought to the notice of the then Governor of Punjab, Dr. Pavate, he expressed dismay at the falling standards. It is appalling to observe, how the public figures, misappropriate the Government property as their own, without as much as by your leave. During the President's rule in Punjab, the pressure of people wanting to meet the Governor increased tremendously. Dr. Pavate had given me strict instructions, that not more than three of four interviews should be fixed for him in a day. One day I asked for his permission to include a few more persons in the interview list. He very honestly and candidly said that it won't serve any purpose. He said that he won't be able to retain, anything which might transpire during the interview, due to his old age.

The family of the Governor staying with him consisted of his wife and two grand daughters. His youngest daughter joined the Medical College at Patiala. Neither the Governor nor his family put any extra demands on the Raj Bhawan staff than what they were entitled to. The Governor did try to learn Punjabi by engaging a tutor. But it did not go very far. However, it did him some good, as he was no longer completely at sea with the Punjabi language.

Imposition of the President's Rule

For political reasons, the Congress party withdrew the support extended to the Lachman Singh Gill Ministry, after a few months. There was no option for the Governor except to recommend the imposition of the President's Rule in the state, till fresh elections were held. The Governor along with his personal staff used to spend the hottest part of the summer in Simla. The entire Punjab Government Guest House was reserved for the Governor and his party at Simla. I along with my wife, Surinder accompanied the Governor to Simla. The arrangements on payment basis were excellent. Even the Governor paid for his family and for himself.

IPS versus IAS : An Unending Discussion

The battles, between the haves and have-nots, have continued, in one form or the other, in almost all spheres of life. The senior officer's boss over their juniors. Juniors boss over their juniors, and juniors over the junior mosts. Similarly in the Government service, the Have Service (the IAS), which is the successor service to the Indian Civil Service has maintained its stranglehold not only on the country's administration but also on all other services. Only its privileged members, can occupy the positions of power. Their cadre structure and postings brings them close to the Chief Ministers and Prime Minister and other Ministers. They get their promotion, with almost clockwise regularity, even if there are no vacancies. The service orders its own promotions and manages its cadre. Only its members, are the cadre controlling authorities of other services. In almost all the States with a few exceptions, the annual confidential reports of the members of the other State Services and also All India Services are written by the IAS Officers.

Punjab is one State where the Deputy Commissioners

did not write the Annual Confidential reports of the District Superintendents. Determined efforts were made by its IAS cadre changing the rules. Most of them felt, that the only way to check the police, was by writing the Annual Confidential Report of the IPS Officers. These efforts had been thwarted by the IPS Officers. One such effort was made during the President's Rule, in 1968/1969 when late Dr D.C. Pavate was the Governor of Punjab. The combined might of Secretariat with the help of the Secretary to the Governor who himself was an IAS officer, lobbied for bringing about this change. Eventually, the Governor passed orders changing the Rules for writing the Confidential Reports of the IPS officers

Before the orders were issued, the Director General of Police as he is called now, and Inspector General of Police as he was called at that time; came to know about it. Infact I had told the IG, about the latest orders about to be issued. He promptly called on the Governor, Kanwar Shamsher Singh, the then IGP Punjab explained to the Governor, that such a step, would deal a deadly blow to the discipline and morale of the force. He also said, that such efforts and suggestions, in the past had been rightly rejected, by the previous popular Governments. He argued, that it would lead to bitterness in the relations, between the two important services in the State. The Governor agreed with the IGP and replied that he was given an impression that he (the IGP) had concurred with the proposal. The IGP himself was shocked and said that this subject was never discussed with him. There was no question, of his agreement, with any such proposal. He advised the Governor, that it would be better, if such important subjects were discussed with him. He also told the Governor, that as the people around him, were from IAS, he was getting only, one-sided version, of any proposal concerning IPS in particular, and other services in general. He informed the Governor that at no time any Chief Secretary or Home Secretary at the Centre or in States had been from the IPS. This was one reason, why the case of the IPS and other services went by default. Here both the accused and the appellate authority were the same. There were glaring differences, in the service conditions, of the IPS and the IAS, though theoretically, both were All-India Services. This was, because one controlled the other, through the Secretariat. The Governor having been a non-IAS saw merit in the argument. He directed, that the matter be kept in abeyance as the elections were hardly two weeks away. The Governor said the matter should be decided by the elected government. There seemed, to be no other way out, except the frontal attack by the IGP. He had pointed out that this service baiting had been going on for a long time and as the head of the Indian Police Service (Punjab) cadre, it was his duty to bring the correct picture to the notice of the Governor.

Powers of DMs and SPs

Under the law, the authority to detain a person, under all statutes, rests with the District Magistrate, all over the country. The exception is, the areas of metropolitan cities like Delhi, Mumbai, Chennai and Calcutta and a few other places where the system of Commissioner of Police, has been introduced. The District Magistrate system functions leisurely. Its pace of work is very slow. The delay in dealing with the sensitive law and order situations can be disastrous especially, when problems require on the spot decisions. It is only for the above reason that the powers of the District Magistrate and the Police have been combined in the Commissioner of Police.

The present policing set up, is based on the Police Act of 1861, framed by the British Government. Despite the recommendations of the National Police Commission suggesting a new Police Act, more than three decades ago, the matter has remained where it was. It essentially boils down, to shedding the powers, vested in the District Magistrate, in favour of those, actually concerned with Policing. The people, who have the power and authority do not want to shed the same. It leads to an anachronistic position. It is the exclusive privilege, of only one service to be the advisors, critical examiners and also the Government. It does not suit it to change. The position has remained unchanged, notwithstanding many reforms, commission or Committees recommendations. A simple problem is made complicated and complex on paper. Only one favoured point of view can be put up.

Despite the difficulties and handicaps, it must be said to

the credit of the Indian Administrative Service, that it has provided a trained cadre of generalists. They have handled, almost any job, assigned to them, reasonably well. Its very structure, enables the young entrants, to be chiefs of their charge, from the day one, after their training. The result is the development of confidence, capacity to handle different and disparate situations. They also function, as impartial umpires, between other services and departments. Their role, is the subject of universal discussion and often condemnation from other services. May be it has its lacunae, but any system better than the existing one has still to be thought and worked out. Several times, condemnation is the result of envy, coupled with a feeling of deprivation, of promotion and other perks not enjoyed by the members of other services. In fact, many officials belonging to services, other than the IAS have admitted privately, that they get better treatment, and fair play from the IAS, than from their own bosses, belonging to their own service. A young IPS officer had excellent relation with a colleague, only one year senior to him in the same service. The senior IPS officer, later on occupied a very important position in assessing and placing other officers in Central Police Organisations. The two officials, had known each other for the last three decades, and were on the first name terms. The junior expected that in view of his outstanding service and record in the most difficult areas of the country, he would have no problems for a job at the Centre. But to his surprise, he found it was his closest friend, who had taken exception, to his being addressed, by the first name. He had taken it, out on him, in the assessment board meeting. He recommended that he was unsuitable for the higher job. The officer mentioned to me, that he did not expect this, from his close friend when the entire board was in his favour. However, the board cleared his name for the higher assignment. Such instances are there in all higher services including the IAS. The major advantage in the IAS is, that it is generally, not a hierarchical service. There is enough room on the top for everybody.

Green Revolution in Punjab

Green revolution in Punjab was almost coincidental with the arrival of late Dr. D.C. Pavate as the Governor of Punjab. The farmers of Punjab, have always been innovative and progressive. The improved varieties of seeds called Kalyan and Sona had been introduced in Punjab in 1966-67. As a result, the yield of wheat, which used to be hardly five quintals per acre, rose to as much as twenty to thirty quintals. The higher yielding variety seeds, were so much in demand, that the Deputy Commissioners of the District used to distribute the same in driblets. My batchmate, K.S. Bains, the Deputy Commissioner, of my District, allotted five kgs of Kalyan variety of seeds, to my father. It yielded a crop of about 20 quintals of seeds. It was enough for our requirements in the next season. The result was that the wheat harvest was a bumper one in the years 1969-70 bringing in real prosperity. There was no looking back, after the green revolution. The prosperity exhibited itself in various forms. There was a construction boom in the villages and the purchase of latest agricultural gadgets, including tractors and tube wells. It also had disastrous effect on the morals and the drinking habits of the neo rich. It increased the rate of corruption in public dealing offices. The corrupt also benefited from increase in money supply, as they hiked up illegal gratification rates. The policemen enjoyed a unique position in the rural area. They were more feared, than respected, for their nuisance value. They had the power to haul up anybody. They were practically, the master of all they surveyed, in the rural area. In view of the generally insecure conditions prevailing, the landed gentry, or "gentleman farmers" depended heavily on the police. Like their city brethren, they all wanted the police, to help in disciplining the hired labour. The labour would take in advance, wages of whole year and then disappear. It was the clout of the "gentleman farmer" with the police, which would put more fear, into them than any legal court processes. Moreover, the illegal distillation is now a part of National culture. Punjab was and is no exception. The bootleggers were scared of the police patrolling. The cottage industry, of illicit liquor was and is thriving, in many villages. It provided gainful occupation to the unemployed though it is illegal.

9

From Punjab to National Capital

Appointment as Chief Security Officer

My wife, Surinder on her selection in 1968, was offered the Indian Information Service. She joined for training in Delhi, in October, 1968. As 90 per cent jobs, of the Indian Information Service, were in Delhi, I made a request to the Governor for my posting in Delhi. It took nearly ten months, to get a job in Delhi in September, 1969 as Chief Security Officer in the Home Ministry. The job involved supervising the work of a Chaukidara force not governed under any law or Statute. The Force called Secretariat Security Force consisted of people recruited from the open market. They had no training and had a trade union of their own.Like other organised Central Civil Services, they performed duty only for the prescribed hours 39 hours per week. Beyond that, overtime allowance had to be paid. In a uniformed force concerned with the maintenance of law and order and VIP security, the job has to be done, according to the task and not according to the clock. My predecessor told me, not to enforce any discipline. He said, that the force never had any training. It was never subjected to any discipline. I should not rake up any controversy by insisting on them to attend the parade or P.T. He advised me that a cardinal principle in life is not to rock the boat. If you do that you may also be thrown overboard. He advised me, to forget all the ideas, of improving the force. The system is so big, and consultations in the system, so long winded and so many, that hardly anything comes out of any efforts made, to bring about the changes for the better. He said that he appreciated my desire for improvements and enthusiasm. Someday later, in the career I would realise, the value of his advice and observations. Since I was his understudy for two weeks and he was still the Chief Security Officer, I kept my counsel to myself. I had no intention to be a dummy.

Secretariat Security Force : An Unarmed Force

The organisation I was heading was called a Force only by courtesy. It was unarmed. It had no weapons, no vehicles and no supervisory staff except the Chief Security Officer. The recruitment to it, was either at the sepoy or peon level. Only its Chief was on deputation. It functioned as a part of the Home Ministry, under the charge of a Joint Secretary. A force to be effective, has to have basics, like smart uniform, weapons and communication, apart from a good command structure. During my checking, I found that some members, were wearing unpolished shoes. I questioned them as to why they did not polish their shoes. I was informed, that the Government was not supplying, the polish and the brush. So no sepoy felt under obligation to spend his own money on the shoes. I initiated a case for sanctioning to each member of the force two tins of polish and one brush per year. It took me six months and repeated visits to the Finance Division, to make them see the need of the above items. The first query was, that what was the neccessity for having these items? Second was, how they had been managing the turn out so far without the polish and the brush. The third was, didn't everybody have his own tins of polish and brush for his shoes? The fourth was as to how it will be ensured that the polish and the brush supplied was not misused. The fifth was as to what arrangements would be made for the safe custody of the above items? The sixth query, was whether it was possible to cut down the supply or defer the purchase of the items to the next financial year? When all queries were exhausted and those asked answered, the Finance Division agreed to the supply of the boot polish. For reasons of economy, it did not agree to supply the shoe brush for polishing the shoes. The repeated pleas, that how could you give polish and not the brush, did not evoke any response. When pressed more strongly to sanction the brush along with the polish, I was informally advised not to press the issue. It was quite likely, that due to economy orders, even the sanction for the two small tins of polish per year, would be withdrawn. I was only a Superintendent of Police. My status in the Home Ministry was that of an Under Secretary. It was difficult even to meet the Joint Secretary, who had no time for small matters pertaining to the security of the Ministry and Government of India Offices. The meeting with the Secretary was almost a meeting with the God Almighty himself. During my whole tenure, I could not see the Secretary, one L.P. Singh, even once. I did attempt in the first few weeks of joining to call on the Home Secretary, but did not succeed. I put a proposal that SSF must have a vehicle of its own to be used for night and odd time checking and for transporting men in times of need. I said that the strong force of 800 men should have its own transport fleet. The proposal was summarily rejected. Instead, I was advised to use my own car, maintain a log book and claim the conveyance allowance on the basis of average three months' mileage. Here I was asking for a vehicle for Government work. No staff car of the Home Ministry was ever made available to an officer of the level of Under Secretary at that time.

I accepted the challenge. I did the checking and started P.T. and Parade for the force. However, except on the first day, when the attendance was good, subsequently, it tapered off because people had to come either by buses or on their cycles for the morning P.T. and Parade. When I called for the explanation of the absentees, a petition was sent against me to the Home Secretary saying that I was cruel in making people attend P.T. and Parade. Instead I had to explain the circumstances under which I started P.T. and Parade for men. I was not deterred by any frivolous and ridiculous complaint against me. I took it as a challenge, to impress upon, the higher ups to discipline such a force. I suggested, that an unarmed and practically untrained force is worse than useless for security duty. I also urged that there were no telephones within the reach of the sentries on duty. The SSF was looking after the security of 32 buildings, including those located in South Block, North Block, Shastri Bhavan, Yojna Bhavan, Sardar Patel Bhavan and others. I was told that I could continue with the parade and P.T. as if it was a personal favour to me. As a result of my pointing out, the deficiencies in the security setup, an order was issued indicating that, in security matters, which needed the guidance of a professional,

I should consult K.F. Rustomji, the then Director General of Border Security Force in 1970. It was a welcome change. I found it easier, to interact with a senior police officer. He knew, more than anybody else, in the Home Ministry, about security and policing. Rustomji was tied down, to putting the relatively newly created force, i.e. the Border Security Force, on a firm footing. I was invited by him, to attend his weekly meetings with officers of the BSF and present my difficulties. At the first meeting itself I convinced Rustomji that if the security duties were to be properly performed, the SSF must be merged with a force created under an Act or Law. It should also be properly trained. There was a bomb blast, in one of the Government of India Offices, outside Delhi. I seized upon the incident, as an opportunity to highlight, the importance of improving the force and security scenario. I suggested that the SSF be merged with the Central Reserve Police Force as it was an armed force of the Union. The advantage would be that the members of the SSF would get a better pay scale. They would be properly officered, commanded and equipped. This proposal aroused a lot of opposition from within the SSF. Its members felt, that they would be subjected to a very rigorous discipline. They would be put through an intensive training. The trade union of the force opposed the proposal. The Home Ministry referred the matter to the CRPF Director General. He did not agree for its merger, as hardly 10 per cent people would qualify to meet its (CRP's)rigorous standards. It so happens in government, that once something is sanctioned or given, rarely it is withdrawn or cancelled. The SSF having been set up, is continuing even now after four decades. But the only difference is that due to security reasons the armed component and the teeth are provided by the armed Central Reserve Police Force. It is posted along with SSF at the gates of the Ministries requiring a high degree of security in New Delhi.

The SSF was charged with the duty of regulating entry to the various Ministries and Departments of the Government of India. Its main job was to check the passes issued to all the Central Government Employees working in the Security Zone and issued by the Chief Security Officer. Those who had misplaced or lost their passes were issued temporary passes by the Reception Wing of the Secretariat Security Organisation. All the Ministries which had the SSF posted to guard and regulate the entry of the visitors also had reception offices manned by the official of the Secretariat Security Organisation.

As per the Government of India instructions, only the officers of the rank of Under Secretary and above, are allowed to receive visitors. The drill was that whenever a visitor came to meet an officer of the rank of Under Secretary or above, the reception officer would ring up the officer concerned to confirm whether he wanted to receive a particular visitor or not. Only if the concerned official was willing, a reception pass was issued to the visitor. The visitor, would be escorted by a peon, to the room of the officer concerned. The concerned official had to sign a portion of the reception pass, in token of having met the visitor. The pass portion, signed by the receiving officer, would have to be returned to the Reception Officer. But in actual practice when a visitor obtained an entry pass, he could see anybody, in the building. This was because each Reception Officer had been assigned only one peon. Sometimes, even that post was not filled up. One peon, could escort, only one visitor at a time. On an average about 150 to 300 visitors used to visit various Ministries and Departments where the SSF was posted. Senior Government officials were reluctant to sport their identity pass, at the time of visiting any building in the security zone. Many complaints were received, saying that harassment was caused by unnecessary checking of the senior officials. Some demanded from the Sentries, the authority to check their identity cards. The identity card in vogue before my arrival was an anachronism. It contained the particulars of the individuals on one side. On the reverse side, was the photograph, of the pass holder. For a conscientious checking, the identity card had to be seen from both sides. This caused avoidable delay. I designed a new card which had all the particulars of the individual as well as the photograph on one side and general instructions and the signatures on the other. I am happy to record, that the same design of the card, I had introduced in 1970-71 is continuing even now. Once a very senior Central Government Minister, who believed that everybody knew him very well in the country, was stopped by a sentry, while entering Krishi Bhawan. He was asked to show his identity card. To be courteous and polite, the sentry first, saluted him and then requested him to produce his identity card. The Minister's personal staff interfered and so he was allowed inside the building on the strength of a temporary reception pass. Immediately a complaint was made to me that the sentry was unnecessaril officious. After inquiry I found that the sentry was not to be blamed and so I politely but courteously informed the gentleman concerned that the sentry had done his duty.

Fear of Transfer

A very senior officer told me that he did not go on tour for fear of being transferred. He said, he had to defend his position, or in other words, the chair he was occupying. He was afraid of his colleagues as well as his ambitious subordinates, who were keen to replace him. He would go on tour only on holidays. He said that the present system of administration was a replica of beheading the head of the ruler, in the old Mughal tradition. He said that his ambition was to retire as the Chief. I asked him, as to what difference, it would make, if he retired from an equivalent position. He had no answer. I told him that all the trappings of his office, would disappear in less than a year. After that none of his subordinates, would take him seriously. He did not believe, that all those, who were fawning on him, and treating his words, as pearls of wisdom would not even receive his phone calls. In fact so keen was he to maintain his importance, that as soon as he retired, he gave his address and telephone numbers to all his old subordinates. He told me, a year later, that I was right and nobody had remembered him on the New Year. Earlier, he had no time to reply to all greetings which he received or even the phone calls. Now, he was almost craving for recognition. After some years of his retirement, he realised the true assessment of the man, is the qualities of leadership and gentlemanliness one really possesses and not the weight of office one is able to throw about for a few months or years of one's life.

Rude Bosses

During my spell as Chief Security Officer in the Home Ministry, I was deputed to study the security arrangements, of the office of the Accountant General of Allahabad, and suggest ways and means for improving the same. The then Accountant General, had confused security with toning up, the efficiency of his office. The two do not necessarily go together. They have distinct and separate spheres. The real problem, as it turned out, was that his subordinates, were neither punctual nor discharging their duties efficiently. The Accountant General, in his desire to improve the running of his office, wanted people to come in time and earn an honest day's wages. He felt that, by introducing strict security arrangements, he could discipline the staff as well as make them punctual. In Delhi, at my instance, the Ministries, having security arrangements, periodically would check their staff, with the help of SSF. For the offices opening at 10 a.m., the checking would start at 10 a.m., The Ministry officials would note down, the names of the late comers. The security staff would check their passes, to confiscate the old expired passes, which were still being used either by the retired employees or by the employees who had not renewed the same. I explained to the Accountant General, that the introduction of the pass system for entry to the office would not necessarily improve either the punctuality or the efficiency or the discipline of the office. When told that the role of the Security was limited to the extent of preventing damage to the office and office equipment, and not of disciplining or coercing the staff, he gave up the idea of introducing security in his office. The Joint Secretary, dealing with SSF was one of the most cheerless and a melancholy person. Those who were working with him for years had not seen him smiling. I was determined that I would break his defences, and make him take interest in the SSF. I asked him for about 20 minutes of time, to discuss the problems of SSF, on any day convenient to him. He put me off for more than a month. So every time I met him in corridors of the North Block, I reminded him that the security set up needed strengthening, and I was waiting to put across my suggestions to him. Ultimately, he relented and gave me time on a Sunday. In the meeting, I pointed out the urgent necessity of procuring at least one light transport vehicle. I also informed him that earlier proposals sent to the Finance Ministry had been turned down at the Under Secretary level. It is strange, but true that anybody at any level can, say no to any sensible proposal. There is no accountability, for rejecting the most urgent and deserving proposal. Instead of saying that the Government cannot afford, the proposals are faulted with by making frivolous piecemeal queries. If you reply to one set of irrelevant queries, another bunch comes, close on the heels. The fate of transport, for SSF had met the same misfortune. The proposal did not go beyond the Under Secretary's level. There is a queer logic in the Finance Ministry. It feels, that its job is to put brakes on all expenditure. It does so, by not saying that no funds are available. It does so, by examining and educating itself, not on the intrinsic merits, but on the proposal itself. Those sanctioning the schemes or the proposals have not seen the field. They have no idea of, what is wanted or required in the field. But they are the paper experts, in picking holes, in the proposals intended, to solve the problems they know nothing about.

The proposal initiated and supported by the then Joint Secretary was turned down. It involved an expenditure of about Rs 20,000 for purchase of a jeep. It made him furious. He sent for the Deputy Secretary Finance and told him that unless the proposal was agreed to he would reject all the proposals of the Finance Ministry. Under the instruction of Government of India, though the Finance Ministry was the Ministry sanctioning the proposals of all other Ministries, its own proposals had to be cleared by the Home Ministry. The Home Ministry, was the Finance Ministry for the Finance. Joint Secretary (Administration), MHA was the Joint Secretary (Finance) for the Finance Ministry. This had the desired effect and the proposal to purchase a jeep was agreed to, post haste. This again proved, that it is not the merit of the proposal which is important. The level, from which it emanates, is more important. The same proposal initiated had been turned down earlier. Now the same proposal, with arms twisting was accepted. This system continues in one form or the other at all levels of the Government even now.

There is no sign of its changing. The only change has been that, the names of individuals have changed. But there is no change in the attitudes and approach. Mind set, is the same even now.

The persistent indiscipline, the attitude of trade unionism and bargaining for duty hours made me impatient. I found that I was unable to bring about any worthwhile improvement and qualitative change. Since in the hierarchy I was only equated with an Under Secretary with eight years of service, I felt frustrated. From the point of view of service conditions, it was an excellent job. Nobody bothered you, if you did not bother seniors, with any proposals for improvements or reforms. I was unable to countenance the situation. I should have realised, I now say, with a hindsight that reforms or improvements, do not take place, because you think they are essential. There is always resistance to change. As young men new in service, we wish to see immediate results. That was the case with me also. Reforms cannot be brought about, only by the youth. Patience and persistence are also required. I was persistent but not patient enough, to wait for years together, with folded hands for the proposals to be sanctioned. This obviously had annoyed Home Ministry senior officials. They planned for my ouster from the job, when I was on leave. On return from leave, I found myself in need of another job, because in my absence another officer was not only posted, but he had taken charge of my job. I was happy to change the job, but not the graceless way it was done, without even any notice. I was to notice the same thing happening to the people who had reached the highest offices in my later career. In one case when a Secretary was away to a foreign country, he on his return found that his successor had taken over his charge. It was with some difficulty and hesitation that he could retrieve his personal belongings from that office. It happened to me again, as Director, CBI, when the then Prime Minister, Gujral, got annoyed with me for not bailing out the President of his Party and the then Chief Minister of Bihar. I did not grumble, on my transfer. It took me more than a month before I could be placed in the Central Bureau of Investigation, as the Superintendent of Police.

Posting in the CBI

I was very excited when I joined the CBI in 1971. Actually the legal name of this organisation was and continues to be the Special Police Establishment. It was created during the British rule, to deal with the offences of corruption, incidental to purchases during the Second World War. But somewhere in 1960's it was rechristened as CBI more to appear like the Federal Bureau of Investigation of the United States of America.

Every organisation has a culture of its own and the CBI's culture was patterned on its head. As an organisation, it has and had a very high standard of integrity and honesty. The officers were expected to be, the models of ideal conduct. About IPS officers in the organisation, it was said that they were totally incorruptible. Inside the organisation, there was no aura of "James Bond". There were tonnes of paper work. Each case was examined, almost with a tooth comb, before being filed in the court.

After the investigation of the case, the Investigating Officer would write his complete investigation report. It would give the complete history of the case, what each witness said, and what documentary evidence was available and what were the main deficiencies. This was called the Final Report Part I. This would be examined by a legal officer, well versed in law. He would advise whether the case had any legal lacunae. He would also suggest, whether any more witnesses, or documents were required to strengthen the case. This was called the Final Report Part I. The case would be remitted back to the investigating officer, for more investigation of the aspects left uncovered, during the earlier investigations. After the investigation was done on the lines pointed out by the legal officer, the investigating officer would write supplementary Final Report Part II. Only after the legal officer had cleared the case and written the supplementary Final Report Part II, the case would go to the Superintendent of Police. The Superintendent of Police would examine the case, go through the case diaries and Final Reports of the investigating and Legal Officers. If he felt satisfied that the case had been properly investigated and had no legal flaws, then he would make his recommendations to his Deputy Inspector General. The DIG would also examine the case and send his final recommendations to the CBI headquarters. Only the DIG had authority to pass final orders in the case involving officers of the Gazetted Ranks, Class two. Even there, the Head Office was kept fully in the picture.

If the case involved senior officers or even junior Gazetted Officers class one, it would be examined again by the Zonal DIG's and IG's called Joint Director's in the Head Office. From the legal point of view, more senior and experienced legal advisors would examine the case. More often than not, they would ask some other aspects of the investigation to be completed, which might have escaped attention. The amount of paperwork was tremendous. The stages through which a case had to pass may look cumbersome. But in practice, the discussions of the major cases amongst the investigating officers, Legal officers, Branch S.P.'s with the DIG's and other senior officers would clarify the doubts.

The Head of Organisation was called "Director". But in the legal parlance, he was an Inspector General of Police. The CBI had to investigate the cases within the framework of Indian Evidence Act and Indian Penal Code and Criminal Procedure Code. They had the same powers as the local Police, for certain notified offences. The Director would apply himself thoroughly, to all the aspects of the working of the organisation. It was this dedication to the work, which has ensured over 70 per cent conviction rate in CBI cases, filed in the court. The CBI had scientifically determined that an investigating officer cannot investigate more than 2.50 cases involving General offences like corruption. 1.25 to 1.75 cases per investigating officer, involving economic offences, was the ideal work load. This was the figure for the whole year and not for one month or so. Unlike the local police, the CBI Investigating Officer, generally of the Inspectors and sometimes Deputy Superintendent of Police level, did not carry any trappings of the office they held. They were generally on their own, or at best accompanied by one or two constables who carried their records. They were not given any vehicles and had to use either the public transport or their personal scooters.

The investigating officers who bore the brunt of the investigation were expected, and rightly so, not to have, even a cup of tea with the witnesses or other parties connected with the case. But still they were not given proper treatment. Not only the non-Gazetted officers, but also the IPS officers were treated as dirt by the top bosses. In fact if an IPS officer wore good clothes, the then Director of CBI, invariably drew a presumption, of malpractices and corruption against him. It was a closed organisation. The Director and other senior officers were, almost autocratic rulers. Some of them had closed minds and views about the cases dealt with by them. They appeared, to believe that they had the divine right of being right all the time. The then Director,while giving the impression of being fair and just was all the time finding ways and means of pleasing the powers that be. In one case a complaint was received against a labour leader of some importance in 1971. The orders were issued from the top that a Preliminary Enquiry be registered.

The CBI used to register two types of cases. The first category of the cases was the regular cases disclosing offences under the Indian Penal Code. These cases were generally registered against the Government Employees and such public men who had colluded with them. Their logical end would be the chargesheet in the court or at least disciplinary action against the Government Employees if there was not enough evidence to prosecute them in a court of law. The second category of the cases would be the Preliminary enquiries. It was a refined version of the inquiries done by the department to establish a prima facie case. After investigation and thorough examination, this enquiry could end either in disciplinary proceedings against the government employees or his prosecution. It was generally, confined to the government employees, who could be asked under the departmental instruction to submit the information about themselves or their families. The preliminary enquiry had no legal basis. It was meaningless to register it against a non-government servant or any labour leader. But it was done by the top man to please somebody still higher up than him. The top man would play, God Almighty only to the people, working in the organisation. But he would bow before anybody, who could show superior connections. I am not mentioning names. Most of the actors of the CBI scene, at that time, are either no more or have retired. They also do not deserve any mention, for their unpleasant role in degrading the organisation. Undoubtedly sometimes political vendetta can make one a victim. But it is up to the civil servants, not to compromise for the sake of temporarily pleasing the powers that be. I have observed, in my over thirty six years of service, that if you discharge your duties honestly and correctly, nobody will bother you. It is the officials themselves who invite interference, so that either they land in cushy jobs or are not disturbed from the same. Once during my later service in the Central Reserve Police Force, one of the Directors General of Haryana Police, under my charge suggested to me that it would be in my favour to consult the Chief Minister of his State for recruitment in the CRPF. I ignored the suggestion. My posting was in the CBI Headquarters. The job involved going through old cases and monitoring their progress. As a Staff Officer to the DIG and the IG, the routine was to carry the files to them, send reminders and convey their observations to the field S.P.'s for further investigation. In a periodical meeting the head of organisation used to review the progress of old cases. This review was, more a review of the memory of the DIG's. Generally the pattern of questions which used to be asked was; what did the witness say in the court of law? Who will brief them and whether arrangements were made to see that they deposed according to what they had stated during the process of investigation.

After a few days in the Headquarters, I was posted in the Delhi Branch of CBI as Superintendent of Police. It used to have two Superintendents of Police and its jurisdiction was confined only to Delhi. The Delhi Branch had a Deputy Inspector General of Police to supervise the progress of work of the two Superintendents. Apart from the normal investigation work, the Delhi Branch was also the equivalent of Kotwali, for the CBI Headquarters. Whether it was a question of getting a railway reservation or liaison with the local administration or the admission of somebody's children or the allotment of accommodation, it fell to the lot of Delhi Branch. This is nothing unusual. In all Departments, it is the local office which caters to the needs of its higher ups.

The DIG and two Superintendents were housed in the same office at Shahajahan Road hutments. All the cases had to be seen and approved by the DIG Delhi. The communication going to the Head Office, which was at that time located in the Indian Express Building at Bahadur Shah Zafar Marg, had to be seen and approved by the DIG Delhi. It was obligatory to mention that the DIG had seen and approved the communication. Once my Private Secretary made a howler which annoyed everybody to no end and perhaps justifiably. The last sentence in the letter used to be "It issues with the approval of DIG Delhi". But he mistakenly only typed it as "It issues with the approval of DOG Delhi." This had happened because in the typewriter the letters 'I' and 'O' are next to each other on the keyboard.

One of the largest contributors, to the registration of cases, in 1971-72, was the Municipal Corporation of Delhi. There used to be a lot of embezzlements and loss to the corporation in the receipt and credit of taxes. The *modus operandi* would vary. In some cases where the dishonest members of the staff wanted to illegally help the parties, they would enter in the records as having received the cheques. Cheques and challans would be written and sent along with hundreds of other cheques for crediting to the account of MCD. Since on one pay in slip more than hundred cheques would be sent, the bank staff would just acknowledge on the Municipal Challan form for having received the cheques. But actually at the time of sending the cheques, the cheques of the favoured parties, would be abstracted and returned to them. The reconciliation of the accounts and the tallying of the cheques, details of cheques bounced or missing would take years of correspondence between the banks and the Municipal Corporation. It would take ages to fix the responsibility, if it was decided to hold somebody accountable. The racket flourished for quite sometime, till the CBI took up above types of cases and advised the Municipal Corporation to rectify its procedures. Whenever any case was finalised, either for chargesheeting in the court of law, or for recommending departmental action, the last para of the S.P.'s report, would always contain specific recommendations, for plugging loopholes in the procedures. It would also give suggestions, for improving the functioning. It would also recommend for taking suitable action as the department felt necessary, against such officials, against whom direct evidence was not forthcoming, but who were otherwise involved. Majority of cases filed by the local police fail, in the courts of law, because of the failure of the witnesses to depose truthfully. Sometimes they are won over, with inducements or threats. The police rope in the nearest available person, as a witness. Credentials, respectability or standing of the witnesses, is rarely verified before utilising their services. This difficulty has been overcome by the CBI. Orders have been issued by the Government, to the departments and ministries of the Government of India, to make available, government servants, as witnesses for CBI cases.

A case is not registered, by the CBI, without proper verification. as it involves the reputation of a Government Official. It may also involve searching of his house and office. Neither rumours, nor hearsay, are taken as the gospel truth. A case is registered only after the basic facts, are verified, for establishing a prima facie case. When a verification of an information, discloses the violation of a departmental rule, and not a cognisable case, the information is passed on to the concerned department, for taking suitable action. The departments, on their own are reluctant to take action against any employee. The departments have no agency to specifically deal with the cases of violation of Conduct Rules. The work of disciplinary proceedings is entrusted to overworked officials, who have no time, or inclination and patience, to conduct the disciplinary proceedings. The result is, that such cases end in exoneration. The CBI has its hands full. Despite its best efforts, due to lack of manpower, it is unable to take up all cases referred to it, for investigation or enquiry. All witnesses in CBI cases are government employees. They are expected to depose, only the truth, about the searches and seizures, which they have witnessed. No witness really has any grudge, that he has been tutored, to say something, which he did not witness. In fact, if anything, the witnesses are careful, not to deviate from their statements recorded in the investigation. In cases which are negligible, the Government witnesses resilence from their statements made to the investigating officers, the witnesses have to explain their conduct to their department. The raid/search witnesses are not summoned except at the nick of the time. For this, a request is sent to the Chief Vigilance Officer of the Department/Ministry to make available witnesses, on a particular day, time and at a particular place. Only after the witnesses have assembled, they are explained their duty of witnessing a particular CBI action and depose the same truthfully before the court or departmental enquiry officer, as the case may be. With a view to ensure that no innocent person is harassed or involved in cases investigated by the CBI, the accused officials at the end of investigation are called upon to explain their defence, for possession of assets disproportionate to their known means of income, or other irregularities. If the accused is able to produce satisfactory defence, there is no option except to either close the case, or investigate it further or take some other view. This defence of the accused is also helpful to the investigating officer. He can investigate the case further, to either rebut or confirm the pleas of the accused. In case the CBI decides to go ahead, its internal mechanism ensures that all points, raised, by the accused are fully investigated. This is a double edged weapon. If the accused is innocent and has the necessary proof, the matter is closed at the investigation stage itself. Many accused, in CBI cases are advised by their lawyers not to give any defence or statement to investigating officer of the CBI. This is to ensure that the clients defence is revealed, only in the court of law.

CBI would trap, corrupt public servants. The drill would, be either to use the marked currency notes, or to put a special kind of powder on the notes, which if handled would leave tell-tale marks behind. On being trapped, the accused is asked to wash his hands. The water would give a particular colouration. The place of trap, and demand of bribe, would generally be fixed in such a way, that the witnesses could see the whole transaction..Delhi Branch of the CBI, during my tenure trapped a number government officials, accepting bribe. But contrary to popular expectations, in no case, the CBI asked for their suspension from service. Court cases filed by the CBI or cases recommended for disciplinary action would take years for completion. Some cases would go on, for as long as, ten years or even more. If an influential and rich accused was convicted, he would go on to appeal to the next higher court, and finally the Supreme Court. There was a serious follow up of the court cases. The review of the court cases was done regularly, to ensure, that no case should go by default. The cases of economic offences, involving Import and Export Trade Control Laws, would go on for years. They would end in a whimper of a fine for a few thousands of rupees or a nominal imprisonment. The violation of economic laws, is not taken as a crime by our society. I observed this trend several times in my career both as Superintendent of Police Economic Offences Wing and as Assistant Inspector General of Police, Economic Offences and later on as Director of CBI. Even now society looks upon the violators of economic laws, with much lesser severity, than on the thieves and robbers. A men convicted of an Economic offence still maintains his respectability in the society as compared to a pickpocket or a cheat. The white-collar crime has gone up.

Even in I970, the CBI took officials from Customs and Excise and Income Tax department, on deputation, to provide technical assistance, in the investigation of offences. They were appointed as Superintendents of Police in the CBI. The lure of easy money is so tremendous. The economic crime has gone up and not come down with the passage of time, both in sheer volume as well as the magnitude of the money involved.

Normally the economic crime is a collusive crime. Always, somebody from within the organisation is either a collaborator or abettor or at best a passive spectator. All this is for a price. The last category generally has bureaucrats, who have neither the time nor inclination or interest to put an end to these kinds of offences. They are content to issue warning circulars or standing orders or inane instructions. The latest scams, in the series, include Securities Scam, in which according to varying estimates, amount varying from Rs 8000 crores, involving one Harshad Mehta, Fodder Scam, Rs. 1500 crores, CRB Scam Rs 1032 crores, Urea Scam, involving Rs139 crores. The sums involved, have disappeared. In all the economic crimes the looser is the Government or the common man. Most of the time it is the Government or government run institutions which have been taken for a ride. Thus, no body feels a personal touch or loss.

Once the son of a diplomat was arrested in Sydney, (Australia), in 1972, carrying Hashish (cannabis). The son had gone to see his diplomat father, posted there. He thought of making easy money by taking the Hashish with him for sale there. But the Australian Police, was too smart for this youngster. He claimed diplomatic immunity on the strength of the diplomatic status of his father. Still, he was not allowed to enter Australia and deported back by the next flight. The father, when questioned, told the authorities, that since his son had committed an offence, he must face the consequences. He was ashamed that such a deed had been done by him. He totally disassociated himself from that incident. When the young offender landed in Bombay, he was hauled by the Customs authorities and prosecuted. He admitted his offence. He was awarded a nominal sentence and then released under the Probation of Offenders Act. The then CBI chief sent a note that let a Preliminary Enquiry (PE) be registered. The legal branch, as well as the Narcotics and Counterfeit Currency Branch, which I was heading advised, that as the accused had already been punished by an Indian Court, there was no legal case against him. He was not a Government official. The registration of a PE had no meaning. The Director felt offended that I, with hardly 11 years service, was advising him. He did not like it and sent me a stinker. I had nothing to lose. I again protested that the advice of the legal branch be followed. I also raised a back query, whether the intention of the registration of the case was to look into the conduct and antecedents of his father. In a period of 2 years and 5 months I spent in the CBI, I had worked as Superintendent of Police, General Offences Wing, Economic Offences Wing, Superintendent of Police, Narcotics and Counterfeit Currency and AIG, Economic Offences Wing (From April 1971 September, 1973). I had four changes or transfers in less than two and a half years. It was not worth staying any more, because of angularities in the then Director. He wanted certain things done on the shoulders of his subordinates.

Before my deputation was to end on 10th September, 1973, I sent a note in writing to the Director that as my deputation was ending on 10th September, the State Government, may be addressed, to indicate my posting. It was something unheard of and totally unexpected in the CBI. Here somebody was asking, to be sent back, on the completion of his tenure. People could stay indefinitely in the Central Police Organisations, including the CBI, as the rules were not very strict for extending the deputation. Many in the organisation, had taken bets, that I would go, cringing and beg for extension, as my wife was also working in Delhi. My transfer would mean upsetting my family life. Her transfer to Bangalore was not easys. They were surprised, that not only, did I not go to see him, but asked to be relieved on the due date. My first tenure of CBI ended in this fashion. I stood firm that the laws be followed to the letter. Nobody had a discretion to tamper with them for scoring points with the political masters.

10

In Karnataka Again

Banglore Tenure as DCP Crime

I left the CBI on the 10th of September 1973, I prepared myself mentally to leave my family—my wife and two daughters, aged four and one year in Delhi. I despatched my scooter in advance. I was posted as the Deputy Commissioner of Police, (Crime) Bangalore, I booked my seat by Air from Delhi. My joining time was ending on 24th of September. As my flight used to leave, early in the morning, and arrive at Bangalore well before 10 a.m. so I left only on the 24th September 1973, the day my joining period was ending.

Straight from the airport, I drove to the office of the Commissioner of Police. As the mess where I was to stay was in the office itself, it took me less than fifteen minutes to put on my uniform and call on the then Commissioner of Police, M.L. Chandershekhar. Chandershekhar ended his distinguished career in the service, as the first ever IPS Chairman of Karnataka State Public Service Commission.

Students' Agitation

The Police Commissioner felt that since I had been out of touch with the Executive Police for over five years, I should first see some action. A violent students' agitation was going on in the state at that time. In a police firing in Hassan District,(the District of the Former Chief Minister and Prime Minister, Mr H.D.Devegowda) where a few students and their sympathizers had been killed. This led to a chain reaction. The Commissioner was monitoring the situation in the city from his chambers. He asked me to observe him. My first day, was spent in seeing, the working of the City Police.

Sometimes it may be argued, that it is a waste of time to just sit and watch. The fact remains that we learn more, by example, and seeing others perform, rather than by any theoretical lessons. There were four Deputy Commissioners in the City Police: Law and Order, Crime, Traffic and Headquarters. The DCP Hq, was also incharge of the City Armed Reserve and Special branch. Irrespective of the broad division, it was the law and order and processions and general *bandobast*, which had priority over everything else. Thirty years later, the number of Deputy Commissioners in Bangalore City Police stands at 14. There are two posts of Additional Commissioner of Police of the rank of DIG/IG. The Commissioner of Police, who used to be a DIG, is now of the rank of Addl.Director General of Police/ Director General of Police. I had been out of the State for nearly five years. I found the attitude of the colleagues all junior to me in service, amusingly tolerant. Somehow they all felt that I had forgotten what policing was. Even the senior officers, barring Police Commissioner Chandershekhar were totally negative. After a wait of two months, a dilapidated Inspector's quarter was allotted to me as the earmarked residence of Deputy Commissioner (Crime). The quarter had the largest lawn available. On my request the Public Works Department repaired and improved it. Each police station in the city had two sub-inspectors, one incharge of law and order and the other crime. A major portion of the police station staff was earmarked for law and order. Less than half a dozen policemen, including a Sub-Inspector were earmarked for crime work. Even that staff, was very frequently pulled out, for law and order duty. I called a meeting of all the crime Sub-Inspectors in the city and ordered them to prepare a list of pending cases. As Bandobast work, consisted of putting on the uniform, and be generally visible, even the crime staff preferred to be involved in that. It was easier, than the laborious and painstaking work of investigation involving property.

I was the senior most Deputy Commissioner of the city. I ordered that no crime staff would be diverted from their work without my permission. It was time that a professional approach was adopted towards the detection of crime, after prevention had failed. As a first step, I decided I would visit the scene of offence of every property crime without any delay. Since my family had not joined me as yet, I was in a position to pay full time attention to my work. One evening, a robbery in a suburb of Bangalore called Indira Nagar, was reported. I sent a message to the Police Station and Sub Divisional Police Officer as well as the Circle Inspector of Police, that I was proceeding to place of theft. I reached there before any other policemen arrived. It seems that all the members of the household had gone out, leaving behind a servant in the house. When they came back, they found the servant tied to a chair. A cloth was stuffed in his mouth. The servant said, that when he was alone, three persons with covered faces came, beat him and tied him up. They ransacked the house and made away with valuables, including cash and jewellery well over Rs 50,000.

I wanted to see the injuries he had suffered in the scuffle. He had none. He showed his torn shirt. On a closer examination I found that the shirt appeared to be cut with scissors. This clue helped to solve the case. The servant, on further questioning, showed signs of nervousness. He was reluctant to say anything about the so called robbers. As soon as the inspector incharge of the area came, I told him that before we go for catching the thieves, let us first concentrate on the servant. The master of the house gave a big certificate of impeccable honesty and integrity to the servant. We had brought some sniffer dogs, who started barking at the servant. This was explained away saying that as there was a scuffle between the thieves and the servant. The scent of the thieves was on the shirt of the servant. Much against the wishes of the master of the house, the servant was taken for interrogation. Sustained interrogation for about five hours broke him. He confessed that he himself had contrived the theft with other fellow servants. He had planned it, in such a way, that it should look like an outsider's job. When questioned about the stolen goods, he replied that his fellow thieves had planned to leave by the 5 a.m. bus for their native place in Madras. He was to collect his share after a month. His accomplices were arrested while boarding the first bus for Madras. This was the quickest detection of a robbery case. It had been possible because of my pushing the case and personally interrogating the accused. Whenever an accused was arrested and property recovered, most of the investigating officers would be content to question him about the crime for which he was arrested. I felt that when the entire city crime was a composite unit at the level of the Deputy Commissioner or Commissioner, the property offences should also be investigated as if all the cases of Bangalore city were being investigated. I directed all police stations of Bangalore city to prepare a master list of all undetected offences for the last five years. I ordered that henceforth the standard routine would be to question the accused and verify his complicity in all undetected property offences for the last five years. Similarly the Circle Police Inspectors and the Assistant Commissioners of Police were also directed to keep the list of undetected property offences, of the areas under their charge with them. This was to be used while interrogating the suspects and property offenders.

Working Style

Every human being has his own style, of working whether in his working place or out of it. For thieves and criminals, their profession and commission of offences is the equivalent of their job. Crime is the only source of their income. Based on the principle that each one of us in the society, whether a saint or a sinner, works in a particular way for their livelihood. The Police have compiled the methods of commission of offences by thieves and other criminals on the basis of their method of operations. Since a offender is not likely to change his method of operation, the habitual criminals are classified as such. Some like to eat at the scene of crime, others defecate, still others enter the house through boring holes in the wall.

Various characteristics distinguish various criminals. Notwithstanding anything elses, the fact remains that the classification based on the method of committing offences coupled with scientific advances and fingerprinting techniques have helped unravelling many a crime.

Third Degree: An Inhuman Practice

I have always believed that it is inhuman to use torture to extract information even out of confirmed criminals. I made it clear that I would not condone or protect anybody indulging in extra legal methods. My approach was not appreciated in this regard. Most of the senior officers had a policy, of turning, a blind eye. They were satisfied, as long as the subordinates produced results. Most people generally follow double standards in their lives. Once there was a property offence in the house of a judicial officer, in the district judiciary. He constantly harassed me to ensure the detection of the offence. I told him that we were doing all that we could. He advised that if we put tight screws on the suspects, and thrash them soundly, he would definitely come out with all the details of the offence. I reminded him that he himself had passed strictures on the conduct of the police for using extra legal methods. I would not be a party to the use of any third degree on any suspect in the police custody. I also told him that the scientific methods of investigation might take a little longer. I would take recourse to them only. He was disappointed with me because I had refused to give instructions to use all methods to detect the case. It is perhaps, true of all of us, that when we are personally affected, we like to use no holds barred methods. Some of the observations of the Punjab Police Commission recorded in its report are worth repeating to indicate the extent and degree of the use of this inhuman method.

An Indian Police Service Officer told the Punjab Police Commission, that third degree methods were still used to some extent to extort confessions. A certain Head Constable was stated to have adopted the method of eliciting confession by making the sister and the father of the accused naked before him (accused). Another Assistant Sub-Inspector said that there was *'Mar Peet'*, but there was no personal motive and that, for the benefit of the public that beating was given. The man would not come out with the truth unless he were treated like that.

A number of people advocated the thrashing of culprits by the police so that in cases against property the goods were discovered. An advocate, president of the bar association of a district, was of the opinion that in Punjab, the Central Investigating Agency was notorious for these methods. It would be better to eliminate this branch and to entrust this work to the Criminal Investigation Department.

A Deputy Inspector General of Police, incharge of a range, admitted that in some cases, third degree treatment was given by the police, even now. Another Indian Police Service Officer said that third degree methods to extort confessions still existed. There might be, some truth, in the description, of the Central Investigating Agency as "*Butcher Khana*". An Inspector of the Criminal Investigation Department, said that, he had not used, third degree methods, that some officers, who lost patience resorted to.

The use of the third degree method had been found to be the easiest way of working out crime. It was noticed that on many occasions a suspected criminal had confessed his guilt readily because of the third degree methods. With greater training and use of scientific methods and scientific aids to the investigation and strict action against the officers responsible for corrupt practices of the use of third degree methods, a reasonable improvement could be expected.

An Assistant Inspector General of Police said that the use of third degree methods, against the suspects and the accused persons, was one of the main irregularities and illegalities committed by the Punjab Police. This method was adopted under a bonafide belief that by doing so they were able to discharge their duties more efficiently. He added that the members of the public complained against certain police officials, that they were not torturing or beating the suspects. No serious effort was being made to detect the crime. To give up these methods would, according to them, result in deterioration of law and order situation. Crime would go up, and criminals would escape punishment in a large number of cases. Government and the people should be prepared, for this and should not be alarmed.

One of the Secretaries of the government said that it went without saying, that such a practice did exist, rightly or wrongly. People had come to believe, unless Station House Officer was strong, there would be deterioration in the Crime situation. He went on to say "When, I say that a Station House Officer is strong, I mean that he is rough and deals with *badmashes* in a manner, which is not considered soft by the people."

A more courteous behaviour, with a suspect may give the impression that the officer is weak. There are no two opinions that this third degree evil does exist and that there is a belief and a very strong one that the maintenance of

Law and Order may become difficult, if this were totally eliminated.

An advocate of Chandigarh High Court said, the only method which the police knew for investigation was the third degree method. He was followed by another advocate of the same court, who described the various methods that had come to his notice—continued beating of the soles of the feet till the swelling levels up the concave space, making him naked, or making him lie on the ground and the placing of heavy ice on the soles. Then he was cured in a hospital so that no injuries could be detected.

A retired Inspector General of Police said that in England suspects were interrogated for days together. In India, the Police officers did not have enough time for such interrogation and thus resorted to third degree methods to achieve quick results. Another senior Indian Police Service Officer said that if a suspect was accustomed to sitting on a sofa but was made to sit tiny on his bare feet, this amounted to torture. The point was the amount of discomfort which a man was made to feel. He gave us the instance of one Avtar Singh, a notorious dacoit. After the Criminal Investigation Department staff had exhausted all legitimate methods of investigation without success, he had got hold of the man, put him in a jeep and had him tied with a rope. He then started driving the jeep very fast and said to the Sub-Inspector on route that as soon as they reached the Jamuna, the man would be thrown into the river. When the suspect heard this, he came out with the truth. Another Indian Police Service Officer said that resort to third degree methods was made in cases in which there were peculiar difficulties in which no evidence was available and in which a witness, was not forthcoming.

The Advocate General, Punjab said that when he was Assistant Advocate-General, he did come across cases, where the police had used third degree methods. One such method was continuous interrogation by keeping the man awake at night. A judge of the High Court said that the third degree methods were more subtle now than before. No investigating officer could leave the investigation just at the questioning stage. He had to use pressure to extract information. Constant interrogation of the suspect during the night without allowing him to sleep in his opinion was cruel and was in the nature of third degree method.

A member of the Legislative Council was of the opinion that without some kind of interrogation or use of force, it was not possible to get clues regarding crime.

The President of a Labour Union said, that there was no use of scientific methods of investigation in theft cases. It was only by chance that a theft case was traced and that too by the use of third degree methods, when these was no other option left. The police were utter failures in the matter of scientific investigation.

There is not a shadow of doubt that for quick results and for short cuts, the third degree methods may be applied by some black sheep in the police force for investigating the cases. But now a consciousness permeates in the senior police officers to at least avoid the same.

Karnataka has a record of taking drastic action against even Superintendents of Police and the Range Deputy Inspectors General of Police for use of third degree. In the year 1992-93 a Superintendent of Police and a Deputy Inspector General of Police, who was working as an Additional Commissioner of Police, Bangalore City, were placed under suspension. A criminal case was registered against them for not taking action, against subordinate. A person had died under suspicious circumstances, in the police custody. It was believed that the death was the result of third degree and inhuman treatment. Action was taken against them for conniving in the use of third degree by subordinate police officials. A few years ago, a case had been registered against the former Home Minister and a Deputy Commissioner of Police for misuse of the office. There was death in Police custody and it was alleged that the above persons had connived in it. The officer was sentenced to imprisonment by the Sessions Cort. He appealed against the same. This drastic action had been possible by the Police itself against the Police officers. Karnataka Police has a specialised wing for investigation called the Corps of Detectives. The people of the state, have developed such a faith in this wing that instead of CBI Inquiry, they ask for an inquiry by COD. It will be too optimistic for me to say that the use of third degree has been totally eliminated in Karnataka. But definitely there is some fear of God in the minds of likely offenders that if they step out of the *Lakshman Rekha*, they ill do it at their own peril.

About the use of third degree, and the type of person, against whom it is used, it is worthwhile to quote from the book *Not Guilty* by Judge Jerome Frank and Barbara Frank, who observed:

"Apologists for the third degree, say that the police resort to it, only in 'emergencies' and that 'no decent man is ever beaten up in a police station.' They imply, that such coercion, is supplied solely, to habitual criminals, or to men whose guilt is already clear. But is this true? Our court report proves otherwise. Some Americans approve of the third degree, because they assume, that it means merely, that the police mishandle gangsters, to make them admit their crimes. But it is precisely, these professional criminals, who are ordinarily, immune from police violence, because they have powerful organisations, backed with lawyers, ready to "spring" them promptly, by writs of habeas corpus. Occasionally, in the case of a lurid crime, when the public clamours for a solution, a prominent citizen may be subjected to the third degree."

But President Truman's Commission on Civil Rights correctly said: "Most of the victims are ignorant, friendless persons, unaware of their rights and without the means of challenging those who violate these rights. As Dean Roscoe Pound once pointedly remarked: "No rich man is ever subjected to this process, to obtain proof in violation of anti-trust legislation, and no powerful politician is thus dealt with, to obtain proof of bribery and graft.

"Those who acquiesce, in the third degree, are saying two things in effect: That the police, in order to detect crime, may themselves, operate outside the law and that civil liberties are, on the whole, the exclusive privilege of the professional criminals and of the so-called upper classes. As a matter of fact, none of us is safe. When a police official declares that he tortures no one but criminals, he unwillingly exposes, the real menace of the third degree. He is asserting, that the police have a right, without trial, to determine the guilt of an arrested person. Once we concede, any such right to the police, we potentially endanger all men. For then we authorise the police to torture any one, they in their, uncontrolled discretion, decide is a criminal. Repeated and under-redressed attacks on the constitutional liberties, of the humble, tend to destroy the foundations, supporting the constitutional liberties of everyone. The test of the moral quality, of a civilisation is, its treatment of the weak and the powerless."

About the third degree, it is difficult to conceive, of methods, more revolting. Sutherland and Cressey in their book *Principles of Criminology* quoted, the statements of two police officers supporting, what the protagonists, of third degree say: "A Police Inspector, in New York city police has said: "There is more law at the end of a police man's night stick than in a decision of the Supreme Court." The Police Commissioner of a large Eastern City said: "I have sworn to protect this community against crime. If there has to be a choice between violating my oath of office and violating the Constitution, I will violate the Constitution every time."

11

Heading Youth Services

The First Ex-Cadre Job

The Karnataka State IPS Association, represented to the Government in 1973, that the promotion prospects of IPS officers, were very poor. The State Government should consider posting IPS officers to non-Police jobs. It pleaded that all the general jobs were mostly managerial. The IPS officers were, as qualified to hold them as others. They also had high educational qualifications and District experience.

The State Inspector General of Police recommended my name for an Ex. cadre job. I was the first police officer, who was posted outside the Home or Police Department, as Director Youth Services and Ex. Officers Deputy Secretary to the Government, Education and Youth Services Department, and Secretary Karnataka State Sports Council in the third week of December, 1973. Ethiraj, one of my Assistant Commissioners, came to sympathize with me on my posting outside the Police. He said that as I was too honest for police, police officials did not like my being in the Police Department. He said that my openly opposing the use of third degree methods and making shirkers work, created a lobby against me. It was this lobby which was responsible, for my transfer. He did not believe me when I said that it is a matter of personal pride and honour to be the first IPS officer in Karnataka to hold a non-Police job. I also told him that my status and position as Director Youth Services was that of a Head of Department. It was the same position, for me in the new Department, as held by the State Police Chief. I also told him that I was happy that the Police Chief selected me for the job. The future postings of the Police Officers, to non-police jobs, would depend upon my performance. This was to prove prophetic. After seeing my performance, as the Director Youth Services, it was upgraded to that of the Deputy Inspector General of Police on my promotion. It was also continued to be held by the IPS Officers from 1973 till now, that is 1999. Also based on my performance and my specific recommendations, an IPS officer was posted as the General Manager of the Karnataka State Transport Corporation. Other non-Police jobs, which were given to the IPS Officers, included, the Registrar of Universities, Director Information and Publicity and Managing Director, Karnataka Film Industries Development Corporation, and General Manager of the Karnataka Agro Industries Corporation and host of others. It all started with me.

Moving to Secretariat

I moved to Vidhan Soudha, as the Karnataka government Secretariat is called, after about three months as the Deputy Commissioner of Police. It looked like a climb down. On 17th December, 1973, I went to my new office, promptly at 10.30 a.m., the usual office timing at that time in Karnataka. The office room for the Director Youth Services, was filthy with no peon in sight. After about, half an hour, an indifferent peon, made an appearance. He glanced at me, with an unconcealed hostility. It was a novelty for an IPS officer to be in the Secretariat as a Deputy Secretary. My colleagues and subordinates, in the Education and Youth Services Department, looked upon it, as a stop gap arrangement, till somebody else was posted. This was the first question, my Special Officer Youth Services, M.R. Narayan asked me. I told him that so far as I was concerned, I was there to stay. My immediate boss was the Commissioner Education and Youth Services. I was given the secretariat work, pertaining to Youth Services and Sports, the Department of Archaeology, Museum, Flying, Adult Education, Libraries, Physical Education, National Service Scheme and Nehru Yuvak Kendras, and National Cadet Corps. I was also the Ex. Officio Secretary of the Karnataka State Sports Council. This council was headed by the then Chief Minister, late Dev Raj Urs. This was the apex body, through which the State Government, released grant to the several sports bodies and associations. A small secretariat was provided which included an Assistant Secretary, and an Accounts Superintendent. Mostly I had to process my own proposals as Deputy Secretary. As Director Youth Services I was the Head of a Department.This work was done by me both for sports and youth programmes, because there was practically no field organisation. At the District level, the few youth and sports programmes, were being conducted through the Deputy Commissioners of the Districts.

Immediately after taking charge I asked my officer to brief me, on the urgent and immediate proposals, requiring my attention. I was told that the State Government was very keen to get the Southern wing of the National Institute of Sports, Patiala to Bangalore. Though there was no formal correspondence, the talks had been going on to get the NIS South Centre to Bangalore. I saw it as a great opportunity to make a mark, by getting the institute in Bangalore. By this time I had put in over twelve years of service. I was very clear in my mind, that apart from the official input, which I would provide, the political push would be required. At my request the then Chief Minister, Dev Raj Urs addressed D.O. letters to all the seven ministers from Karnataka in the Union Cabinet to use their good offices to get the Institute to Bangalore.

The Chief Minister also addressed a personal letter to the then Education Minister of India, Professor Nurul Hassan to use his good office to set up the South Centre of National Institute of Sports in Bangalore. I had voluntarily undertaken the responsibility. I was on trial. I realised that as the Head of the Department, my days of looking to others for guidance were over. It was I, who had to provide guidance. Nobody was going to tell me, as to what to do, and how to do. I was my own boss and it was up to me to prove that I could set goals and achieve the same. I also discovered that I was the government for my own work. I had to send proposals as the Head of the Department, to myself as Deputy Secretary and then process and sanction the same in consultation with Finance or Law or General Administration Departments. Most of the time what I proposed as Director of Youth Services, was approved by me as Deputy Secretary.

Collusive Corruption

When I visited Delhi, for getting the NIS, South Centre, I was very surprised to notice, that no officer was in a position to say either 'Yes, or 'No', straightaway unlike the State Government. In the State Government, the 'Yes' or 'No' of the Chief Minister was a clear answer. A strong and a clear-headed Chief Minister, like late Dev Raj Urs or Gundu Rao, could give a decision and that would be final. But in the Central Government, a simple proposal was subjected to the rounds of several officials, Ministries or committees. When all possible avenues of consultation had been exhausted and almost everybody had said 'Yes', then only a final 'Yes' would emerge. I tried to meet the members of the committee, which was to recommend the setting up of the South Centre of the NIS. They felt that by meeting me, they would be laying themselves, open to the charge, of having been influenced by me and the Government of Karnataka. They suggested that I meet them collectively in the meeting. My brief from the State Government was to get the Institute to Bangalore at any cost. It was a farsighted idea of the then Chief Minister. He felt that with the arrival of the Institute in the State, the interest of the youngsters in the sports was bound to increase. This would also give, a fillip to the sports activity in the State. He told me that as and when the Institute comes to Bangalore, it would outbeat the original at Patiala. Because of the salubrious climate of Bangalore, training camps would be held throughout the year. With a massive investment over a period of time, the city would become the top sports centre of the country. His vision has come true because as on date more than Rs 125 crore have been spent in Bangalore for creating new and updating old sports facilities in the NIS South Centre. At the National Stadium in Delhi, I appeared before the Committee to decide about the location of the Institute. I had all the plus points like the climate, availability of a sports complex at Kanteevera Stadium for starting the Institute. I also informed the Committee, that we would give land, free of cost up to 75 acres in the new Bangalore University for the permanent complex. I also explained that the State Government would give a grant of Rs 25 lakh for the institute. This totally swung the balance in favour of Karnataka.

G.V.K. Rao, a distinguished civil servant of Karnataka cadre, whom I had known as S.P. Bidar since 1965, had given me a valuable piece of advice. He said that promise anything to Government of India for getting any project for the State Government. Once they sanction a project, they cannot take the same back. Secondly the memory, of any promise made, is so short that with the transfer of one of the two parties, that is one promising, and the other promised....the sanctity ends. And transfers are quite frequent in Government. So I gave a commitment in writing about the free allotment of 75 acres of land and Rs 25 lakh cash. The Chief Minister of Karnataka, fully stood by me, and honoured my commitment later on. I had also committed, on behalf of the Government of Karnataka, rent free use of the sports facilities in Kanteevera Stadium and also hostel facilities in the nearby Government College of Physical Education, for the new Institute for seven years. The entire exercise was gone through a number of times. After the initial meeting, the committee members came again to Bangalore. They were dined and wined and looked after. Ultimately we won. I drew a line that beyond excellent hospitality we would do nothing more. I was aware, that some State Governments, have taken care, of the shopping of the Central Government functionaries. It was for getting, their schemes, running into hundreds of crore through. The shopping had included, the sale of expensive sarees and carpets as seconds or rejects, at the cost of the State Government Corporations or other gifts. This is unfortunate but true. The tragedy is that, it is almost the top civil servants who are involved in this free for all loot. As it benefits both the parties, i.e., the receiver and the giver, so there is no chance of complaint. Neither the receiver looks upon it as a bribe, as he has made some token payment, nor the giver feels a pinch because it is not his own pocket which is pinched, but of an abstract entity called the Government or one of its Corporations. As it is a collusive corruption, there are no individuals who feel they have done anything wrong. The game merrily continues but in forms and shapes and with different actors.

The difference between exclusive corruption and collusive corruption is, there is that: only one beneficiary, like a corrupt policeman, taking money to let off a traffic offender in exclusive corruption. Here there is likelihood of complaints because an individual's pocket has been touched. But in a collusive corruption, like an Engineer passing a substandard construction and making full ment for work not done, no individual is affected. It is the State treasury which has been robbed and shared. So everybody, robbing public money stands to gain.

Sports Coaches Training

Finally after months of labour, a representative of the National Institute of Sports came down to Bangalore and signed an agreement with me as the representative of the Government of Karnataka. The broad clauses were that the Government of Karnataka would give them, existing facilities, in Kanteevera Stadium to start the sports activities. We were keen that the Institute should start functioning, quickly. For training, as coaches, the trainees had to travel thousands of kilometres away from Bangalore or other states of South to Patiala. Later on, a formal function was held where the then Chairman of the National Institute of Sports, Ram Nivas Mirdha in the presence of the Chief Minister Dev Raj Urs and the Minister of Youth Services, R. Gundu Rao made the formal announcement of starting of National Institute of Sports, South Centre. A retired, Army General, a member of the board felt cut up and upset with me because he had not been provided a seat on the dais next to the Chief Minister. He had forgotten that whatever he had achieved was only a recognition of his past. People after retirement tend, to forget the reality and not realise that they are now only "Has beens."

My contribution was openly recognised and acknowledged by the Chief Minister. He said that it was my dogged determination and perseverance, which was responsible for bringing the sports coaches training Institution to Bangalore. I was nominated as a representative of the State Government, on the Board of Governors of the Institute as well on the then apex sports body, called All Indian Council of Sports.

Working Style

Since Chief Minister, Dev Raj Urs, was both Minister of Sports and Youth Services and Chairman of Karnataka Sports Council, it was very easy to see the proposals through the impenetrable wall of the Finance Department. In the first instance, all the proposals sent were turned down, on the grounds of economy and lack of funds. I devised a method, of first discussing the proposals with the Chief Minister. Then I would record that this was discussed with the Chief Minister and he had approved the same. Most of the time this method worked, but not without resistance. Getting exclusive time, with the Chief Minister was difficult. Meeting him at functions and official dinners, was frequent. It was on such occasions, that I would corner him and discuss all my subjects, projects and proposals. Dev Raj Urs was a fine, Chief Minister. He never said 'No' to any of my proposals. He always had a kind and encouraging word for me. Once during a function to honour the Karnataka artists, I suggested to him that Karnataka Sports Council should also honour outstanding sportsmen. The Youth Services Department should honour students, getting first ranks in various examinations of all the universities of Karnataka. I also suggested that we should give a 'State Award' to any sportsman or sportswoman from Karnataka winning a National Championship. He promptly agreed with me. So in my capacity as Head of the Sports and Youth Department, I sent a proposal to the Government. I said that the matter of recognising Sports and Academic Excellence had been discussed with the Chairman of Karnataka State Sports Council and the Minister of Youth Service. He had agreed to the proposal, that State Government should sanction to any sportsman from Karnataka who wins national championship, in any item, a sum of Rs 1000. Similarly any student getting the first rank in the Universities of Karnataka would be sanctioned a cash award of Rs 1000. This cash reward would be accompanied by a memento, as a State Award and a certificate. As usual, the Finance Department kept quiet on the proposal for sometime and when pressing reminders were sent, a classic reply cum query was received which asked "Whether the Chairman of the Karnataka State Sports Council, which is only an advisory body, has the power to sanction such a proposal." I was aware that all powers are exercised by the various departments in consultation and with the concurrence of the Finance Department. No such power had been delegated to the State Sports Council. So I gave an equally classic reply saying that "As Director Youth Services and Secretary Karnataka State Sports Council, I was not aware whether the Chairman of Karnataka State Sports council has any such power, but a Chairman who also happens to be a Chief Minister would have all the authority of the State Government." I also said if the Finance Department had any doubts about the powers of the Chairman of Karnataka State Sports Council, who also happens to be Chief Minister, the matter could be referred to the Chief Minister, for any clarification. This ended any further debate, and the flexing of muscles, on the file. The proposal came back with the usual noting "Finance Department agrees." May be the Finance Department was right, because any proposal, which aims at improvement, costs a lot of money. With limited amount of money available, it is not possible to satisfy the needs of all. But if any results are to be achieved, the only way is, to get one's proposals sanctioned. I noticed that there never was lack of funds in my charge. It was only the lack of push. May be, all the proposals were not agreed to in one go, but ultimately whatever has been required or needed has been made available.

Karnataka's Peace Corps Volunteers

As soon as I joined as Director Youth Services, I noticed that a major scheme pending implementation, was the appointment of youth volunteers. Karnataka State had started a scheme of enlisting the services, of young unemployed graduates, for various fields of social services. A committee headed, by the Director Youth Services with three other social workers was to select, young men and women out of the applications received by the Youth Services Department. A budget provision of ten lakh was made in the budget. The scheme envisaged, that the young unemployed graduates, would be paid a stipend, of Rs 200 per month. Their services would be utilised, in their native districts, so that they did not have to incur heavy expenditure on boarding and lodging.

Instead of asking the candidates, to come to Bangalore for interview, I suggested that let the committee, interview the candidate in the Divisional Headquarters of Gulbarga, Belgaum, Mysore and in the State capital. This was promptly agreed to. All the members of the committee, including myself, headed by me, travelled in the only vehicle of the Youth Services Department. The other members of the committee, were unhappy, to travel in the milk delivery van type of vehicle of the Director of Youth Services. They satirically asked me, as to for how long, I would be working, as Director Youth Services. Out of courtesy, I was polite. But they thought I was a doormat. I told them, that it would be better if they direct the same question to the government. So far, as I was concerned, I was there to stay for a full tenure. It had become essential to take a no-nonsense attitude, as even most of the people working under me took me lightly. They felt, that I was only a stop gap arrangement.

We interviewed about 5900 candidates and selected only 400. I ordered that they must have training. I had noticed the same defect everywhere. We recruit people and position them. But in most of the departments nobody is trained, specifically for their duties. So I drew a syllabus for the young volunteers. The idea of the training, was to sensitise them, to the problems facing the society. Some volunteers were to work, as socio- medical workers, in the hospitals. They were expected to talk to the sick and ailing, give them succour and help, as well as guide the new patients to the proper places for treatment. They were expected to write letters, for the patients as well as read out, and generally cheer them up. As they were graduates, it was expected, that their presence, will strengthen the hospital administration. They were at liberty to leave their assignment, at any time, for any regular job or even otherwise. This exposure was aimed at making them humane, kind and conscious of the society's needs. Another set of the volunteers was assigned to the various voluntary organisations and orphanages for assisting them in their activities. They were generally to help the organisations, in organising programmes and functions.. Amongst the volunteers, a number of them were not only graduates but also B.Ed. and B.P.Ed. So we utilised, their services, as Auxilliary Teachers, in the schools having shortage of staff. Those who were good in Physical Training and fitness programmes were asked to take sports and games classes for such schools. Another group of volunteers, was assigned to the District Youth Services Officers, for activating the youth clubs and youth and sports programmes. The volunteers were given the choice of the activity, where they wanted to work.

As Director Youth Services, out of the 27000 villages in

the State, I had organised 8000 youth clubs, in the viable villages. To be in touch with them and to involve them in celebrating, national festivals like the Independence Day and Republic Day was very important. A token grant was sanctioned for the building of the youth club, for sports and cultural activities. The youth club had to raise an equal matching contribution for its activities. Matching contribution, has been a very important factor, in involving people for their continued interest. Karnataka is a big State. Most of the people, had no idea of the potential of their own State. It had been formed by integrating areas from old Hyderabad, Bombay, Madras and Mysore State, apart from merging the Part C State of Coorg. If an official was posted ,from Mysore to Gulbarga, a distance of about 500 kms, he would consider it a punishment. Food habits varied in different parts, as well as the dialects of spoken Kannada. Many old Mysore officials, posted to the Districts of Gulbarga, Raichur and Bidar would say that they had done their deputation outside the State, as if those areas were not part of Karnataka. One senior officer promoted to the IAS , when asked to give his willingness, for Central Deputation, replied that he had done his deputation, by working in the above areas. I felt that the best way for the National Integration of the country was to have integration of the State. They should first see their own State, to realise their oneness, as Kannadigas. I got a scheme sanctioned, under which the youths, from different parts would be taken for a Karnataka sight seeing or Karnataka Darshan. It was on the lines of Bharat Darshan for the All-India Services. Karnataka Darshan was confined, to the developmental projects in the State. I also gave a fair share, to the extent of 30 per cent, to the fair sex, on such tours. I wanted to treat, all youth leaders, whether men or women alike.

Winds of Change

The then Chief Minister, Devraj Urs expanded his ministry and inducted R. Gundu Rao as the Minister of State for Youth Services. As long as the Chief Minister had held the Sports and Youth Services portfolio, after a few wrestling bouts on the files, the Finance would agree to the proposals of my Department. Thinking that now only a young first time Minister of State was heading the department, it started rejecting, all worth while proposals, on the ground of acute financial crisis. Incidentally from the year I joined service in 1961, the economy instructions, based on the prevailing acute financial crisis, have been issued with clock wise regularity every year. Hence they have not been taken, seriously by those who wish to produce results. I was one of them.

The Youth Services and Sports Department, had no field organisation of its own. It was dependent for its activities on the District Panchayat Officer who was also designated as District Youth Services Officer. The government in 1976 abolished the posts of the District Panchayat Services Officers. I immediately mooted a proposal for the creation of a new cadre of District Youth Services Officers. As I was only a Deputy Secretary in the Government hierarchy, it was rejected. I had clearly urged, that in the absence of any officer, to work for Sports and Youth Activities , it was as good as closing the Department. When I found that my pleas and all the logic had no effect, I told the Minister for Youth Services, that we would have no option but to cut our activities at the district level. We did not have, any functionary, at the District level, for implementing our programmes. This conversation took place during the lunch time. He telephoned the then Finance Secretary, asking him to see him immediately. The Finance Secretary, on his arrival, was asked by the Minister; 'Is their any problem in creating infrastructure for the Youth Service Department?" The Finance Secretary replied "No problem Sir". He asked me to send all proposals to him. He claimed, that he had not seen any proposals, of the Youth Services and Sports earlier. Before he could reach his room, I dictated a note, to my Private Secretary, a proposal for creation of 19 District Youth Service and Sports Officers, four Deputy Directors as Youth Services at the Divisional level and the supporting staff for each one of them. The entire proposal was received back the same day, with the magic word "FD agrees." I immediately, issued the sanction, as Deputy Secretary creating posts, as well as four cars I had asked for.

A Unique Publication

Sometimes I felt, that even as officer, I did not know about the various schemes for the benefit of the public. Even, I was, at mercy of the custodians, of the files to know, how the public could benefit from those schemes. At no place, details of any scheme were available. I felt that the position must be the same for the public wanting to know, what the Youth Services and Sports Department could do. So I decided to bring out a publication under the title *What can we do for you?* both in English and Kannada. The publication contained details of all schemes, how they were implemented and who was the competent authority to sanction? This did away, with the power of the petty bureaucrat.

So impressed was the then Chief Minister, with this idea, that he asked me as to why, such a booklet, containing all schemes, for the benefit, of the poor and deprived sections, could not be published. I kept quiet and thanked him for the compliment. I said that it was for the government to take such a decision for other departments. I passed on his observations to the concerned officials. But the wishes of the Chief Minister remained unfulfilled and only on paper. Not only in Karnataka, but all over country, as well as in Government of India, there is no single publication, detailing schemes of any department, for improving the lot of the people. There is a crying need, to spell out the schemes, available with details of the procedures.

Gundu Rao: A Dynamic Leader

Though the schemes of the Youth Services and Sports involved expenditure running into few thousand rupees, there appeared to be, some perverse delight, in stalling the same. Even petty sanctions running, into five hundred to two to three thousands were deferred or outright rejected. It was shocking, but true that even where the Youth Services Minister, had announced grant, of one thousand rupees for some societies and organisations, their rejection was a routine affair. I would put up all rejections, before the Minister. One day he called me and said that, what was the point of his being a Minister, when even an Under Secretary in the Finance Department could reject his proposals? I tried to explain to him, that an Under Secretary may convey the rejection of a proposal, but actually on file, the orders of the competent authority, may be Secretary or Minister may have been taken. I also said that the Finance Department had its own files. It did noting on its parallel files, to preserve the anonymity and independence, of its officials. Some how it did not convince my Minister. So he rang up and fixed a meeting with the then Finance Minister, Ghorpade. The meeting with the Finance Minister started on a cordial note but it heated up with the Minister of Youth Services, Gundu Rao telling the Finance Minister: "I do not tell you how you should run your Finance Department. So why should your officers, or even you, tell me how to run the Youth Services Department or its schemes." He pressed for the demand for the suspension of the Under Secretary, who had rejected the proposals, approved by him .

When late Gundu Rao, was in a fighting mood, no power could come in his way. The meeting ended with an understanding, that in future if any proposal of the Youth Services Department was to be turned down, it must be first brought to the notice of the Finance Minister. The Finance Minister also told his officials that since it was a very small department with the smallest budget in the State, a sympathetic view must be taken of its activities and proposals. He gave me an unusual liberty, that if I felt that any proposal had been unjustly turned down, I could come to him and discuss the same with him. This made a *persona non grata* with the Finance Department.

No Typewriters for Typists

The Government of Karnataka had sanctioned the posts of stenographers, for the District and Divisonal level . But for getting their tools of trade, that is the typewriters, we were asked to procure the same from the Director of Printing and Stationery. So I sent a request for the same. In reply we received a communication, that the request had been registered and we were assigned a registration number of 508. I was told, that we would be supplied, on our turn. On further informal inquiries we came to know that due to economy orders the budget of the Director of Printing and Stationery had been drastically cut. On the reduced budget, he could procure only fifty to sixty typewriters, per year for all the government departments.

In other words, it meant that if the same rate of procurement continued, and if there were no jumping of the queues, we could expect to receive the typewriters not before a decade. So till that time we would have to keep the staff idle. I inquired, as to why we could not purchase the approved typewriters, ourselves at the same rates and from those firms who were supplying to the Director of Printing and Stationery. I was informed, that it was against the established procedures. It had neither been done, nor allowed, for any government department. I did not agree with the logic. It amounted to not doing any work and keep on paying the recruited staff, for ten years just to follow the procedures. So I prepared a note to the Finance Department asking for special dispensation to permit us to purchase 23 typewriters at the same rate as were supplied to the State Government. I also said that we would purchase the same model, which had been approved. I took the file personally to a Deputy Secretary Finance and explained to him the reasons behind our proposals. It took me just fifteen minutes to convince the justness of our proposal. He agreed but to safeguard himself said that "Finance agrees provided the Commerce and Industry Department agrees." So my next visit, the same day, was to the Deputy Secretary Commerce and Industry. He also agreed with my logic but noted on the file that "Commerce and Industry agree provided the Director Stores Purchase Department agrees." It took me about two days to get a "Yes" from that Department. So I myself promptly issued Government orders, permitting the Youth Services Department to purchase typewriters for its staff.

Visit to Iran

The then Chief Minister had been a wrestler in his younger days. Even after becoming the Chief Minister, Devraj Urs continued his interest in sports and games in general and wrestling in particular. The Asian Wrestling Championships were being held in Iran, in 1974. He wanted Bangalore to host the next Asian Wrestling competition. He felt that the interest in wrestling had dwindled and needed to be revived. He also felt, that Karnataka had the best wrestling talent, provided it was fully exploited. So when an invitation came from the Wrestling Federation of India to visit Tehran, the State Government accepted the same. It deputed the then Minister of Youth Service and Chairman Karnataka Sports Council, R. Gundu Rao and myself, as Director Youth Services and Secretary Karnataka State Sports Council to visit Iran in December 1974. Those were the days, of great scarcity of foreign exchange. It used to be released, by the Ministry of Finance, on a case-to-case basis. The proposal to release £140 each, for seven days trip, was rejected. Devraj Urs had to plead with the then Finance Minister, before the proposal was sanctioned. The sanction for visit was issued on the same day, we were to leave for Iran. So the foreign exchange was purchased, from the airport itself. Earlier, I had written a personal letter to my batch mate, Prakash Shah, of the foreign service. He was working, as Counsellor in the Embassy at Tehran. I had told him the possibility of my visiting Tehran, with my Minister. No date was indicated. Due to the shortage of time, the intimation from the Ministry of External Affairs reached Tehran after we had reached there. There was no body to receive, or guide us. Another problem at Tehran airport was that most of the people working there, knew only Persian or French. I asked the Minister to guard our luggage. I went in search of a telephone, and a person who could understand English. After about half an hour of futile search, I found an English passenger, who was just leaving for London. He could speak both Persian and French. I explained to him our predicament, especially when an Indian Minister was with me. He spoke into the telephone and found for the Telephone number of Indian Embassy. It was snowing in Tehran. Through Indian Embassy I got the phone number of Prakash Shah and told him how we had been stranded at the airport without any guide or assistance from the Embassy. He told me to take a taxi and come straight to the Embassy.

Prakash Shah, whom I have always affectionately called the "The Shahanshah of India" offered us steaming hot coffee. It took a couple of hours, for the Embassy to find two rooms, for us in a hotel. Each room was costing, £12 a day, leaving only £8 per head for transport, meals and other expenses. At that time, each pound was equal to Rs13.75 as compared to nearly seventy five rupees in 1999. The telegram of our arrival was received, just when we were about to leave the Embassy for the Hotel. The lunch was quite expensive, costing £ 9 per head. I requested the Minister that it was difficult for us to live in that expensive hotel and eat our food there. Mercifully the hotel had accommodation for us only for two days and later we shifted to a slightly more reasonably priced hotel, where we could both live and eat.

Minister Trapped in Hotel's Bathroom

On the first day, the hotel had only one room and so Gundu Rao and myself shared the room. Next morning, as usual, I got up early. I had my bed tea outside the room, in the lounge, so that the Minister might not be disturbed. I had my bath. With a view to give privacy to the Minister, I went out again. The Minister got up later on, and had his tea. I again went out of the room, so as to give him privacy for using the bathroom and getting ready. Four hours passed and the Minister did not open the room. I was little apprehensive as to what had happened. One of the hotel employees remarked, that possibly a chamber maid, had been trapped inside, with the Minister. He said that he was saying that on the basis of past experiences of the guest VIP's from many countries. He also added, that the chambermaids, did not mind, making some extra money, for an easy virtue job.

I knocked at the door violently and said "Sir, please open the door." For sometime there was no response. Then I heard a faint response, as the TV was on. After more knocking and shouting, I heard the booming voice of the Minister, over the noise of the TV, that "I am stuck up in the bathroom and the bathroom door is not opening." I went to the Reception and told the Manager that the Minister from India had been stuck up in the bathroom. The door had closed automatically. It was not opening from inside. It happened to be a Friday, which is a holiday in Muslim countries, including Iran. The Reception Manager expressed his helplessness in securing a locksmith on a Friday. I pressurized him saying that it was a Minister from India who had been trapped in the hotel bathroom. He had already spent four hours trapped inside. I said, it would be adverse publicity for the hotel. I would ensure that not only Indian Embassy, but other Embassies too, blacklisted the hotel. I said that they would have to pay, very heavy compensation, for the inconvenience caused. I used both bullying and pleading tactics. The hotel did procure a mechanic. The mechanic had to struggle for an hour, and use different gadgets, for opening the electronic automatic lock first to the bedroom and then from the bedroom to the bathroom. He took the help of the trapped Minister by passing on the screw driver, from under the door, for opening the lock. Ultimately after about five hours of being trapped the Minister was rescued from the bathroom. But when rescued, Gundu Rao came out with a smile and took the incident in his stride. He did not change the room, when the hotel manager offered to shift him, from there. I played safe and moved to a separate room.

For promoting sports and good health consciousness among the Iranians, the then Ruler of Iran, Shahanshah Mohammad Raza Pehl, Arya Mehar had spent more than 400 million dollars. Indoor and centrally heated stadiums with seating capacity of over 25,000 and outdoor football stadium which could seat over a lakh of people had been constructed. The stadia had the latest timing equipment and the best available sports facilities which money could buy. For wrestling, special mats and equipment had been installed. Well built wrestlers from Asian countries, gave very fine display of their skills. Indian wrestlers, were nowhere performance wise. Seeing poor performance of Indian wrestlers, I told Gundu Rao that we would be wasting our money, if we host any championship in Bangalore. I said there was no point in spending money, for the glory of other countries. It would be better spent in our own country.

Adopting Wrestlers

During his visit to Delhi in 1976, the Chief minister came across a promising young wrestler. The wrestler, who staying in Delhi, belonged to West Bengal. The CM felt, that irrespective of the States, Karnataka should take a lead in promoting National Integration and talent. He asked me to work out a scheme where we could select and adopt wrestlers. Their expenses would be paid by the State. His idea was that wrestling talent, should be trained and well fed, so that in Asian or Olympic Games, India, could show excellent performance. As per the Chief Minister's wish, a scheme was prepared. It involved an expense of Rs 100 per day, on the diet of a trainee wrestler. The diet would include butter, chicken, eggs and other necessary nutritious items. In return the wrestler would have to spend at least 8 hours a day in training. The State was also to pay boarding and other incidental charges amounting to Rs 500 per month. Estimated expenditure was to be Rs 3500 per month per wrestler. This was the amount, which the Chief Secretary of the State, earned as his salary. The Finance Department considered it as an extravagant expenditure. The total expenditure in the proposal was Rs 1.40 lakhs per year, for covering the expenditure on four wrestlers. But since the proposal was the brain child of the Chief Minister himself, the Finance Department was overruled. The money was released to the Secretary Karnataka State Sports Council, that is myself, in another incarnation, for implementing the scheme.

As the Chief Minister and the Minister of Youth Services, had already selected, the young wrestler, Anand Roy, from Delhi, so he was invited to Karnataka. He came to Bangalore and spent some time in the State Sports Council. But he was more keen for his training in Delhi. He made request to the Minister for going back. This was agreed to and he went back by air. After a few days he came back again. Every ten days, he kept going back and coming back, by air. Karnataka State Sports Council was required to foot his bill. When this was repeated too often and with no apparent dedication to the scheme, I suggested to the Minister, that it would be better, if he were to be trained by the National Institute of Sports to organise his training in Patiala, as per International Standards and with the best of coaches. Training expenses would be reimbursed by Karnataka directly to the NIS. So the young wrestler, was asked to proceed to Patiala for training. He attended the training for a few weeks. The training was vigorous, and under strict discipline. The young wrestler left the training, on the pretext of going to Delhi. He neither continued his training under the NIS, nor did he come back to Bangalore.

Apart from him, we wanted to give, a chance to three promising Karnataka wrestlers, to join the scheme. In response to the advertisement, we received hundreds of applications, accompanied with recommendations from influential public men, including MLA's, and Ministers. Some accused me of extending patronage to a non-Kannadiga, as I was from North. I kept quite as the file was clear that it was the Chief Minister's idea to adopt a non- Kannadiga. As a civil servant, I kept my mouth shut taking all the flake for the decision taken at the political level. The pressure continued mounting for adopting one or the other wrestler at the State cost. I felt that the pressure was too much and in those circumstance, it was impossible to do any independent and fair selection. So I kept on postponing the selection. Informally, I told the Minister, that it would be better not to implement the scheme, as it would lead to more criticism and discontent. He also said that a number of ministers had spoken to him and recommended a few names. He himself was not in a position to decide anything. I advised him, that as the Department dealing with the youth we should not only be fair but also appear to be fair. He agreed with my assessment and did not press for the implementation of the scheme. I informally explained the strategy to the Chief Minister who remarked: "We the politicians, have not even spared sports from politics. It is for this reason that we are faring so badly in the arena of international sports."

Ladies Cricket and Politicians

Once when I was away on a foreign tour, in my absence, a State Ladies Cricket Association, obtained a sanction of over Rs 3 lakh, for organising a match, between a visiting, nondescript Australian ladies cricket, team with the State team. The amount was sanctioned, to the State Sports Council, for releasing it, to the association. It was to be subject, to the scrutiny of their expenditure. As the match was over, I, as the Secretary of the State Sports Council, insisted on getting a statement, of expenditure with full details, duly audited by a Chartered Accountant. My experience had shown that many sports and cultural or Non Gazetted Organisations prefer, to have influential people, either from the bureaucracy or senior politicians or their wives as their titular chiefs. It makes their job of securing funding easier. It so happens, that the honorary chief of such bodies, do not have the time or the inclination to thoroughly check the details and sign whatever communications are put up, by the professional office bearers. This was confirmed to me by a Union Cabinet Minister, adorning many honorary offices. Not only the Union Minister but many State Ministers are requested to be either the patrons, or the honorary chairman of associations. As soon as such dignitaries cease to hold office, they are ignored by the professional office bearers. I had also noticed, that many sports and cultural organisations had been captured by persons of doubtful antecedents. Their full time activity, as well as the means of livelihood, was through such organisations. Many of them had been abroad, numerous times at the cost of their association or the government. In the case of Karnataka Ladies Cricket Association the organisers had very thoughtfully made the wife of a very influential Member of Parliament, Mr N. as their President. "Mr. N" was, one of the closest friends of Minister of Youth Services and Sports. The same worthy, had slapped the then serving Commissioner of Police, Bangalore, as per press reports. When I got the statement of account, I found several totally unacceptable items of expenditure. For example, the visiting Australian Ladies team had been put up in a hotel, which was not even half a kilometre away from Bangalore Cricket Stadium. Yet, the expenditure running into thousands had been shown as incurred on their transport. I, as the officer, authorised by the State Government and accountable to it, for the Government money, was in no position to accept the statement of account. So I returned the same, seeking detailed clarifications, as well as the original receipts of the expenditure incurred.

Again a request was received, from the President of the Association, for early passing of the accounts and release of the grant. But no convincing replies, were given, to the basic queries, over which, the audit would hold me responsible, later on. I wrote back to her, that the matter was pending because my queries were not rectified. At the same time, I put up the file to my Minister pointing out all my objections on statement of account. After one month, "Mr N", husband of the President of the Woman's Cricket Association, 'ordered' immediate release of the grant, on the strength, of his proximity to the Minister. I explained to him the reasons, why it could not be done. He was not in a mood to listen. He complained against me, to the Minister that I was unnecessarily withholding the grant, already released by the Government. I cleared my position to the Minister, who agreed with me. After a couple of weeks, I received a call in the evening summoning me to the residence of my Minister. He upbraided me for not attending to the requests promptly. I asked him who had complained against me. I saw the President of the Ladies Cricket Association sitting with the

Minister.

I requested the Minister that I wanted to have a word with the President of the Association privately. I took her aside, away from the hearing of the Minister, and other persons . I asked her, whether she had doubts, about the integrity of any body in the Sports Council. She answered in the negative. She also agreed that I had no favourites. She also accepted that she was aware, that I could not even speak the Kannada fluently, and there was no question, of my having any motive, other than following, the office procedure and the rules. I told her, how the professional hangers on, in the sports bodies, were make a living off the government grant. I also told her, that she was not the first one, to be used like this. My five years stay, as the Secretary of the Sports Council had made me, fully aware, of all the tricks of trade, indulged in by unscrupulous people. I said that if she insisted, upon the Minister, to release the grant, against my advice, it would perhaps mark the end of his career in politics. The opposition parties would exploit it, on the floor of the Assembly. I advised her, that so far as this grant, was concerned, she should consider it a poison, for the political career of late Gundu Rao, the up and coming politician. I said that after this meeting with the Minister, I was not willing to engage in any fight on the file, with the Minister . But then I would not be able to defend anybody, for any wrong decision. After fifteen minutes of conversation, we came back, to the Minister. I told him, that we have sorted out the matter and in near future he would not hear any more on the subject. Afterwards, as long as I was the Director of Youth Services and the Secretary of the Karnataka State Sports Council nobody ever enquired for the grant.

Protest of the Students

In 1974 a students' unrest broke out in Karnataka. The Chief Secretary instructed me, to go around the whole State. I was to discuss the issue, and try to find out a solution with the Principals of various colleges and the Vice-chancellors of the Universities of Mysore, Dharwar, and Bangalore. In the new Karnataka Universities Act, the Director of Youth Services had also been made Ex-Officio Member of the Syndicates, of all the Universities, in the State. A quick visit to various colleges, revealed that the causes of the student's unrest, were varied from lack of toilets, to the abnormal number of vacancies of the lecturers. Toilet facilities, where existed were only for the boys. No toilets were there for the women lecturers and students. Due to large number of vacancies, no courses were completed, leading to poor performance in the examination. The delay in filling the vacancies, in the government institutions, was due to the procedural delay. The selection was to be made, through the State Public Service Commission.

In private colleges, the vacancies were not filled up, due to lack of funds and non release of Grants in Aid, which was 95 per cent of the expenditure, by the Government . Other causes, were a sporadic incident of a road accident, leading to a student being injured, or a quarrel between the bus conductor and the students. During my detailed discussion with the Vice-Chancellors, I requested them to identify the causes of students' unrest college-wise, so that remedial action could be taken. They replied that such a study, would involve meeting all the Principals, of the colleges affiliated to their Universities. Only detailed discussions, could unravel the causes and the steps to be taken in solving the issue. I sent a proposal to the Finance Department, saying that "Due to students unrest in the State it had become essential to conduct an in-depth study. The four Universities had agreed to the same and the total financial implication of the proposal was about Rs forty thousand." I also said that this had been discussed with the Minister of Youth Services and the Chief Minister who had approved the proposal. The proposal in the first instance was rejected at the Deputy Secretary's level. Second time when I sent it to the Joint Secretary, Finance, it was tersely, turned down observing, that "Finance has no reason to revise its stand." Third time at the Finance Secretary's level it came back rejected, saying that I should not have sent it to the Finance, which had twice rejected the proposal. It also advised me that the "State was passing through a financial crisis and such proposals should not be sent in future." After exhausting all channels, I sent the file, to the Secretary to the Chief Minister, saying that as the proposal had the approval of the Chief Minister the matter may kindly be brought to his notice lest he should feel that his orders have not been carried out. I also said that as advised by the Finance, after the Chief Minister had seen the file, the matter would be closed. The Vice-Chancellors would be informed, that due to financial stringency, the matter relating to study indepth causes, of students' unrest had been dropped. When the file was put up to the Chief Minister, he was wild. He wrote in his own handwriting that "The state is not going to become bankrupt with an expenditure of rupees forty thousand. Finance should agree." The file came back through the Finance Minister's noting "We agree" through same channel which had rejected it earlier. This raised my stock, in my department. I had earned the permanent hostility of the Finance Department, for my getting them overruled. Once a Joint Secretary (Finance) very sarcastically remarked that, "I had very high connections and I did not need the concurrence of Finance Department for my schemes." I told him, as you were interested in your department, so was I. If you sanction my proposals, I would not go higher. But if you don't section them for me, sky is the limit.

Bangalore's Guru Nanak Bhawan

In 1969, for commemorating the quincentenary of Guru Nanak, the Union Ministry of Education had sanctioned a scheme of construction of Student Centres in each State, to be called Guru Nanak Bhawans. A grant of Rs 2 lakh was sanctioned to the States desiring to implement the scheme. Under the scheme a Student Service Centre for students' activities including a library, an auditorium and a hall for indoor games, was to be built, on an area of 5 acres. Karnataka had received, a grant of Rs 2 lakh, for the construction of Guru Nanak Bhawan, at its request. It was impossible to get a plot of 5 acres of land in Bangalore .The matter remained under correspondence for a long time, without any fruitful results. I felt that with high land prices, it was just impossible, to get 5 acres of land, within the contemplated budget. I wrote to the Government of India, that it would not be possible to secure 5 acres of plot for the project. We would meet all the requirements, laid down in their order, in a Central area, of Bangalore. Scouting for the land began in all earnestness but without much success. In the meantime, Bangalore City Corporation had a new dynamic administrator, Lakshman Rao.

I requested him for a plot of land for constructing Guru Nanak Bhawan. He asked me to spot the land. I had already done that homework. I told him that we would be satisfied with a 500 x 200 feet plot in the Akhitmanhalli Tank bund area. It was just half a kilometre, from the Vidhan Soudha. He said that I should see him next day for joint inspection of the area. The area had some encroachments from unauthorised persons. I said that matter might be left to us and we would deal with it. After joint inspection at 6 a.m, the same day, he passed orders allocating that plot to Youth Services Department. The Minister of Youth Services had a still better idea . I told him that we had been successful, in getting land, for the Guru Nanak Bhawan. It was after six years of the receipt of Government of India's grant. He said that the Bangalore Guru Nanak Bhawan should be the best in the country. It should not look like a stereotyped, government building. I reminded. him about the limited budget and the necessity to go through the State Public Works Department as per the State Rules. He felt that if we insisted on getting the project completed through the PWD, it would be inordinately delayed. He also said that the best architect should be invited to participate in a competition. At his instance, a high power committee consisting of the Secretaries of the Departments of Education, Finance, PWD and the Chief Engineer Buildings, and myself as Member Secretary was constituted. The Government authorised the Committee to accept public donations. All payments were to be made by the Committee directly, from the government grants and donations. This was a unique experiment undertaken for the first time. For the first time, a work was taken out of the purview of the Public Works Department. They were asked to give measurements, of the work done, for enabling the committee to make payments. They would also certify about the quality of the work done

Ultimately when the building was completed, after six years, the government had spent, more than 50 lakhs over the project. I could get the project pushed through on the tip of a small grant, sanctioned by the Government of India. I had to do a lot of running around, for following it up vigorously. Gundu Rao was really a force to whom nobody could say 'No'. But for him, the present Guru Nanak Bhawan, in Bangalore would not have come up.

Youth Programme in Manila

Karnataka was a pioneer, in Youth Programmes. It was the first State, in the county, to have set up a full-fledged department. I won international and national recognition for the work done. A request was received from the Central Government, Ministry of Commerce, for nomination of an officer, to attend a youth programme organised, by the United Nations Asian Development Institute, Bangkok. Chief Secretary, G.V.K. Rao, nominated me straight on the letter of the Government of India. I had found out, that my police batchmate, A.A. Deshpande had joined the Asian Development Bank at Manila. After joining the IAS in 1963, he had moved to the Asian Development Bank, after a stint in his Maharashtra Cadre. I informed him about my arrival in Manila. I was getting in touch with him after nearly 14 years. Deshpande was very cooperative. He promised to receive me at Manila airport. The KLM flight left Delhi two hours late. When the plane reached near Bangkok, the Captain of the plane announced, that the passengers bound for Manila, should get down in Bangkok, as the plane would not land there. He also said that KLM Airlines would provide hotel and meals for that day, as well as the next, till the connecting flight to Manila. I was upset, because unless, Deshpande was intimated about the change in the plans, he would arrive at the airport. Next day when I actually reach, there would be none to receive me. I would be stranded at Manila airport. I was told that Manila was being skipped as the flight was already late. It was a must for all planes to reach Tokyo well before I0.30 p.m. The reason was, that no flight was allowed, to land at Tokyo between 10.30 p.m. and 5.30 a.m. to avoid disturbance to the Japanese. So if the plane were to land at Manila, it would not be able to make it to Tokyo, in time. It would disrupt their schedule and destroy the credibility of the KLM Airlines with Japan. It was a small price, for them to pay, to keep two dozen passengers at their cost in Bangkok. Moreover, from the business point of view, Japan was more important than Philippines. The airline did not mind upsetting the schedule of the passengers for Manila. The KLM put us up in a five star hotel, in Bangkok.

Incidentally, my friend and classfellow, Ajit Kumar, and

his wife were in the Indian Embassy in Bangkok. He had been with me in Government College, Ludhiana and was a topper of the Punjab University. He had joined IAS in 1964 and married his batchmate Kamlesh of the Indian Foreign Service. I telephoned, after getting his number, from the Indian Embassy. He picked me up for dinner, at his house. We had a quick round of the city in his car. Bangkok is the city of sex and massage parlours, by petite Thai Women. Tourists flock to it for the freely and easily available sex. It looked as if the whole city was full of brothels. There were a number of statues of Buddha, like the Golden Buddha, Jade Buddha, Sleeping Buddha, and a lot of other Buddhas in temples. I did not know that the Buddhists monks freely ate pork. In India we associate Hindu, Buddhists or Jain holy men with complete vegetarianism. I was also informed by a monk that Lord Buddha had passed away as a result of a bone stuck up in his throat. This looked incredible to me, because one of the Edicts of Buddhism was "Not to kill".

In Manila

Next day, the Air France flight, took me to Manila. Luckily Deshpande had been intimated about the change of my travel plans, by KLM at my request. I did not have details of the venue or the hotel, where the programme was being conducted. Deshpande had done all the home work for me. He took me straight to the venue of the programme, which was the same, as the hotel earmarked for our stay. As English was freely spoken, it took care of discomfort and misery one faces, when one is in a country, where nobody understands you and you do not understand anybody.

Thirty-five participants from several nations were participating in the programme. It consisted of lectures, demonstrations and field visit. A representative from India, from a non-governmental organisation, painted a gloomy and poor picture, of the country. He condemned the imposition of emergency, though night curfew was imposed in Philippines, for the last ten years. I told him, that by condemning, of our own country, before the representatives of other countries, we were only condemning ourselves. Representatives of other countries and organisations, could not do anything, about our own internal affairs. He claimed that he was working in a voluntary organisation dedicated to the cause of the youth.

Free Loaders of Our Society

After a few sessions of conversation with him, I discovered that he had attended a number of international conferences. He had got an impressive letter-head printed something like the "National Council of the Future of Youth for India". The letter head showed his name, as the President. He was sending letters to a number of international organisations, as the President of the so called Youth Organisation, which was only a one man show. On the strength of his letter head, he had managed to secure a number of invitations to a series of conferences abroad. His livelihood was dependent only, on attending conferences, where the organisers paid for the ticket as well as the boarding and lodging. He would purchase foreign goods and sell them at an exorbitant profit in India. He especially welcomed trips to the duty free areas, like Hong Kong or Singapore to criticise everything Indian including the youth and sports programmes. In my later foreign visits to West Germany and other countries, I was to meet a horde of such free loaders, not only from India, but also from Pakistan and other Asian countries. Free loaders are a part of the phenomenon of life one meets them in the form of classfellows, friends, strangers and relations. A classfellow, Jetka (name changed) specialised in free loading from the college days by joining marriage parties especially in five star hotels. He graduated to borrowing shirts, shoes, ties and cash. He also specialized in entangling girls, on the promise of, getting them roles as film stars in the glamorous world of Bollywood.

Another prince of free loaders, I have met, had specialised, not only in parking himself, where he could for days, but also insisted on the host in providing him nightsuits, tooth brush, toothpaste, which would travel with him, to his next destination. The free loaders live, in a make-believe world, of their own. They thrive on, the gift of the gab, whether it is to extract, a drink or spend the night or borrow jewellery or clothing. So beware. My niece Golu told me that her elder brother Bikram keeps everything worthwhile, in the locked cupboard of his room. His friends come to him and say "Can I borrow your pants as I have to go for a wedding."? After screening his room, they select the best of the clothing.

The items, once borrowed, are never returned. Now he has started keeping all his good clothes in his sister's room.

The Philippines currency of Peso, was very cheap. We were paid enough to live well. Within the allowance given, we could go around Manila. Manila had a floating Casino, in a ship, anchored , five kilometres away in the sea. It was open only to the foreigners. You had to show your passport, to be ferried, to the ship free of charges. No Philippinos were allowed to visit it.

Memorable Visit to a Casino

The organiser decided, to let the youth, group attending the programme, visit the Casino. My wife, Surinder also joined me. Hers was, a private sight seeing first visit abroad. She also accompanied us, to visit the, Floating Gambling Den. We were given a royal reception by the Ferry Staff. They took us to the ship, after checking our passports. An equally royal treatment was extended to us on the ship. Obviously the people of the ship, were not aware, that we were on a shoe string budget. I politely refused the invitation, of card game, by saying that I was ignorant. I have never played cards, which is true. I saw the slot machines for the first time. These machines had a place for inserting the coins. After the coin of a fixed denomination was put in the machine, then you could pull its lever. If after pulling the lever the machine stopped, on a predetermined number, then you could win a prize. It may be, one hundred dollars or even more, depending upon the slot machine. I had the beginner's luck and won about thirty dollars, in the Pesos. Later on, not only did I lose what I won, but also another twenty dollars. There and then, I had decided on an unwritten rule, to stop gambling when my loss or gain equalled 20 dollars. I have stuck to this self-made rule, during my visits to Casinos, in Monte Carlo , Kuala Lumpur, France and United States. I and my wife, went around Manila, in the evenings. It was a mini America, in so far as the culture or behaviour of the people was concerned. The public parks were full of necking couples, doing everything normally done in the privacy of a closed bedroom. You could hardly find any public place, where the couples, were not glued to each other. Indian public culture was different in 1970's, though in 1999-2000, the younger generation has absorbed lot of Western value.

Kissing, was something you could observe only in English movies. Indian ladies of old generation do not find it easy to stomach public love making. One evening when we were roaming around, a siren blew at 9 p.m.. I had heard it earlier and ignored it. I asked a Philipino its significance. He told me that it was a signal to indicate the commencement of the curfew time, after one hour. It was a warning to people to go back to their homes.The curfew from 10 p.m. to 5 a.m., was a permanent feature, in the regime of President Marcos. The Philippino, in turn asked me, as to what were the curfew timings in my country. I told him that we did not have any curfew in India. He found it rather incredible, that a country, of the size of India, beset with numerous problems, could run, without the imposition of a curfew. I noticed that even biscuits were imported, like most other goods of daily use. It made me feel proud of my country, that we had become self sufficient in most areas of industry and agriculture. An attractive tourist draw, was the open bus ride, on Roxas Avenue. It was a two kilometre drive by the beach side. The bus had very broad windows. It also had fixed chairs on the roof itself. One could enjoy the view of Manila as well as beach at a slow speed. The passengers had the choice, of sitting on the roof top, or inside the bus. As in India, urchins were selling local delicacies, to the tourists. I inquired as what was the delicacy. It turned out to be a half boiled eggs, with half-formed chick in it. In India, we recognise, such eggs, to be bad eggs, unfit for human consumption. In Philippines it was a great delicacy. Roxas Avenue was full of Saunas. Saunas, and massage parlours were, only a cover up, for prostitution. It was legal and nothing to be ashamed of or conceal. Five-Star hotels, having saunas and massage parlours, were thriving,on the Roxas Avenue.

I drink plenty of water with my meals. One day, during lunch at a restaurant, I drank seven glasses of water. The head steward, was quite amazed as he had not seen any customer drinking so much of water. He came to my table after the meal was over. He politely enquired whether I had enjoyed my meals and the water. I said "water is water everywhere." He said he could understand, my drinking, plenty of water. He had seen on TV, the acute scarcity of drinking water in India and dire perpetual poverty. The only news about India, was either the floods, or drought, or lack of drinking water and illiteracy. These were the features of India, shown on Philipines television. I dispelled his impression, that I had not come thousands of miles, just to quench my thirst. We had plenty of water in our country and the stage had not come that we had to travel to Manila to drink water. I also told him that unlike their country we in India were manufacturing everything, from needles to aeroplanes. He did not believe what I told him. Philippinos are generally happy and smiling people.

In Hong Kong

After the training phase, in Philippines was over, we were flown to Hong Kong, for the next and final phase, in June, 1976. We flew by, one of the best airlines in the world, Cathay Pacific. It provided memorable in-flight service. Landing of the aircraft at Hong Kong airport itself was a thrilling experience. The aircraft seemed to be landing in the sea itself. The fact was that land-starved HongKong, had retrieved the land from the sea. An area equivalent to the required runway had been filled up in the sea itself. So the plane had to make an accurate landing and taking off. The safety track record of Hong Kong, despite a precarious run way jutting into the sea, was one of the best in the world. The aircrafts, had to land and take off in the sea. Hong Kong has two parts. The newly developed area is called Kowloon and the old part is old Hong Kong. We were put up in the Young Men's Christian Associations building in Kowloon. It was well furnished, cheap and located near the shopping centre. With all big and tall buildings built alike, the whole of Hong Kong is a concrete jungle.

The youth programme, in Hong Kong, included a visit to licensed slums. For the first time, I came to know, that slums were also licensed. Due to shortage of space, the Government of Hong Kong felt hat it would not be possible to meet all the housing needs of the people. So it had provided electricity, drinking water, and street lighting in the slums, which were the areas of cheap housing. They were just like *jhuggis-jhomprees* in India. The people living in the licensed slums, were not very poor. But the expensive flats of Hong Kong, were beyond their reach. They were the workers, engaged in building Hong Kong. They were the ones, who were providing basic services to run the city. Since both the husbands and wives, generally work in Hong Kong, the government had encouraged all the members of the extended families and their relations to live together.

A bewildering array of electronic, and other types of goods are available, in Hong Kong. Many departmental stores had escalators, taking the customers to seventh or even other higher floors. I was exposed to the escalators, or moving staircase, for the first time. I must confess, that I visited many departmental stores, not to purchase anything, but to have the thrill of enjoying a ride on the escalator. Since as a Sikh, I was easily distinguishable, by my turban, moustache and beard, I took care not to visit the same departmental store again and again the same day. The shopkeepers, especially Chinese, were quite abrasive and to the point that on seeing Indians, their ire would go up. It was, because most Indians, on a visit to Hong Kong, were tough bargainers. They would go to numerous shops, cross check the prices, before making any purchases.

One day when I entered a Chinese store, the shopkeeper immediately asked "Want to buy or see". I was in an equally defiant mood and replied "Want to sell or close". He was taken aback. I asked him the reason for his offensive behaviour. On seeing me, speaking polished English, he apologised and said that most of the Indians, who came to his shop, spent hours without making any purchases. Seeing the shop full of Indians, no other customers would come. So he had made a point to avoid selling anything to the Indians. Such is the reputation our countrymen had in the eyes of the Chinese. When I mentioned this incident, to the Director of YMCA, also an Indian, he confirmed what the Chinese shopkeeper told me. He advised me, to avoid the Chinese shops, if I wanted to avoid any unpleasantness, He said that "If you buy something from Indian shops, you can at least tell him what you want." He gave the address of "Esquire" departmental store for purchases. Indian shops sell goods matching the Indian conditions and in the case of electronic goods, the voltage. The old Hong Kong and Kowloon were connected, by a quick ferry service called "Star Ferry". It was available from both sides, at fifteen minutes interval. In fact in the Ferry not only you could ferry yourself but also your vehicles and personal goods, over the sea, which separates two parts of Hong Kong. Hong Kong has done something unheard of at least, in the rest of Asia, in 1960's. It had built a tunnel road under the sea. The tunnel was water proof, air-conditioned and was more than three kilometres long. Over the tunnel, the ships in Hong Kong Port, were plying. Hong Kong had also planned an underground metro and the work was progressing without any traffic or disrupting the life of citizens, in 1976. I had the pleasure of using the underground, metro train during my next visit to Hong Kong in 1983, on my way to Australia. It was quick, smooth, and very fast and had connected every corner of Hong Kong with the rest of the colony. Probably the idea of building an underground link between England and France in English Channel must have been encouraged by the success of the under sea tunnel in Hong Kong.

Choose Reptile for Eating

Hong Kong has a vast number of eating joints. Some times, eating places, display live snakes, lizards, fish, crabs or tortoise. The customer can indicate his choice of the animal for eating. In minutes, it would be cut in your presence, and boiled or fried. I and my wife, were content with the food we were used to. We relished the Indian food, much more in Hong Kong. For three weeks, in Manila, we had not eaten anything resembling the Indian meals, except in the house of my friend Deshpande. We lived only on toast and bread.

After the programme was over, I decided that might as well see Bangkok, Singapore, Kuala Lumpur and Sri Lanka on our own. In any case, the visit was possible within the fare already paid. From Hong Kong to Bangkok, it was less than four hours of flight. We stayed, for the night, in a hotel in Bangkok. I traced my IAS batchmate, Ranjit Singh who was with United Nations Wild Life Fund. He took good care of us in the evening and took us for dinner to his house. Bangkok in 1976, did not have any sewerage system. The traffic was so chaotic. From the airport to hotel, hardly a distance of twenty kilometres, it could take two to three hours, depending upon the overcrowding on the roads. I saw an interesting newspaper report, and the Statements of Thai leaders, expressing resentment over the thinning of the American Army presence in Thailand. It was apprehended that it would affect the sex business of Thai girls. One editorial comment, pointed out the bleak future, of Thai sex industry, if the American went away. It was accepted, that one of their biggest foreign exchange earner was and is even now, the free and safe sex. It attracts more tourists and more dollars than many commercial business enterprises.

Singapore: A Well-Organised State

After Bangkok, the visit to Singapore, was a transition, to a new well-organised world. The taxi drivers were polite and would take you by the shortest route. Prominent boards were displayed at all public places, in case of any complaint, the tourists should contact Singapore Tourist Promotion Board. The complaints were attended to promptly and taken very seriously. The taxi drivers or the shopkeepers, dreaded any complaints against them. The city was impeccably clean. Throwing of litter, in the public places and parks, entailed a prompt fine of 500 Singapore dollars. With a population, of about two million, at that time, it had one of the lowest crime records. Possession of drugs like heroin, etc., were Punished with death penalty. It was not only on paper. A number of criminals were executed for these offences. During another official visit to Singapore in 1985, I found a lot of building activity going on. The independent houses were very few. Mostly, there were multistoreyed flats. I asked an official, whether they had any problem of stay order from the courts, coming in the way of construction activities. He did not understand, the word "stay order". When I explained to him, that it meant the court giving the stay order on any activity, till it finally decided the case. He asked me, what was the legal basis of the same. I replied, that to the best of my knowledge, there was no legal basis for this. At the best it could be compared to the equivalent of "bail" in criminal cases or it could be argued that it was done, with a view to prevent injustice. He said, that it was not in the purview of the courts, to stop any activity, unless it contravened any law or statute. The judiciary had never interfered, in Singapore to stop any development. Singapore, like Hong Kong being a 'duty free', city was cheaper. It had massive departmental stores, like Hong Kong, where for a price, you could procure anything from a needle to an elephant. It was also great attraction for Indian tourists. Tamil was and is still one of the official languages apart from the Chinese Malay and English. The other attractions were small islands, which were a part of Singapore. As Indian food was freely available in Sarangoon area, we felt at home in Singapore. After two days of sight seeing and limited shopping,we flew to Sri Lanka skipping Malaysia, in between.

A visit to Colombo, after Singapore was a climb down. I had written to my batchmate Bhupat Oza, the Acting High Commissioner there, about my visit. He had picked us up, at the airport. Colombo airport in 1976 had only dilapidated buses and ramshackle taxies, like itself. The roads were full of potholes. The Colombo market was, like a small bazaar, in the Trans-Yamuna colony of Delhi. There were no supermarkets or big departmental stores. We had planned, to stay there, only for two days. The shops in Sri Lanka in 1976 had much lesser goods than in any decent shop in Delhi and many shops in State capitals back home. A lot of effort was required to clean the town. Sanitation and hygiene appeared to be worse than many towns in India. A month of absence, from my own country, had made me homesick. It was with a great relief and joy that myself and my wife boarded the Indian Airlines flight from Colombo to Madras. The first thing I did on landing at Madras was to kiss the earth of my motherland. It might appear as an unabashed demonstration of love for the country, but I did bend down and kiss the soil or tarmac. It surprised and astonished many passengers, as to what I was doing. When I explained my rationale for doing so, the people just nodded, silently approving what I had done.

Youth Programme in Solo (Indonesia)

The Adenauer Foundation of the then West Germany invited, the Government of Karnataka to send its nominee for a Youth Programme, to be conducted in Solo in Indonesia, in August, 1976 . The Government of Karnataka nominated me to attend the programme. When the matter was referred to the State General Administration Department, it advised that the approval of the Union Education Ministry should be obtained, first. It was pointed out that the invitation had been sent by the United Nations Development Programme (UNDP) and as such did not need approval. However, a senior official of the GAD than a Joint Secretary, had a lot of tiffs earlier. He thought it was a good opportunity to cut me to size. So on his insistence, a reference was made to the Central Education Ministry by the then Education Secretary, P.R. Nayak. He sent a number of personal messages, through telex, to the concerned Joint Secretary, asking for formal clearance. The courtesy of a reply was not even extended by the Joint Secretary, who was very junior to Nayak. Nayak, the education secretary pointed out again that there was no outflow of the foreign exchange or even expenditure either by the central or state government.

In the meantime the UNDP sent a prepaid two-way ticket in my name. As I had returned only a fortnight back from Manila and Hong Kong and other countries, my official passport was still valid. I did not receive any clearance from the Government of India, till 5 p.m. on the day, previous to my proposed departure. The State Government offices used to close at 5.30 p.m. I went to my Secretary, asking as to what should be done. I told him that neither the state general administration department, had issued orders, deputing me to Indonesia, for the reasons, he also knew, nor the clearance of the Central Education Ministry had been received. He pondered over for a minute and asked me to proceed to Indonesia. I told him that I did not want to embarrass him, in the absence of any formal orders. He said "Does not matter. You go. At the most I will get a rap. I am prepared for the same." Then I told him that some kind of Government orders should be issued, which would indicate my credentials to represent the Government of Karnataka. He asked me to get a Government order typed, on the same lines as GAD order and he would sign it himself.

He signed the order, on behalf of the Government of Karnataka, deputing me to Indonesia.. This is one of the few instances of boldness, in my long career, by a senior officer, who did, what he felt to be correct, notwithstanding any quibbling over the formalities. After my return from Indonesia, P.R. Nayak, later on submitted the file to the Chief Minister, detailing the circumstances under which he had deputed me, requesting for the ratification of the action taken by him. The Chief Minister approved.

After my Secretary had signed the order deputing me to Indonesia, I came back home at 6 p.m. In anticipation of proceeding abroad, I had already done my packing. Government permission always comes at the last minute. If one were to await for the formal Government approval, before completing the pre-departure formalities, then the visit is not likely to take off. Next morning at 8 a.m. I flew to Madras from Bangalore, so as to catch the evening flight from Madras to Singapore. There was no connecting flight available to Jkarta from Singapore, I was put up in a five-star hotel, at the cost of the Airline. Next morning I flew to Jakarta from Singapore.

Distance between the two Airports

On the flight to Jkarta, I met a lady of Indian origin, settled in Jakarta. I told her that I had to catch another flight to Solo in less than an hour of my arrival at Jakarta. She said that it would not be possible, as the domestic flight to Solo, took off from another airport. It was 30 kilometres, from the International Airport, where my plane was landing. After arrival, I tried to get quick immigration and customs clearance. The formalities took time, as Indonesians were working rather leisurely. I changed 100$, into the Indonesian currency, and took a taxi to the domestic airport. By the time I reached there, the last flight to Solo, for the day, had taken off. I asked the taxi driver to take me, to Air India Office. I wanted to meet the top man. I showed him the ticket issued by their Bangalore office. The issuing office did not take into account the distance between the two airports. This left no time gap between the arrival of the flight from Singapore and the departure of another flight to Solo from another airport. First he tried to bluff me off. When I told him that it was no fault of mine, he very reluctantly, gave me accommodation and meals in a newly opened five-star Hotel Sari Pacific, Jakarta. Only after I had settled down in the hotel, I telephoned my friend, Mangalmurthy, Minister in Indian Embassy. He was surprised to find me in Jkarta. He promptly came to the hotel to see me and took me to his house for dinner.

Enjoyment and Fun in Jakarta

After dinner I asked him to show me around Jakarta. He took out his Mercedes and along with his wife, took me for a long drive through the well illuminated streets and highways of Jakarta. After that he drove me through the famous amusement park called "Anchol Park". For the first time I saw a dog race. Dogs were made to run along side a mechanical rabbit on a mono rail. People would bet, which one would win. Later he drove me, through the rest of the amusement park. It was full of soliciting, naked, half naked and semi-naked charming, young Indonesian girls. Seeing me tongue-tied, his wife told me "not to feel out of place." Mangalmurthy said "Don't worry. You are not the only Indian to have come to this place. In fact many senior officers and Ministers have also visited this place in our company. But it was just a visit and nothing more." I asked him, as to how a predominantly Muslim country, could encourage a park like this. He said that the Governor of Jakarta was very "progressive". He was aware that a lot of foreign tourists, including Indonesians, were going to Bangkok to have some fun and sex there. So he decided to have a kind of free and unrestricted area.

Thus, Anchol Amusement Park, is a kind of a Free Trade Zone, for the sex. The entry fee, to the park was the equivalent of about two dollars. This amount was used for the development and beautification of Jakarta. As Herpes, a disease contracted, due to promiscuous sex, had affected some men, the business was adversely affected. He told me that corruption was rampant in Indonesia. In every deal the money had to pass hands. The salaries were not high and were not even on the subsistence level. Next day, I reached the airport well in time to catch the only flight leaving Jakarta for Solo. It was a brief flight, of one hour. Solo was a new world in itself. Language was a big problem, even for getting ordinary services. The programme was conducted in Spartan rural surroundings. It was the only programme, in which the accommodation provided was not only bare, but also the cheapest, with no air conditioning. It was very humid and hot. Except for the fact that the programme, was conducted in Indonesia, it might have been better to have it in Chandigarh or Bangalore. The programme in the oil rich Indonesia was for one week. I returned to Bangalore, via the only route of Singapore to Madras and Bangalore. In Singapore, except for visiting the High Street and some departmental stores, there was nothing much to be done. I had returned from Singapore, only a fortnight back. There was no shopping to be done.

National Cadet Corps

The strength of the National Cadet Corps was limited by financial constraints. The cost on it, had to be shared between the Centre and the State. The NCC, training for the college and school students, prepared them for a disciplined life. It also enabled them to have a small taste, of defence services. The NCC training itself was devised on the pattern of Army, Navy and Airforce. The holders of the NCC "C" Certificate, could appear for direct entry examination of the Indian Military Academy. Their success in the examination would lead to their joining the Army training, for passing out as Second Lieutenants. People from Karnataka, especially old Mysore, were not inclined to leave the state, for any service. Only few districts like Coorg or South or North Karnataka or Old Bombay or Old Hyderabad district, contributed to the uniformed services. For the rest, the uniformed services, held no attraction.

The Government of India, also started centrally assisted scheme, called NSS (National Service Scheme) to involve the university students, in social service. The main objective, of the scheme, was to make the students conscious of the various socio-economic problems. They were to be encouraged to take part in community building activities, like constructions of the school buildings, laying of the link roads rural sanitation and desiltng of tanks and aforestation. The students had a choice of joining, either the National Service Scheme or the National Cadet Corps, to involve in building up a new society. The only constraint was money. The Government of India would pay Rs 35 per student per year and the State Government Rs 25 per year. An amount of Rs 60 or Rs 5 per month was not sufficient even to purchase implements and tools for the tasks expected to be done. For the annual camps, held during the vacations, an amount of Rs 100 per participant, was sanctioned. This was to cover their expenses on transport, food and tools for working. The net result was, that only the projects in the nearby villages, would be undertaken. This was the only way to keep the expenses within the sanctioned amount. Sometimes the same village would be visited by more than one group of National Service Scheme volunteers, but from different colleges. One day, during my visit to a camp, a villager asked me as to why the students were coming again and again, to their village. They did not need any help or advice, as the students were coming in their way, instead of helping. In a meeting with the University Co-ordinators I told them, that the formal compliance, of holding camps and taking up projects, in the same village, again and again, by different colleges must stop. It had made the villagers sceptical about the whole scheme. I suggested, that the projects be taken up, wherever they were needed or welcomed. The same practice was prevailing in other departments. Whenever a VIP visited the State, he was shown the same model village, or the same project, instead of developing similar projects elsewhere.

Departure of Gundu Rao

In the 1977 General Elections, the then Prime Minister, Indira Gandhi was defeated, and her Congress party was decimated. Janta Party came to power and Morarji Desai took over as the Prime Minister. My Minister, R. Gundu Rao was quite close to her. He was becoming, a parallel centre of power. In the reshuffle of the State Ministry, which was headed by Dev Raj Urs, he expected to be promoted as a full fledged cabinet Minister. As he did not get cabinet rank, this upset him. He came to Delhi and met the powerful politicians to canvass his case. He had earned a name for himself as an effective and a go-getter Minister. He was dedicated to the cause of the youth. But the differences between him and the Chief Minister had affected the functioning of the department. The Secretary to the Chief Minister in the Chief Minister's Secretariat advised me that I should neither meet Gundu Rao nor put up files to him. I told him, that as long as he was my Minister, I could not refuse, to see him, if he sent for me. I added, that I have not done, anything out of the way or against the Rules. He was disappointed, with my reply. He conveyed it to the Chief Minister. My position had become unenviable. On the one hand, I was to keep the Chief Minister happy, by not maintaining any relation with my Minister, on the other I had to keep running my department, in top gear, as it was going on. It was impossible, without the help, of my Minister. I was mentally prepared, for my transfer, for not complying with the orders, of the Chief Minister. The expected transfer did not come about. I had done tight rope walking. I kept a fine and correct balance in my relationship with all concerned. In the next Cabinet reshuffle, Gundu Rao was elevated to the cabinet rank and given the portfolio of Transport and Housing. I had worked with him for over four years. I felt that his departure, would be a great set-back, to the Youth Programmes. He asked me whether I would be willing to accept the job of the Chief executive of Karnataka State Road Transport Corporation as the General Manager. I thanked him and felt honoured. I told him, that my heart was in the Job of Director of Youth Services. He was succeeded by another young Minister, who was no comparison with the bulldozing ways of his predecessor in getting the proposals through. The new Minister did not appear too transparent in his dealings. But I had the satisfaction, of putting youth programmes, on a sound footing. I had codified all the schemes and had the staff sanctioned at the Taluk, District and Divisional levels. The Ministry of Rural Development, Govt. of India, nominated me for a Youth Leadership Programme in West Germany at Herrshching, near Munich from 14th June to 5th July 1978. The nomination came directly, as a result of the Ministry's Officials, having seen the work done for the youth in Karnataka.

Visit to Germany

The State Government deputed me for the programme, after the last minute clearance and sanction from the Government of India. International flights are much longer and faster than domestic sectors in our country. The Swiss Air flight, took me to Zurich, after nine hours of non stop flight, from Delhi. I was the only Indian, in that flight. I had no visa for Switzerland. When I explained, that I was staying only for one day, in Switzerland the Immigration officials, instead of giving me a visa, kept my Passport and air Ticket. He gave me an acknowledgement for the same. I was told to come, in time for the next day's flight. My passport and ticket, would be given at that time, to enable me to board the flight. Since I had the whole day, I did some sightseeing. I was impressed by the superb cleanliness of the city. One of my cousins, DP Singh came and picked me up. He was in the travel trade. He guided me where to go and what to see. I bought some cheap plastic watches from him and paid him in dollars. He said that I had paid him too much. But he did not return any excess amount paid. Next day I flew from Zurich to Munich in than West Germany. I was advised to take a train to Herrshcing, 40 kms from Munichen or Munich. Since I had reached Munich in the morning, I went straight to the railway station and put my luggage in a locker. I took the city tour in a bus and saw the Olympic Stadium and a few museums. In the mining section of the Museum, I saw a miniature of actual mining being done on a model. It would show a lift being lowered with dummies, the dummies excavating the material to be mined and loading the same in the material lifts. One could see the physics phenomenon, of prism or the halogen effect, or three dimensional pictures. The Germans had also preserved, the gas chambers, where millions of Jews, were gassed to death by the Nazis.

In the evening I boarded a train to Herrsching. My room-mate happened to be a fellow Indian from West Bengal. He was representing a non-government organisation. When I was told to go to room number 26 on the second floor, I hauled up my luggage there. I found a slip on the room saying Zimmer 26. I thought Zimmer had already occupied it. So I knocked and knocked without a response. When there was no reply, I just pushed the door open and made myself comfortable, waiting for Zimmer. Instead of Zimmer, it turned out to be one Mukerjee. I inquired from him about Zimmer. He had no reply. Then we came to ground floor and found that on every room the word Zimmer was written. The mystery was solved, by the Course Incharge, when he explained, that Zimmer meant room in German language.

Life in Germany

Herrshcing was a small village with a population of 2000. The village had only five taxies. The taxis would respond, at the dot time requested. Some German taxis charge by the time and not the distance. Punctuality is the hallmark of German life. One day, I asked my German Course Director, as to what they do, when electricity fails. He told me that electricity had never failed in their country. We were 65 participants from 50 different countries. The largest group was from Africa. One participant from a small African country, boasted of the high position he was occupying in his country. The African participant, was all the time asking the German organisers, for money for his expenses. When I questioned him, as to why he had not been able to get some foreign exchange from his country. He said that his government had sanctioned him 5000£s. But when he went to the Federal Bank of his country, he was told that the total foreign exchange available that day was only 100£s. The Bank refused to release the same on the ground that even the amount had been kept, as reserve to be utilized only on the orders of the "President" of the country. Amongst the participants were nationals from United Kingdom, Ireland, Norway, Sweden and Germany. The English participant, Brown, was free with the information, on the western style, of living. One day, the discussion centred, on the subject of arranged marriages. I told that I did not know my wife before marriage. Most of the westerners were shocked. They wondered how could one live with somebody, one did not know at all. A German girl, Susan, said that she had five boy friends and all of them were keen to marry her. But it was she, who felt that she did not know them sufficiently. She lived with all of them as husband and wife. It was she, who had declined to marry any of them. She had them, one at a time and discarded them, one by one, on grounds of incompatibility. She said that as per the traditions, she left her parental house, at the age of 18, to be on her own. She said that boys and girls, after the age of 18, leave their homes, to fend for themselves. They earn their own livelihood by taking up jobs. Even the children of the multimillionaires and high up people seek their own fortune. Only in few cases, children stay in the families, to manage the family empires. It was so all over Europe.The Englishman said that everybody has to pay for the services utilised, in western society. He said that he was a very good father. He was not charging anything from his daughter, though she was earning a good salary. and living with him. I told him, that in my country, one is not expected to charge anything, from ones children, even when they are earning children. He said that in western society, many parents charged their children, for staying with them.

We were put up in a hostel belonging to the training institution. It was not a hostel in a sense of a hostel in India. It was a three star establishment, with central heating, swimming pool and a big dinning hall. The programme, included discussions, debates and visit to German institutions concerned with the Youth programme. The programme also included spending one day with a German farmer to know about the latest, in airying and agriculture. One of the best methods used for energy conservation was in vogue, in the Hostel. There were timer lights, of thirty seconds to two minutes, depending upon the requirement. While crossing the corridor you needed to put on the light to dispel darkness. The light, will automatically, go off after one minute or half minute. It was programmed, as such. If I get a chance, I swim every day. I found the swimming pool, of 16 x 12 feet, a big disappointment. I felt, there was no point in using a swimming pool meant for kids. My German friends insisted that I should give a try and swim. I was warned that I will not be able to complete even one length of 16 feet. I laughed and jumped into the swimming pool. The Germans were proved right, I could not even complete one length. The swimming pool was a piece of engineering marvel. Powerful jets were fixed inside the swimming. The water entered the pool at a great force. The swimmer, had to swim, against the jets. It was the swimmers might against the jets. It turned out to be only stationary swimming, as the jets would push you away. The German ingenuity had devised the pool in the smallest area available. It was capable of giving you, as much exercise as you wanted. The swimming enabled you, not to only to do swimming exercise, but also get massaged by the powerful jets. The breakfast was punctually at 8 a.m., tea break at 11 a.m., lunch at 1 p.m. and supper at 7 p.m. The official training programme was from 9 a.m. to 6 p.m. Germans were so punctual that, if you did not reach, in time for your meals, you could miss them. The kitchen staff, would simply throw away, the un-consumed food and the left overs. The breakfast was generally boiled egg, toasts, butter, plenty of tea or coffee or milk and juice. The lunch was some boiled vegetable, or beef. I told the course incharge that I was not a beef eater. So at my request, either chicken or lamb meal were added to the menu. Our meals were cooked by two German girls. They would get up early, not only to prepare breakfast, and serve it but, also lunch, and dinner. Coffee and tea was served in between. They were very hard working, putting in 14 to 18 hours of work every day. Since the participants did not know any German girls, the same girls, would join for social dancing and other social get togethers outside the hostel. In India, cheap domestic help, is available. It is normally the servants, who remove the plates or utensils after the meal. I was no exception to Indian culture. I found, everybody after the meals, removing his plates and keeping them, near the automatic dishwasher. One day I asked my course incharge, why we should be expected to do the work of the persons who are paid for it. In western culture, nobody uses the word 'servant' or 'subordinate'. People come and help in work and get their wages for the work done. The German replied "Mr. Singh, there are only two girls who get up at 4 a.m. They prepare your breakfast, lunch and dinner in time. A little help, from the participants, would go a long way, in lessening their burden. For each one of you, it is not even one-minute job. Also, some of you, expect to dance, with them, or take them out, after dinner. So what is the harm in giving a helping hand. Moreover, in German and Western Society, nobody minds doing his own dishes and other chores. It was an eye opening advice, for me. Since then I have tried to be as helpful as possible. After every meal, I make it a point to keep my utensils in the kitchen.

Joseph, a member of the faculty, from USA, told us to prepare our hopes and expectations, through the pictures in the magazine. We were given old magazines and scissors and told to present our hopes and fears. Some of the participants cut pictures of German Blondes, wine and liquor bottles, Mercedes cars, yachting and skiing in their hopes and expectation category. Others, cut the picture of factories, farms, and night clubs. In the fear category, some cut pictures of road accidents, beggars and poor homes. Another method, taught to us, was that the participants were asked to pair themselves. Each participant was asked to talk to the other for about fifteen minutes. He would introduce him and answer all questions about him or his family or any other matter, other participants may inquire. This ensured, that we knew every participant, his family and problems sufficiently well. Every week, we were asked, to evaluate each guest faculty member. We were to give our views about the quality of his presentation, the indepth preparation of the subject, and whether he was able to answer all the questions. Participants were also asked to assess, whether he was fit, to be invited for the next programme. It was a unique system, in which the participants were the judges. The lecturers could not get away, just by whiling away their time, or bluffing if they wanted to be invited again, for any other programme. One day, a Secretary to the Government of West Germany, addressed us, in clear English, as if he was an Englishman. During tea break we chatted with him. I was surprised to find him sharing his tea table with his secretary, his chauffeur and other staff. With the Indian culture and traditions behind me, I asked him, as to how could he have tea with his subordinates, as he had to get the work out of them. He said that was no problem. Each member knew, what was expected of him or her. They performed their duty, without any complaint or fuss. He also said, that taking tea together, did not mean, that he would not sack them, if they were found amiss, in their duties. He asked me; "Don't you do the same in India?" I replied in the negative. He asked me for reasons. I said that first of all we would be misunderstood. Secondly, it is quite possible, that staff so extended the hospitality, may misuse the generosity. They may give, a wrong impression, to outsiders. Thirdly, even the common people are likely to get an impression, that the officer is clay, in the hands of his personal staff. The German official said, that they had no such problems. After the office hours everybody was equal. I told him that even my attending social functions, like wedding receptions of my subordinates, had invited complaints against me. It was alleged that I was favouring some and ignoring others. The result was that to avoid controversies, I had stopped going for all such functions. The German official smiled and said that some of his employees earned double his salary and the overtime to which they were entitled.

Agriculture and Dairy System in Germany

As part of the training, a bachelor German farmer, picked me up along with other participants, to show us farming and dairying. He first took us to his well furnished house. He had the latest gadgets, music and TV system to make his life comfortable. Later, he took us to see his Dairy farm of 35 cows. I asked him, as to how he could, take care of these cows, he demonstrated it to us by taking his cows to his 40-hectare farm. He himself rode on the horse back. The cows ate lush green grass, and drank water from the constantly replenished trough of water. The animals were trained, to go straight, to the water trough, for drinking water on their own. Barbed wires had been put around the parameter of the farm. Animals did not have any opportunity to stray out. There were enough of partitioned compartments, for the animals to enter in, for resting and for their fodder. Electric milk extractors were used to milk the animals. The milk from the udders, of the animals would be piped directly to milk containers. The electric milk extractor would function gently and also massage the udders of the animals. The extractor, was capable of milking the last drop of the milk. At one go, all the 35 cows could be milked. The farmer took the help, of only one part time worker-a young lady. For feeding hey and grains to the animals, the electric lift would transport the same, from the stored bins, to the feeding place, of the animals, in their respective enclosures. The water supply was so piped, that it would be stored in front of the animals. For cleaning the barn, the press of another button would extend a cleaning gadget. It will sweep the floor, wash and clean it. There was no physical handling, of milk. The milk would be collected by the dairy agency every day. While taking away the drums of the milk, freshly cleaned and disinfected containers, would be left behind so that next day's milk, collection could be stored in the same. The entire operation, from the milking of the animal, to its collection, was mechanised. I enquired from the host, about the consumption of milk, for his personal use. He replied, he did not keep, any milk from the animals, for personal use. He purchased, whatever was needed, by him from the market. No farmer in India would purchase any milk from the market, if he has, his own 35 milch animals. I asked him what did he do when he was not well or when he wanted a holiday. He said, that the District Farmers' Association, was committed to providing help, for 15 days in a year, for his vacation. The help, so provided, would competently, look after his work, during his absence. Similarly, during emergencies and sickness of its members, the Association provided workers. Of course, the workers had to be paid well.

Later he showed us his workshop. He had a variety of tractors for harvesting, ploughing, cultivating and grass cutting. He said that he did not have to look elsewhere for the repairs of his machinery. The German Machinery was robust and did not need any repairs. Some repairs, he could do the same himself. I asked him where did he learn all this from. He said, that his country was running a Farmers' Training Institute. Those desirous of becoming farmers, could undergo training there, for two years. The training included all aspects of agriculture, horticulture, maintenance of machinery, looking after the milch animals, seeds, irrigation, etc. It was a full fledged course. It took care, of every aspect of farming. It was something new so far as I was concerned. In our country we have Bachelors of Agriculture Science degrees awarded by the Agriculture Universities. But I have not come across, any farmers' institute, for training the ordinary farmers. Coming as I do from the rural background, I have noticed that all agricultural operations, and skills are learned from experience and by observing others. Later on we were taken to Farmers' Training Institute, where even manual milking techniques were taught. But most German farmers preferred mechanical milking. As some pigs were also in the Institute, I asked the official showing us, around, to tell us, whether they taught their trainees, milking of the pigs. It created a flutter of laughter and smiles.

An Honest Living

We looked forward to the week ends. We would visit Munich, on those days. Munich was the second largest town of Germany, after Frankfurt. It took one hour to reach there by train. The railway station, at Herrshching, was a one-man show. The tickets were sold through the automatic machine. You had to put the requisite amount, in the machine, and the ticket would pop up. The fare to the prominent places, connected from Herrshching, was displayed, near the ticket vending machine. There was no collection of the used tickets at the end of the journey. I asked the lone Railway official at Herrshching, about people not purchasing the ticket, he replied that rarely anybody cheated or underpaid. If somebody did not have, the requisite amount, he would indicate it to the Railway official. He would pay the same, next time. Trust begot trust. On some selected railway stations, video cameras had been installed, to check whether all passengers were purchasing the tickets or not. Those found travelling without tickets, which was very rare, were fined 500 marks. The German can be called, cleanliness maniacs. So much so, that even when you visited green forests or side roads, you got an impression that somebody had already come and cleaned. The trees were methodically and symmetrically planted and trimmed. The Germans are also physical fitness fanatics. Even when they were to travel by train, they would cycle down to the railway stations . They would keep their cycles there. In the evening after returning by train, they would pick up their cycle and ride back to their houses. On some railway stations, I found hundreds of cycles, just left, unlocked and probably unstolen. Nobody perhaps thought of stealing. The problem in Germany, was the problem of prosperity. When once an item had outlived its life or a new model was available, it was just discarded. I saw a number of televisions, radios, and tape recorders just lying on the roadside. Nobody even looked at the old discarded items. You had to pay charges, for removal of such junk material. Frankly admitting I was tempted to pick up a few left over of the electronic goods. But I did not have the courage, to do so, as it would create, a very poor impression.

During my later visit in 1983, an official who was posted there, told me that when he initially came, to West Germany, his wife saved even the old newspapers and plastic bottles. His house, had become full to the brim, with the items, which would be the delight, of the junk dealer in India. He found no takers. He had to pay, for their removal. Even when a young boy or girl were dating, they would share all expenses on fifty-fifty basis. Even when living together, without marriage, as husband and wife, the girl would insist, on paying for her share. Nobody accepted other's obligation. The German women like their counterparts everywhere had the main responsibility of looking after their home, children and the meals for the family. Some menfolk, would assist their spouses in household chores. Engaging a full time domestic servant was an unthinkable facility for most Germans. The wages being very high, everybody did his own shopping, cleaned cars, and maintained the own lawns. The life had been made comfortable by the gadgets, but still the gadget did not do all the work. After you cut the grass, you still have to throw it out. Even the riches preferred to get part time help for domestic chores. Even the richest, have conservationist and a saving streak.

Visa Problem in Switzerland

After the programme was over in West Germany, I had already planned to return to India after visiting Geneva and Paris. I took the morning flight from Munich to Geneva. I did not have visa for Switzerland. I felt it would be easy, to go for sightseeing, the same way, I had done in Zurich, on my journey to West Germany. I arrived at Geneva Airport at about 10 a.m. I had tied up with an official of UNDP dealing with the Youth Programmes, to receive me at the airport. He was to take me quickly, to the office, for discussion. I had also an understanding with him, that after lunch and discussion, he would take me around Geneva, for sightseeing. He would drop me, at the airport, in time to catch the evening flight to Paris. I went to the Passport control, Geneva Airport. It is there, they stamp the passports, and give temporary visas, or permission, to go out of the airport, into the city, I found the man behind the counter gesticulating me to go to another side. I went to the next counter. The reception was no better there. I got the impression, that I was refused, permission to enter Switzerland. I telephoned the United Nation's Officer. Sakaguchi, my contact. He reached the airport. I explained the position and asked for his intervention. He said that he did not know Swiss language. I tried my luck, with six more different counters for temporary visa. Every time, I was waved off, to another direction. I did not understand, what exactly they were wanting me to do. I asked an English speaking passenger, whether he could explain to me, as to what the immigration incharge or passport controller was telling me either in French or German or Italian. I told him, to advise, the Swiss Official, that I was a holder of an Official Indian Passport. I wanted to go out for a few hours, to meet the United Nation's officials concerned with the youth programmes. He translated, what I had said. He told me, that the controller was saying that I should check in for evening flight and come and give him my passport and the ticket. He would then grant me the temporary permit, to enter Geneva. What all of them, had been telling me, was to check in and give them the ticket with the boarding card. Then they will have, no objection, to my going out. I pointed out that the flight was at 9 p.m.

How could I check in, ten hours in advance? In India, the Airlines expect you to check in only one hour in advance for domestic flights and two hours before the international flights. I got another surprise when I was told that in Europe for domestic or international flights, you could check in days in advance. You did not have to wait for the flight timing. After the planned programme for the day, minus two hours wasted, due to misunderstanding, of the language, I was taken for a quick sightseeing of Geneva and its beautiful lake. I was dropped at the airport, in time for the evening flight to Paris. The Immigration officer, asked me whether I had a visa for France. I said "No" because I had planned for less than 72 hours of stay there. The official asked me to wait. He inserted my passport in a machine. I asked him what was he doing. He said that he was checking my antecedents whether there was any look out notice for me any where in the world. I asked him how he did it. He said, that the particulars of all undesirable persons, against whom there was either a look out notice, or on entry denial list, had been fed into the computers, linked to the scanners. In this way, all the particulars, in the passport, are fed into the machine and scanned.

Visit to France

In less than a minute, I was cleared. The official told me, that he had given me, a French visa for one week. On arrival at Paris I was welcomed by a batchmate, Raman. I had requested him, to meet me at the airport. I walked out of the Orly airport, without any checking, or stamp on my passport. I became apprehensive. I asked Raman to find out, as to why I had not been checked by the Immigration. I said that I would not go out. I did not want to appear, as having illegally, entered France. I did not want to be arrested by the French Police, at the time of my departure from Paris. He found, that since I had arrived from Geneva, by a Swiss Air flight there was no need for a double checking. He told me, that a part of Geneva airport, was a French territory. I had already entered France, at Geneva Airport. When I went to collect my baggage, the Swiss Air staff apologised and said that my luggage had been sent to Charles De Gaulle Airport. Charles De Gaulle Airport, was 50 kms. from Orly Airport, where I had landed. They offered to pay the taxi fare, for going to the other airport for collecting my luggage. They also offered to pay for a night suit, toothpaste, tooth brush and other essentials for the night's stay. My friend told me to forget it. He drove me, to Charles De Gaulle Airport; I collected my luggage there. I told him, that the airline, had given me two days hotel stay at its cost in France. He insisted that I stay with him. I accepted his hospitality. It turned out to be a wise decision due to the language difficulty. Raman was and is still a bachelor even after his retirement. He had a full day's job, next day. He put his valet, at my disposal, to show me around Paris. I was so starved of Indian food that I asked him, whether his Indian domestic help, could prepare Chapatis for me. He said that he could prepare nice puris and aloos. I welcomed it. I told him, to tell his servant, to go on making puris, till I had my fill. Next day I was taken around to see the landmarks of Paris like the Eiffel Tower and Lourve Art Gallery. Eiffel Tower looked very ordinary at a distance. I felt that I could climb, without the use of the lift. I did it. I was one of the few to do so. It provided a beautiful view of Paris. The famous Champs Elysees had a big gate, which resembled India Gate in Delhi. When I commented that it was just like the India Gate, I was corrected by saying, that India Gate, was its copy. I rushed through Lourve Art Gallery. I saw the world famous painting of "Mona Lisa" painted, by Leonardo Da Vinci. I did not find "Mona Lisa" attractive at all. In the evening my host, took me to the "Lidos". It is a restaurant, with a number of exciting night shows and cabarets. I pretended to enjoy it, though actually, I did not. The reason was that my friend had spent a small fortune on the tickets for seeing Lido show. I did not want to give an impression that all his money had gone waste. After this, Raman took me to the night life area of France called "Pigalle". It was a curious combination of night clubs, prostitution and gentle extortion. As soon as you entered bar, and ordered a drink, some semi-nude girl would come to your table. She would ask you, for a drink, and expect you to pay for it. The cost of a ten frank drink, would be, inflated to 200 franks. The remaining deal and the price for the night, was left to mutual negotiation. Soliciting for prostitution is an offence in France. The lady would be complying, with the laws of the country, by not soliciting, She would only ask for a drink. I noticed several young girls were standing under the street lights in areas close by. I was told, that they were standing, so that people interested in sex, could solicit them. So here was the French compliance to the oldest profession in the world. Sex is something not hidden in a closet in Europe. The *Newsweek* dated, 13th April, 1993 carried the following item;

"Free Sex: Italy's War of the Prostitutes. Today is free – try and see. Cars screech to a halt when they see the road sign; Drivers crane their necks for a glimpse of the give-away. Wine? Cheese? No, Sex. Streetwalkers in the northern Italian town of Biella recently spent a Saturday offering their services free of charge, in an effort to win back customers from the growing numbers of less expensive North African prostitutes, invading their turf. "It was hard to explain it to clients – the first guy did not believe me and left". A streetwalker who called herself Laura told a reporter for La Stampa. "A few wanted to pay me anyway, but I refused. I am not a scab."

Streetwalkers from this small industrial town in Piedmont don't like being pushed around. They have been working, without pimps for years and about a year ago, they banded together and developed their own code of conduct: dress must be "Striking and tasteful, condoms are mandatory and all customers pay the same rate (40 in a car, 120 dollar for house calls)".

Everyone was happy, until dozens of poor North African immigrants, many lured to Italy, by false promises of nursing and factory jobs, showed up and began working for pimps and charging as little as 17 a trick. Tensions exploded: this year, there have been several clashes between local and foreign streetwalkers as well as a recent shoot-out between the husband of a Biella prostitute and the pimp of an Africanne. The day of freebies, boosted business, for the locals, but times are tough and they can't afford to do that very often. "You must be nuts", said one Italian streetwalker named Moana. "I wouldn't do it for free with my husband."Obviously the technical compliance to the French Law does not have to be followed in Italy.

My unwritten rule has been to go to sleep latest by 11 p.m. After the outing for the evening, we took the underground tube to his house. He was scared that lest we be mugged. He said that we should occupy the compartment, which has some passengers in it. A number of robberies and snatchings had taken place on the Paris underground. In my bravado, I told him that being a Sikh police officer I will not give way easily, without a spirited fight and he need not loose courage. This cheered him up and we reached his den safely. He was a bachelor and had been a man of character and integrity throughout. So I felt quite happy in his company being of the same brand as myself.

Next day, Raman dropped me, at Charles De Gaulle Airport. It was an architectural crossword. All the boards and signs were in French. Even if a French man knew English, he would speak only in French. I would have been, totally lost, without my friend in Paris. Finding your way about, the then newly opened, "Charles De Gaulle" Airport was almost impossible. It was more so, for an outsider, who did not know French. Airport was an Engineering marvel .I had planned to take a flight to London from there, London was about 45 minutes, by air. Due to the heavy traffic jam, I missed the flight, for which my booking had been done. I was apprehensive, that I would have to purchase a new ticket, making a big dent in my foreign exchange purse. My friend said; Not to worry. I could take, the next Air France, flight, on the same ticket. He told me that as it was an international flight, the same ticket could be used for the next flight.

Visit to England

Arriving in London, was like coming, to a second home. I had been a student of both English history and English literature. I had travelled umpteen times to London and other parts of England in books and imagination. It was a dream come true that I had landed in England, which had produced great poets, novelists and dramatists like John Keats, Robert Browning, William Wordsworth, Shelley, Alfred Tennyson, John Milton, William Shakespeare and Charles Dickens. I had dreamt to visit the places associated with them. This wish had come true. England was the home of British rulers of India. It was not a pleasant experience to be reconciled to the former rulers. Proceeding to England for studies or jobs was the fashion in the fifties. The "England returned" people were considered a unique breed. They were looked upon with awe and admiration. A series of Punjabi folk songs by Ramta had popularised the life and sex in England. Since my imagination had already predisposed me favourably to England, I presumed that every single person living there was either a Lord or Lady and there was no working class and everybody would be fabulously rich including the Indians settled there. My first cultural shock was to see in the form of an Indian sweepress near the bathrooms at the Airport. I asked her for how long she had been working on that job. She said that she was working for the last ten years. She was getting a fabulous salary equivalent of Rs 8000 per month.

I asked her whether she would have worked as sweepress in India. She was indigent. She claimed that she belong to a high caste. She had not told her people back home that she was working as a scavenging woman with the British Airways. Her relations in India were only told that she was working with the British Airways. Free Air passages to India boosted her position. It was buttressed with the lot of gifts. Like everybody else, she had a car of her own, in which she travelled, for her duty. She also explained, that only Indians, had a concept of high and low jobs. In western society, no job was looked upon as an inferior type of work. The western society was egalitarian. I had been given tips, before departure from India that, it would be useful to consult the Information Counter. I was sceptical whether the information, or the enquiry would be just like, what, we have, back home. The Airline at its cost, had given me, three days free stay in London, in one of the cheaper hotels. This is one of the attractions, that airlines, including Air India, offer for travelling, by their carriers.

The information counter gave me the location of the hotel, and the easiest way to reach it. It also gave me information about the places of tourist interest, in London. The tourist literature was available in plenty, just for the asking. I took the underground and trooped into the hotel with my luggage and the airline voucher. After checking in, I phoned up

Colonel John, whom I had known during his visit to Karnataka, in 1977. He had led a 250 strong Commonwealth Youth delegation to India, and some other Asian countries. They had extended me a standing invitation, to visit London, and spend some time with them. I had earmarked one day for discussions and sight seeing with Col. John. I had heard a lot about Orator's corner in Hyde Park. It is a unique place, where there is total freedom of expression. Anybody can speak, on any cause, whether Pro or anti-British. A number of speakers, from Africa, had brought their own little podiums for their lectures. The speakers were condemning South Africa, for its apartheid policies. They also condemned the British for their support to South Africa. Every speaker had few listeners surrounding him. In another place, the wisdom of Karl Marx was being expounded. It appeared to be more of an amusement park, than a place, where you could build up, any public opinion. Still Orator's corner had become an institution by itself. It continues to be so even now.

A batchmate, and a good friend, R.K. Puri, who was posted as Director Tea Board of India at London, played host on one day. He showed me all the places worth visiting, in London. Puri was in the Police. Later on, he left Police to join Indian Railway Traffic Service. During Christmas, the departmental stores have big discount sales. One departmental store in London, Debnehm, had the best sales attractions. It offered goods, worth 5000 pounds just for one hundred, to the first entrant to the store, on the first day of the sale. People would sleep in the open for days together to be the first or second or even third entrants, as all of them had some attractive prizes. Puri's office in Oxford street was the vantage point of having a look at Oxford Street. Senior bureaucrats, used his office, for dumping their purchases, before going for the next round. Most of the big departmental stores have four to seven storeys, in U.K. The food restaurant is generally, in the basement. All other floors have only one type of goods, like electronic, household, or linen or toys or stationery. There is no salesman breathing down your neck. Nobody insists that having come to the Store, you must buy something. You can amble leisurely and pick up whatever you want. The prices are printed on each item. There is no haggling. The stores have their detectives roaming about to nab shop lifters. The bigger stores, have video cameras, installed at strategic places for surveillance. Some departmental stores have gone so hi-tech, that they videograph every single visitor entering and departing with the exact time of entry. Despite all these precautions, a colleague, in my course, in the University of Manchester in 1981, never purchased socks, pencils and pens. They were the items, which he euphemistically explained, was a British Departmental Store's contribution, and small homage to his stay there. He would walk in, with a supreme self-confidence and complete his shoplifting operation with great aplomb. Once, on the pretext, of trying a new suit, in the clothing section, he left his old suit there. He walked off, with a new one, without anybody noticing it. London traffic is smooth and orderly. One does not hear blaring of any horns. No shop displays any board, proclaiming, what it is selling. Only big departmental stores just display their names. In some departmental stores, even one day would not be sufficient, to have a look, at all the objects, displayed there. All the variety available, all over the world, can be seen in some places. The prices are printed on each item. In the 1980's an IAS officer doing a course in United Kingdom was caught shoplifting in a departmental store. He was proceeded against departmentally, but let off, by the fellow IAS brotherhood on the ground of racial prejudice. The shoplifting is not confined only to the visitors. Even the local whites, try to take a pot shot, whenever they can . Harrods is a very high class and the most expensive Departmental Store, in London. The British queen does her shopping there. I was reluctant even to step in there. But at the suggestion of my friend, R.K. Puri, I did visit it, with him. I purchased the cheapest available. necktie there. A visitor confidentially, told me that most of the Indians purchased the cheapest items, for presentation, back home. But they took care to take a lot of empty polythene bags of Harrods and other Stores. The items were presented in those bags, showing off, as if they were purchased from there.

Southall: A Part of India in England

I was jocularly told that a part of India was in England. I was desperate to see it. So I was driven to Midd-X. It did not appear to be India. But it was India, with the Indian tandoori restaurants, Curry restaurants and sweet shops. Punjabi Hindi and Urdu were being spoken freely. The presence of the turbaned Sikhs, roaming about, in the market, added a home touch. Some hawkers had displayed, their goods on wheeled carts. You name anything you wanted for your Indian household, or personal use and it was available there. There were a number of Gurudwaras, temples and mosques for the mixed population of Sikhs, Hindus and Muslims. I asked a shopkeeper the difference between India and Southall. He said "plenty". He explained that the enforcement of the laws was very strict. You could not, keep your shop open, beyond the prescribed hours. If you did not follow the rules, you had to pay very stringent fine. You had to maintain very high standard of cleanliness and hygiene. If you did not, your establishment could be closed down. The most important difference was, that you could not bribe anybody, to ignore infringement of laws. Nobody accepted or offered bribe. Neither the bribe nor recommendation worked there. The people of Indian origin in Southall had their parallel Indian political parties,including Indian National Congress, Bhartiya Janata Party, Akali Dal and Muslim League. They also had their groupisms. Even the Sikhs of different sub-castes had their own Gurudwaras. The tradition of earning their own bread and butter was quite common in the youngsters of Asian origins, like the western youth. In some cases, the youngsters worked for their parents, during summer vacation. The Indians preferred to marry, in their respective countries of origin. Indians found, the womenfolk from back home more adjusting, accommodating and willing to extend all help in the family business, than the local girls. That is the reason, for tremendous demand of Indian girls, by the Non Resident Indian Families and people working abroad. Even the NRI girls prefer to marry the boys from India. It suits both as the girls get a suitable match and the boys get work permit, for working abroad. London is the only airport where I heard announcements being made in Punjabi language, for an airline leaving for Kenya, Uganda and some other African countries. Before leaving London, I saw Oxford and Cambridge Universities. I also visited the birthplace of William Shakespeare at Strat-Ford-Avon. I also saw the tourist sex spot of Piccadilly Circus, the area that is the counterpart of Pigalle in Paris. The local girls also have many matches of conveniences, arranged for persons desiring to settle down in United Kingdom. On my way to England during a later trip, I was requested by a fellow Indian to fill up this disembarkation card, for check by the immigration authorities at Heathrow. One question printerd on the card was the duration of stay in England? So, I inquired about the details to be filled for answering. He said in pure Punjabi, "Asian thann wapis he nahin anna, Viyha kara ke uthe he tikk jann hey." (I will not come back. I will get married and settle there).

Such cases were reported regularly in the London Tabloids. Most of the labour class entering United Kingdom did not know English. For the convenience of Punjabi/ Urdu/ Hindustani knowing passengers, both Indian and Pakistanis, a few Immigration counters were manned by officials knowing those languages. In fact, London was the only airport where I heard an announcement being made in Punjabi for an airline leaving for Kenya, Uganda and some other African countries. After my visit to England, I had planned to go to Italy.

Network of the Sex Shops

Piccadily circus, like Pigalle had a number of sex shops. A sex shop is commonplace, in Europe. The free sale of pornographic literature, gadgets, stimulants, blue films and peep shows, are tourist attractions. Pornographic literature and blue film industry provides livelihood to a large number of people. A lot of criticism was made of such establishments in United Kingdom. A demand was pressed, when Margret Thatcher was the Prime Minister of England, to close such joints. The feminists, were of the view, that a woman Prime Minister would be more than willing, to concede their point of view. During her regime, a law was passed, which banned the entry of the young persons, under eighteen years, to such shops. However, neither the British nor the Europeans, make much fuss, about such establishments. They look upon such establishments as commercial enterprises. Pornographic and blue film industry sustains a large number of people. In Germany, the biggest owner of the chain of sex shops is a multi-millionaire lady. However, even those countries, expect a fairly high standard of character and conduct from their rulers. In a case of 1970s, a Minister of the Crown, John Profumo was accused of cheating on his wife, by having an affair, with one Ms Christine Keeler. He committed the indiscretion of making payment of 500 pounds, by a credit card. It was traced to him. He admitted his liaision, but pleaded he had not compromised the secrets of the Crown. To get out of the scandal, he resigned from his job. There is nothing stealthy about the areas like the Pigalle or Piccadily Street or Soho or the sex shops of Denmark or Netherland. They are often located in the prime area and have thriving business. Some hotels, in places like Bangkok and Philippines list the telephone numbers of their massage services or/ and escort services. Escort service is a very discreetly arranged affair with a beautiful female, who doubles up as a guide, cum secretary, cum a temporary mistress. Newspapers, in Europe and America carry advertisements like "Available young attractive escort, very beautiful and pleasant company, terms negotiable." Such services are generally rendered at very steep rates.

Visit to Rome

After spending three days in London, I flew to Rome, Italy, for another round of sightseeing. The Italians are lively, boisterous and extrovert like the Punjabis. The Italian women are buxom and attractive. They are more aggressive than other European women. Some of them are the greatest bullies and keep their husbands under their thumb. As I was staying only for 48 hours in Rome, I kept my luggage in the cloak room, at the airport itself. I just took a handbag containing one change, and boarded the bus to the city centre.

I had been booked in Hotel Canada, by the Swiss Air, at my own cost. I wanted to reach the hotel quickly, so that after checking in, I could go for sightseeing. I asked a taxi driver whether he could take me to Hotel Canada. He agreed, but demanded $ 75 as the fare. I said, I would be damned, rather than spend $ 75. I had only $100 left with me. I went to the Information counter to find out, as to how far was hotel Canada. I was told that, it was just 20 yard away, on my right. This was nothing new. I had been warned to be careful when making purchases or using public transport. They were, just like, our own people, back home. I walked to the hotel, in much less time, than I had spent in arguing with the taxi driver and inquiring about the hotel from the information counter. So I started walking to the hotel. On the way, the same taxi driver asked me whether I wanted his services. I told him that I could walk twenty yards. He sheepishly laughed, and said that he also had to make a living. Sometimes he succeeded in getting suckers, sometimes not. It was his bad luck that I missed being the purveyor of the meals for the day, as well as his family, in one trip only. I was reminded of a tip given to me by an Indian colleague in the Embassy that while in Italy you must count the change if you purchase something. You are likely to be short charged if you are not careful. This was advised only for Italy, unlike the rest of Europe, where normally nobody would under pay or cheat you.

A Wonderful City

I took a conducted tour bus for seeing Rome by night. Rome is not only full of history, but has a host of architectural wonders. We were taken to a wish fountain. It is said, that if you throw a coin in the fountain water and wish something, that wish comes true. I also visited Vatican, which is considered "a State within a State". It is the seat of the Popes the head of Catholic Christians. The Pope stays in Vatican and is regarded as a living representative of Christ. The cathedral of Saint Paul, is probably the only place in the world, which displays the best of architecture and paintings from the ancient masters, who gave their life, for the works therein. I saw the building of 'Senate', where Julius Caesar, was stabbed. The well preserved ruins of the palaces, and the Roman building and art galleries, were spread all over Rome. The amphitheatre, where the gladiators, fought for their lives, had become a great tourist attraction. During my visit, I was living Roman history in my imagination. I inquired, whether Jesus Christ had ever visited Rome. For the Christians, especially Catholics, it is the holiest, of the holy. I was told that Jesus had never stepped out of Israel. It is only his teachings, which had spread far and wide. Protestantism was born in the refusal of Pope to grant divorce to King Henry the Eighth, from the woman he disliked. The climate was ripe for a change, because of the various evils, which had crept into Christianity. The Catholic Priests, were selling the places in Heaven for huge amounts. Henry the Eighth, declared himself independent of the Vatican. He proclaimed himself as Defender of the Faith and granted divorce to himself. Even now one of the many titles, of the British sovereign is the "Defender of the Faith". It is how personal a reason led to the birth of Protestantism. Italians are just like Punjabis. They enjoy their Parathas, with their different stuffing's. The only difference is that their Parathas are called Pizzas. Pizzas, instead of having, stuffing inside, like the Indian Parathas, have their's outside. Their women are much more beautiful as compared to their European counterparts. At the same time, they are much more dominating.

I also saw a Roman amphitheatre, where the prisoners had to fight with lions for their lives. It was more so with the early Christian Missionaries, who were considered a good bet for the hungry lions. However, no record in Rome is available, to show whether one Christian Missionary was a sufficient meal for the lion, or the diet had to be supplemented by more Christians. It is also not known, whether the lions were happy with feeding on the missionaries, or whether the missionaries expressed happiness and joy in being of some use to the lions. In the modern times, the game of throwing the prisoners to the lions has been replaced by bull fighting. In the bull fighting, a fighter shows a red rag, or cloth to the bull. Then both the man, and the bull, try their luck, in gorging each other. Mostly, the bull loses. It is a lively sport, but far less lively, than seeing a lion, feeding himself on the poor emaciated prisoners in the ancient Rome.

Back to Delhi

I felt that more than two month stay abroad, was more than sufficient for me. More than that would have been only repetitive visits. My ticket had included a visit to Greece and Athens also. But I chose to return straight from Rome to Delhi by an Air India flight. Rome Airport is not as busy as Heathrow, where every minute there is either a landing or a take off. The passengers were security checked with the help of x-ray and decoding machines. After luggage was security checked and screened, the baggage machine wrapped it in the transparent polythene, and security sealed it. From there it was conveyed, straight to the hold of the aircraft. The flights going to Israel had the heaviest security, with gun toting Italian Policemen guarding the aircraft. There was much tighter security for the passengers proceeding to Tel Aviv.

On return, I decided, that evaluation of the training programmes must be done on the same lines, as I had seen being done in Germany. This was not welcomed, even by my own officials. They opposed the trainees evaluating, the guest lecturers, and youth services faculty. I overruled and made even the trainees themselves take few classes, to fill in for the absentee faculty. I introduced this evaluation for the first time in Karnataka in 1978. It is a standard practice now, to evaluate the quality of lectures and lecturers. A few weeks after returning from Europe, I took the annual leave to visit my parents. During my absence of nearly three months to Europe my wife Surinder had done the impossible, by completing the construction of our house in Indira Nagar. My contribution had been limited, to the securing of the site, getting loan from the government of Rs 80,000 and Rs 40,000 from Metropolitan Co-operative Society. I had opened a joint bank account in my name and her name, so that she could, spend the money on construction. I had also purchased wood in auction in Karwar District and brought it to Bangalore. The teak wood logs were available at that time for Rs 25 per cubic feet. Not only did she complete the construction, before I returned, but she had also rented it out. The company paid a monthly rent of Rs 2000 per month. It was sufficient to pay the loan instalments and all taxes, and leave a few hundreds to supplement the two salaries drawn by us. Karnataka Government rules required, that if you had your own house at then government accommodation had to be vacated. I was staying in a Government house at Vasanthnagar in Bangalore. I promptly vacated it, and shifted to a rented flat on the fourth floor in Vyali Kawal area of Bangalore. Many colleagues were surprised at my prompt compliance of the government rules. A few advised not to vacate the centrally located accommodation, allotted to me, at a pittance of a rent. It was only Rs 70 per month. My reply was, that as senior government officials, we should be an example to others, in following all the rules and laws of the country. I also told them that I did not believe, in double standards, one for my self and one for others.

The Accountant General in Karnataka generally used to act as a policeman. I was not paid my salary as Director Youth Services, for six months. There was an objection to my posting. The AG wanted to know why I had been posted and wanted a speaking order. The Chief Secretary, sent a stinker to the AG that when officers are posted to any jobs, the reasons do exist on the government files. If every order was to be made a speaking order, it will lead to litigation. This tendency continues even now. The basic question is that nobody posts himself. It is done by the Government but the punishment is given by the AG to the posted officers. The Government is an abstract entity and is not able to protect the interests of the suffering employees.

12

Back to Police Department

After putting the training on sound footing, I proceeded on two months leave to visit my parents in Punjab. I had made the Youth Services Department vibrant and important. It had excited both jealousy and envy in the Police Department. People starting propagating that I had been out of Police for a long time. The real reason was that many were keen to occupy the job, which had become high profile due to my taking interest. On return from two months leave, I found that within a week of my departure, another colleague had been posted as Director of Youth Services. No posting was indicated for me even on return from leave. I had to cool my heels, for a couple of weeks, before I was posted as Deputy Inspector General of Police (Headquarters).

The Inspector General of Police, Albert Manoraj was a thorough gentleman. He was not petty, unlike some of his successors. I was the senior most staff officer, to the IG, next to him in running the State Police Headquarters. Before I joined as DIG headquarters, the State Inspector General used to be literally buried in the routine files. I felt that there was no use of my being a senior staff officer, unless I could lighten his burden . Within a couple of days, I cut down drastically, the number of routine files being put upto the IG. One day he called me and asked very politely how his work had been reduced drastically. He wanted to know the mystery behind this. I told him that I was disposing off the routine work. Only the matters requiring attention of the Inspector General were put up to him. But I had made it a point to apprise him, of the work done by me. Once somebody thanked him, for some prompt official work. The IG smiled and later on asked me why he was thanked. I said that a communication had been received, for immediate help. I had got the matter attended to urgently.

Mass Transfers

As DIG (Headquarters) Bangalore, I noticed that a bunch of letters would come from the Chief Minister's secretariat, directing the posting of the officers, of the level of Inspectors and Sub Inspectors to particular police stations. When I asked the IG whether he was resisting the same, he replied "Where is the question? Instead of the government issuing the orders, they are requesting us to do the same". Only in very bad cases where the persons of proven dishonesty, had been recommended for posting to "lucrative police areas", he would take up the matter with the Chief Minister . He attempted that such a direction was either withdrawn or modified. He rarely met with success. The result was that all orders of the Chief Minister, were immediately complied with. I told the Inspector General, that this would seriously compromise the efficiency and discipline of the Police Department. He replied that he had tried his best to explain the ruinous effects, of such interference, in the Police force, but without much success. He also said that he did not believe that it was only his responsibility to keep the Police free from the political influence. It was also the responsibility, of the State Government.

A few years later, I asked the Head of State Police, now called, the Director General of Police, how much of his time, he spent on transfers and postings and how much on professional police work, for improving the efficiency of the Police Department. He replied that he spent his 95 per cent of his time on transfers and postings and meetings with the Ministers or the Chief Minister, 4 per cent in answering the Assembly or Parliament questions and hardly 1 per cent on professional policing. I also interviewed J.F. Ribeiro, IPS as Commissioner of Police, Bombay and asked him the same question. He showed me a drawer full of such letters, which had been just kept there without any action. He said that worst that could happen to him was that he would retire as Commissioner of Police in the rank of DIG or Additional IG and he was prepared for that. He also said that Government had conveyed to him the adverse remarks, made in his annual confidential report. He told me that he was not bothered and was not even going to make any representation. I was to witness the same spectacle of mass transfers in the late 1980's when I was staying in a police officers mess. In my neighbouring room, I saw the then Director General of Police, and the Home Minister of the State doing the exercise of transfers and postings. I had a funny spectacle of an officer coming and complaining to me that he had lost Rs 50,000 I, out of curiosity, asked him, as to what he meant by that. He said that he had paid the amount to an MLA, to get a plum posting. In that place, he recouped, what he paid, in one month. He was posted to the station he paid for. He went and took charge. But within 48 hours he was shifted to another "dry" police station. Technically, the Legislator had got him posted, where he wanted. But his posting was short lived. He had not taken the assurance while paying money that he would not be shifted, at least for one year. In that sense, he had suffered a loss. It is quite common to manage recommendations for posting and transfers. For what consideration the recommendations are made, whether for sheer love or desire to help or hefty cash or for some other "weightier consideration", can never be proved either in a Departmental Inquiry or in a Court. The person offering the bribe is only offering his slush money. The person receiving, will never admit, in a court of Law, that he got the money for getting any posting or license or quota or permit. So the game goes on.

13

Posting in Commerce Ministry as Director Vigilance

Longest Tenure

I received orders, in December 1978, of deputation to Government of India. I had been posted, as Director in the Ministry of Commerce and Foreign Trade, New Delhi. I flew from Bangalore to Delhi, on relief from Karnataka, on 23rd December 1978. Finding a place, to stay, can always be problematic, in the first few days, at a new place. Karnataka Bhawan was our sanctuary for first few days. Later, I shifted to the house vacated by FTR Colaso. He could keep the house for two months, on his transfer. Colaso, a cadre and a batch mate, had finished his tenure with the Government of India. At my request, he agreed to lodge me in the house vacated by him. I was responsible to make payment for the rent. On my reporting to the Ministry, the Commerce Secretary, Krishanswamy Rao Sahib, introduced me to all senior officials, of the Ministry, that is Directors, Joint Secretaries and only one Additional Secretary, P.K. Kaul. Kaul later on became the Cabinet Secretary. Finding him not toeing the line and signing on the dotted spot, the then Prime Minister shifted him, as India's Ambassador to the United States of America. Kaul confirmed this himself. The Commerce Secretary told me to go through the annual reports of the Commerce Ministry for the last three years, as well its attached and subordinate officers and the corporations under its administrative control. This was a good way of familiarising myself, to the work of the Commerce Ministry. The commerce Ministry had divided the entire world between its officials.

The detailed allocation of work, amongst the officers, was based either on the handling of a particular commodity, like tea or coffee, or certain territorial areas like the Western Europe or USA, etc. The officers dealing with a particular territorial area had an opportunity to visit several countries, falling in their charge, either for annual trade talks, or signing of fresh trade agreements, or for leading or joining, any trade delegation, proceeding to their territorial jurisdiction. The officers handling the European countries and USA were in great demand. They were mostly abroad at least for six months in a year. The officers of the Commerce Ministry, appeared to be, the blue eyed boys, of the government. But the job of the officers was and is to promote, foreign trade. It just cannot be done, sitting in Udyog Bhawan, the headquarters of Commerce Ministry. Especially in 1970's and 80's, there was a lot of trade on the Government account, especially the import of items, like the newsprint or edible oil or fertilisers or petroleum products. In that scenario, the foreign trips, were not only inevitable, but was also absolutely essential, to meet the basic needs of the country and industry. This was apart from the trips, which the Finance Ministry officials made, for raising the loans, from the international organisations. The system in Commerce Ministry was that, almost all the Directors had to report to the Commerce Secretary through the Joint/Additional Secretary. But the Director, dealing with Vigilance, had the privilege to put up his papers directly to the Commerce Secretary. This had been done, with a view, to give him complete independence. The corruption or malpractice charges were also to be looked by the Vigilance. The Director Vigilance, was subordinate only to the Commerce Secretary. An IPS officer, of the rank of DIG had held the charge of the post. Since he had left before I joined, on completion of his term, the Vigilance work, was being looked after, by another Director belonging to the railway service. An Under Secretary designated as a Deputy Director was running the show. For the first few days, no papers were put up to me, though I was the Director, incharge of vigilance. On seeing the files, I noticed , that the Under Secretary, most of the time recorded a note on the file, that the Director need not be troubled. Despite advising him, that all the papers relating to Vigilance should be put up to me, the same practice continued. There was a total lack, of compliance of the orders. It was also a way, to keep me ignorant of cases, I was expected to attend to. This is an old trick, which is played by every office on every new officer who joins. Keep him off the work as long as possible. It is because, new brooms sweep clean at least initially.

I called a meeting of all the officials dealing with the Vigilance. I told them, that no disposal of the papers, would be final, till I had approved . I also said that for the first one month, I would like to see every single paper, either being received or being sent out of the Vigilance. The Deputy Director-cum-Under Secretary did not like it, as all his authority had been taken away. His method of functioning had almost closed down the Vigilance department. Whatever reports were received, he would recommend their acceptance. I noticed that quite often, he did not even read the papers. Another trick he had adopted, was to refer the particular lapse to the concerned administrative section. In his parlance, the vigilance matter was disposed off. I changed the method of functioning of the Vigilance. I said that the matter was not over till all the aspects had been examined and the Central Vigilance Commission consulted wherever the consultation was required. My working in the Central Bureau of Investigation, came in handy in dealing with the Vigilance cases. I taught all the officials in the Vigilance as to how to examine the complaints and the inquiry reports and if necessary to have the person accused of lapses questioned by his superiors. I also said that anybody could see me for discussion or clarifications irrespective of his rank. I also started a weekly meeting with my staff. They were asked to prepare a list of pending case's, office-wise and corporation wise and do a regular follow up. The result was that within a month, I knew what cases were pending against whom, and where was the bottleneck.

Corruption Cases and the Role of Vigilance

There was a general belief about the existence of corruption in the various offices under the Ministry of Commerce. Especially cases concerning the issue of Import and Export permits, or the distribution of scarce commodities, had a bad reputation. But, in actual practice nobody ever sent any signed complaint against any senior or junior officer. The reason was that the sender of the complaint had to be necessarily a businessman. He would be interested in getting his work done. He would generally not have either the time or the inclination to make complaints. That would tie him down either with the courts or in deposing before the Departmental Inquiry officers. The complainant would unofficially be considered as black sheep by the entire office and even his genuine work would not be done. The entire system had been rusted by a plethora of rules and regulations. I asked a businessman why he was not making complaint about the prevailing corruption. He replied that he was in the business to make money and not enemy. Nothing came out of the complaints made by anybody. He would rather use the time, in making more money, rather than waste it in complaints and follow-up. He also felt that except for some limited officers, most of the people were poorly paid. He did not mind helping the needy as long as "the so called needy" came to his assistance. He said that however honest the senior officers may be, it was the junior most functionary who had to put up the file. He also said, that anybody who had made any complaint, had badly suffered. The import-export policy was so rigorous that even the missing of one coma or full stop could lead to the rejection of their applications. Even the lower division clerks had such authority that, unless their officers were hard working and honest, nobody had guts to overrule even the most frivolous objection put up by them. The system, had become too large, for one person, however high he may be, to adjust or break, or make it serve the needs of the society. The Government systems rooted in precedence, traditions and old rules tend to be conservative. It is not to say that the system does not respond. It does respond, to the requirements of the high and the mighty. It is the ordinary mortals, who have to stand and wait.

In one Indian Administrative Service Association, my friend, S Santhanam, IAS (1958) did some plain speaking in 1970. He told me himself that he had become *persona non grata*, for criticising the Secretaries to the Government, who had subverted the system, due to nepotism and favouritism. He said that all the plum postings went to the sons and son-in-law of the senior bureaucrats. He said that "you show me the man and I would show his postings without even asking anybody." I received a complaint from, Chander Kant Baljee of Hotel Harsha in Bangalore, that he had earned a lot of foreign exchange, from the foreign tourists staying in his hotel. As per the rules, he was entitled to the purchase of a certain quantity of imported whisky. The tourism department of the Government of India had recommended the release of imported whisky for the consumption of the tourists from the duty free shop. Instead of getting the import permit, he had got a reply that "your permit had been endorsed in the name of Hotel (name withheld) in Delhi." He also complained, that he had never made a request, that the liquor quota earned by him, should be endorsed in the name of any other Hotel. Nobody replied to him. I called for a report, from the Chief Controller of Export and Import. Only a vague reply was received that a mistake had occurred. Not satisfied with the reply, I summoned the concerned file. It was not only dealt with callously, but also in utter disregard of rules. I summoned all the officers who had dealt with the file. I asked them to explain how, when a person, had not asked his license, to be endorsed in any other person's name, was given a reply, contrary to the facts. They had no reply except to say, that it was a mistake. Later on, I learnt that the beneficiary five star hotel, had been bribing the officials in the CCI and E, to get such quotas, on account of the hotels far away from Delhi. The hotels would claim the imported liquor, but would receive neither any reply, nor any permit. This was the logical conclusion, but it was not sufficient, to start disciplinary proceedings. However, I had the necessary orders passed, for making adverse entries made in the Annual Confidential Reports of the defaulters. There was a strong protest that I was victimising the "poor employees" of the Office of the Chief Controller of Imports and Exports. The Chief Controller, an Additional Secretary level, IAS officer came to my room and pleaded for taking a lenient view. I explained to him that, what came to the notice, was less than the tip of the iceberg. If we become charitable, for such serious lapses, than we might as well close the shop, and forget all efforts at keeping minimum norms of honesty and integrity in the government. The Chief Controller of Imports and Exports, reluctantly agreed. He said that he had come to see me, as his subordinates had pressurised him to do so. I told him that as the Chief of the Vigilance, I had to take a principled stand. It could not be whittled down, only on the ground that it did suit any organisation.

Sugar Deal, Pocket Kickback

In a case involving, import of sugar, it came to light that a Chairman of the State Trading Corporation had been paid 2 million US dollars, for awarding the contract. The money was also credited, to his Swiss account, as desired by him. This was a case of 1975-76. There was a telex message recovered about the payment of kickbak. The CBI registered a criminal case. But the Swiss did not pass on the documents to prove the case in a Court of law, despite the then Prime Minister of India taking up the case at the highest level. The Estimate Committee of the Parliament, was apprised of the position. The Chairman of the STC lost only his contract appointment. The entire system of appointing the Chief Executive to the Government Corporations had been changed in 1970's. Under the system, people from Private Sector and Open Market were selected to head the Government Corporations, transacting business, worth millions of dollars. The people from the open market not only carried their culture, of non-observation of any rules, with a view to show results; but also the culture of kickbacks. The offerer of kickbacks in private sector, became the recipient of the same, when heading Government sponsored business houses. Some proved their mettle and showed outstanding results. But a large number only lined their pockets, during their tenure of three to five years. They were also susceptible to political pressure for the sake of further extensions. (Urea Scam of 1996, where 139 Crores was paid by the Fertiliser Corporation under political pressure, by such appointees is a glaring case.)

Before the split of the USSR, there was a lot of trading by the State Trading Corporation, with the USSR and other East European Block countries. No private trade was permitted. The Government Corporation, did not manufacture items, like shoes and shoe uppers. But they would permit export on their account and officially earn a small commission. But the big cut was earned by the persons doling out the quota. One exporter mentioned to me that a particular Director, had fixed a rate of fifty paise per shoe/ shoe upper, for permitting export of those items, against the account of State Trading Corporation. Nearly eighty million shoes and shoe uppers used to be exported. He made a huge pile of money, more than what the STC earned. I brought this complaint, to the notice to the then Commerce Minister, V.P. Singh. I suggested that since nobody would depose openly against him, for fear of losing his business, the corrupt official, at least, should be shifted from Delhi to a far-off place like Madras. The Minister agreed. But the Chairman of the Corporation had developed a soft corner for this official, for the reasons which are not difficult to guess. The official was boasting that he was giving a share to the Chairman. The orders of VP Singh were not obeyed for a long time. I pointed it out, in a meeting. The Minister was wild. He gave fifteen days time for implementation. The Chairman took the plea that no post outside Delhi, was available, in the pay scale of the officers to be transferred. I gave the solution that the officer could carry his pay scale to the place he was transferred. The post in the lower pay scale, could be transferred to Delhi. The Chairman tried every ruse to make sure that his earning did not lessen through the corrupt official. But I was more than a match. Ultimately, the official was shifted to be brought back, after I and VP Singh had left the Commerce Ministry.

When corruption and malpractice are visible even to the half blind eye, sometime our "Chief Executives" are so full of "milk of human kindness" or are so myopic that they can not see , or do not see what is obvious. Perhaps, some of them make hay while the sun shines.

Kingdoms within Kingdom

There is another brand of Chief Executives of Public Sector undertakings, who are result oriented, Some are only rule oriented, to the last letter. The result is a total distortion of the objectives. Some executives are very scared of the Vigilance cases, being instituted against them. It is common to send anonymous and pseudonymous complaints. Taking advantage of suspicious nature of the then Minister VP Singh, it had become a free-for-all to throw mud, on the seniors and even upright officers and indulge in character assassination. The easiest way in the Government, to ruin anybody's reputation, is to send a spate of anonymous and fictitious complaints. This way, either the innocent person, would be driven away from his job, or will stop taking any initiative. Some Chief Executives, of the Corporations under the control of Commerce Ministry, complained to me, that commercial activity had come to a halt. Their officials were scared, of being involved in any CBI case. I assured them that the objectives of the Vigilance, was not only to haul up the guilty, but also to protect the innocent. I also explained, that as long as the transactions were done in a bona fide, and transparent manner, the government would back them, to the hilt. But they, on their part, would have to ensure, that the corrupt were weeded out. If that was impossible, at least such elements should be posted to non-sensitive places, minimising chance of doing any mischief. A bona fide commercial decision, going sour, will not be the basis of any vigilance inquiry. But, the Head of the organisation would have to satisfy himself about the bona fide of such an action.

Despite the apprehension, that they may be involved, in any case, many of the corrupt officials were not scared of any vigilance enquiry. One of the reasons, was that many big deals, were shrouded in mysteries. They were rarely publicised. The secret of the strength of bureaucracy, is to keep all the procedures and orders under wrap. If the methodology of decision making is made transparent, it would go a long way in rooting our corruption and resolving grievances of the public. The knowledge of working of the government, rules and procedures for getting for licenses and permits had a premium on it. Former Finance Minister, Manmohan Singh observed that officials had made fortunes, interpreting the provisions of Import and Export Policy. In fact in 1980's the officers dealing with the interpretation of the policies were a powerful lot. As nobody wanted to take a chance, on the interpretation of the import police, the easiest course, was to refer the file to Policy cell, to confirm whether the subject matter, was covered under the rules. The interpretation of the policy was not a "dry" seat. One word from them, could either enable an industry to run or be closed down. The allegations, often without basis, were quite common, that while some industrial houses were favoured, others engaged in similar business, were denied the raw materials and import licenses. One of the top industrial house, based in Bombay, had all the benefits under all regimes. When its chief was interviewed by a magazine, he is reported to have said that "I am a business-man and it is my job to make money. I salute anybody who is in power". A retired Secretary to the Government of India, told me the following story. He said that the same businessman, was rebuffed by the government, more than two decades ago. He could not get any interview with the Prime Minister of the day. He paid a generous donation to an organisation, which had invited the same, youngest PM of the country for a function. His condition for payment of Rs 25 lakhs was, that his chair be kept next to the VIP, at the function. He reportedly whispered some magic words into the ears of the then PM about a huge cash donation. But afterwards there was no looking back for his industrial house. It is said that only V P Singh, and later on, Manmohan Singh, with both whom I have worked, did not meet the business man individually. They met them either in a delegation or at functions organised by their organisations. This may be an over simplification. But the facts remain, that those in position of authority have to guard both their front and rear. They do not only have to be upright and honest themselves, but appear to be so.

Exports and Obstacles

Both exports and imports are governed by a lot of formalities and procedures. During my domestic and foreign visits, I invariably used to ask the various officers of the organisations under the Ministry of Textile and Commerce, any difficulty in their functioning or pending matters. Once in Hong Kong, the local Manager of State Training Corporation, mentioned to me, that he had secured a contract for the export of shirts from India to Hong Kong. The only condition was, that the cloth for the shirts, was to be sent from Hong Kong. The shirts after stitching were to be exported to Hong Kong. The matter had been pending, for over one year, over the quantity of the cloth to be utilised per shirt. According to the calculations, done by the office of the Chief Controller of Imports and Exports, five centimetres more cloth, was being sent to India, per shirt. It felt it unjustified, as the excess cloth could be used for fabricating about 200 shirts, which might not be exported. The order was a million of shirts. Here for the sake of a few dozen extra shirts, the Babus had held up the proposal. So no import of the cloth, was allowed. On the other hand, buyers in Hong Kong, were clear that they wanted a particular design for the shirts. They did not want their orders to be delayed. So there was a stalemate. It was ridiculous that a big export order, with a buy back agreement, was jeopardised over five centimetre of cloth, per shirt. So I promised that within one week I would have the matter sorted out. A private business house could have bribed its way through the maze of bureaucracy. But Government organisations, generally do not bribe other Government Departments. On return to Delhi, at the next senior officers, meeting I raised this subject. I said, that on one hand, we were keen to increase export, but on the other, we were quibbling over five centimetre of cloth, per shirt. It was the first opportunity, of exporting shirts fabricated in India to Hong Kong. The deal was almost off, due to official quibbling. Both the Chairman of the State Trading Corporation and the Chief Controller of Imports and Exports said they did not know why, and where the proposal was pending. I told the Chairman, that it was for his officers, to have brought this matter to his notice. It only showed that even he did not know, what was pending and where. I did not want to indulge in the debate to apportion the blame. I suggested that the clearance be given quickly. It was given in one week's time, as I had pursued it. Some of my colleagues, asked me ,as to why I had taken so much interest in the work, which was not under my charge. I replied, that it was a question of the overall interest of the country. It also highlighted the need to simplify with transparency the rules and procedures. The procedural wrangle, over five centimetre of cloth, had not only stalled the export, but it also made our country the laughing stock of the trading community. This also highlighted that, when it came to the foreign visits, all the Chief Executives and the Senior Officers of the Corporations and the Ministry, were more than keen to go, ostensibly for increasing exports. But when it came to the basics and solving the problems on the ground, nobody was interested. Unfortunately, the position continues to be so even now.

The State Trading Corporation had a number of foreign offices including in Kuwait, Singapore, Paris, New York, London, Sydney, Hong Kong, amongst other places. I noticed, during one of my foreign visits, that new officers were posted frequently. I asked, the then incumbent, the present postings of his predecessors. He told me, that all of them, either after completing their tenure or even before, had resigned. They set up their own business in the place of their previous posting, whether Hong Kong or London, or Singapore. Most of them had become middlemen, for dealing with the State Trading Corporation and other Government of India agencies. This is nothing unusual. Even Government officials, after resigning or retiring have taken up jobs with some companies. Mostly, it is, with those companies, whom they had obliged, while in Government. Many have accepted the Chairmanship or the Directorship, and where rules come in the way, the same job has been accepted as consultant. Being a consultant requires, no approval of the government. The rule regarding non-acceptance of the jobs, after retirement, have been more observed in breach than in compliance. It is because, there is no machinery in the government, to check the compliance of such rules, in respect of retirees. To dodge the rules, a number of senior retired officials, including the retired Secretaries to the Government of India, have been accepting jobs as consultants, with companies and industrial houses. They draw no salary. But the company gives them a car, a telephone and a bungalow in a posh locality at a fabulous rent. They also get an unlimited expense account ostensibly to promote the company's business and a paid membership of one or two clubs. All the travel within the country and abroad is, at the company's account. A couple of years after the retirement when the contacts and influence dry up, with the new arrival of officials, such people have been shown the door. So much so, the Chief of the company who according to the retired officials used to "lick" their shoes, even refused to meet them. A Petroleum Secretary had actively promoted the interests of a private company and lined his pockets while in service. He was persuaded to join the parent company. But he was treated so badly that within six months, he resigned. Such stories are galore.

The same malady had spread, in the State Trade Corporation. Key officials on foreign posting would oblige prospective employers and then join them. The Corporation employee, before proceeding abroad on a foreign posting, had to execute a bond, that he would deposit an amount of

Rupees ten thousand, with the Corporation, if he quit the service, within three years of completion of his foreign posting. Rupees ten thousand, in most cases, was less than their 15 days foreign salary. I suggested to STC, that they should, prohibit their employees, from resigning while on a foreign posting. They should also take a bond, that each foreign posted employee would be bound to serve the corporation for five years before resigning, after the completion of his foreign posting. I also requested STC, to raise the bond amount, to Rs one lakh. This amount was to be forfeited, if somebody still left his job against the conditions laid down. The State Trading Corporation agreed to raise the bond value to Rs 75,000, in the event of somebody prematurely resigning, while posted abroad. The officials were clever. They would resign, at the end of their tenure, after settling the terms of conditions of joining other foreign companies, and making a pile wherever it could be managed. The raising of the bond amount to Rs 75,000 was resented by the STC staff. I was accused of an undue and unwarranted interference. I explained to the Chairman that he could make it clear, to officials, to be posted abroad, that they can decline foreign posting, in case they felt that the condition of executing the bonds was not acceptable. I added, that the corporation, was entitled to safeguard its interests. It should not happen, that its employees establish contacts and experience at its cost, and then leave for greener pastures. Not even one person declined foreign posting on the ground that the bond amount of Rs 75,000 was on the high side. Despite the bond which required them to serve the corporation, some of them, still on completion of their tenure resigned. They settled in the country, of their foreign posting for their own business or higher paid jobs under foreign employers. They happily paid amount of Rs 75,000. Hardly anybody came back to India, to serve the Corporation, for the period specified in the bond.

Colours of Cheating

After returning from Australia in 1982, from an official programme, I had planned a two days private stay, enroute to Delhi in Singapore. It was a private stay and I did not have the kind of money required for expensive hotels. I wanted cheaper accommodation. I was told by an official, that I could stay in the flat of the Manager of the State Trading

Corporation. The flat was vacant, as somebody had still to be posted. Their only requirement was, that it was needed from 7 p.m. to 9 p.m., well after the official hours . I learnt that the flat was used, by the STC officials for conducting negotiations, for purchase of vast quantity of edible oil (Palmolein). Everything did not appear to be straight forward. I decided to visit the flat unannounced in the night. The STC official did not expect the Director (Vigilance) and were surprised to see me. I told them to go ahead and not to interrupt their work just because I was in their midst. I told them, that I only wanted to educate myself, as to how they went, about making purchases for millions of dollars for the country. I just sat on a chair and saw, frantic phone calls being made to Malaysia, as well as locally. After their work was over, I asked the Chief of the State Trading Corporation, Singapore office to explain to me how they made purchases. He told me that the Singapore office would keep Delhi apprised, of the prevailing prices of commodities, which India might purchase, in Singapore and Malaysia. As Singapore was an international marketing centre, with all major International Companies having their office there, everything could be purchased there. In 1980's, purchase of edible that is Palmolein oil, was the main item on India's agenda.

The major source of supply of Palmolein oil was Malaysia. The drill was that the STC office in Singapore would telex to the Head Office in Delhi the spot as well as the forward prices given over a specified period. The Board of Directors would determine how much to purchase and at what price. For instance the Board could communicate to the Singapore office to purchase half million tons of Palmolein oil at a price say 210 dollars per metric ton. The branch office might have communicated to the board that at a given time the oil was available for 210 to 214 dollars. The Board sitting in Delhi would go by the advice of the branch and would indicate the purchases to be made at a price say not exceeding "210 dollars per metric ton." I asked the Branch Manager that if by the time he received the orders to purchase at 210 dollars the price went down to 207 dollars, what prevented a dishonest person in purchasing the item at 210 dollars and pocketing, balance of 3 dollars per metric ton. This, would be shared, with the staff involved in the purchases. Moreover, the Head

Office was not sitting on his head all the time and the prices varied from hour to hour. He reluctantly agreed, that it was possible to pocket a substantial amount without appearing to be dishonest, even at the price approved by the Board of Directors. He also said that sometimes even before the official communication for the purchases was received, the sellers in Singapore and Malaysia knew in advance, the item, the quantity, to be purchased, and the price approved. He himself received, a number of requests from the prospective sellers, even before he received the official communication. He also told me that some of his predecessors had resigned after their tenure was over. They had helped themselves considerably, during the era of high purchases and canalised imports. The Chairmen of the State Trading Corporation did approach me to suggest ways and means to ensure that no unauthorised messages for the purchase were passed from the telex room of the Corporation. I said that it was not difficult. He should request P&T department to record the telephone number and telex number to which all messages were flashed by the STC telex room. Any message, going to any telex, other than the official telex number, indicated by the STC, would give away the game. In very sensitive cases, where purchases, say over a half million dollars were involved, message should be telexed from the Chairman's personal telex. Moreover, no board member should be allowed to leave the board room till such a message had been flashed either on telex or telephone. This would prevent any possibility of leakage from the higher levels. It should especially be applied, in the cases of the staff, attending the important meetings. The communication in 1970's and 1980's used to be by telex. Fax had not made its appearance. Leakage of information for consideration of different kinds was and is quite common even now. The interested parties know in minutes, the decisions taken, concerning them. So much so that some official knew, or even now know, the contents, of their Annual Confidential Reports, through their different networks, including the Private Secretaries or despatch. This was equally true of the decisions taken in connection with the Industrial approvals as well as the matters involving Import and Export. The liaison officers of the Industrial and Trading houses, are on the look out, for the needs, expectations and demands of the seniors, in the upper echelons of power. On the occasions of festivals when it is customary to offer gifts and other presents, they would make their presence to fulfil their needs. Sometimes, any excuse or even no excuse was good enough to meet their demands.

One evening I got a frantic phone call from the Commerce Secretary, C.B Krishnaswamy Rao Sahib, in July 1979, late in the night. He asked me to go immediately, to the house of a Joint Secretary, Mahesh Prasad. He said that "something very serious had happened". I immediately went to the house of Mahesh Prasad. The husband and wife (Mr. and Mrs. Mahesh Prasad) were in a dazed and a dishevelled condition. I asked Mahesh what had happened. He told me that he had been invited, to a reception by the Embassy of a foreign country. He went there because of our trade relations. He had taken the staff car of the Commerce Ministry. The Embassy officials told him that the reception may take a long time. They would drop him, at his house, in Pandara Park. It was not a problem for them, they explained, as one of their officials lived in the close by locality of Sunder Nagar. Mahesh agreed and dispensed with the services of the car of the ministry. He told me that he discussed the subject of trade, and the necessity to balance it between the two countries. The balance of trade was in favour of that country. At the time of dropping him at his house, a gift parcel was presented to Mahesh by the embassy official. He accepted the parcel. He opened it in his house. He found in it, a few quartz clocks and a huge bundle containing currency notes in denominations of Rs 100. He counted the currency notes and found it to be Rs 90,000. I was foxed and felt that the amount in such cases would be a round figure of Rs. one Lakh. I had my suspicion that somebody had kept back Rs 10,000.

Usually in the case of slush money, nobody would count the amount or even notice if it was short or even complain about it. Being unaccounted money both from the giver and taker's side, such transaction is usually a hush-hush affair. To set all doubts at rest I asked for the package in which the amount was given. When I put all the money back into the container, I noticed that it had the space, exactly for bundles worth Rs 90,000 which had been presented to him. It was apparent, that probably the giver, had given Rs 90,000 and had kept back Rs10,000. I immediately informed, all agencies dealing with foreign and domestic matters and asked them to depute their representatives, for finding out the truth. The matter had to be handled delicately as a foreign country was involved. We need not have been to secretive about the matter. Hours of interrogations of Mahesh Prasad only brought out the fact that as he was handling North Korea, for trade and commerce relations, probably an effort was made to soften him.

Next morning, I rang up the Commerce Secretary, Rao Sahib and apprised him of what had happened. I urged him that we must take a very serious view of the effort made to bribe a Joint Secretary, to the Government of India. He agreed with me. But, a high powered meeting, presided over by one of the Secretaries in the foreign office, played down the incident. I urged in the meeting, presided over by one Eric Gonsalves, that we should not take the matter lightly. Most of the officers, from the External Affairs Ministry said it was a normal practice to bribe people. Some also said in reply to my persistence, that it was for the Indian bureaucracy to stand up to such challenges. I emphasised that we must give a lot of publicity to the incident. The idea was that we should show to the country, that there still were, honest people, who would not brook such temptations. I also said that such honest officers should be commended. An excuse was trotted in the meeting, that it was difficult to link the money with the Embassy officials. I took out my magnifying glass, and with it read out the stamp, the name of the branch and the bank, from where the money had been drawn. I said that as the notes were stapled, the Bank Employees would definitely be in a position to identify the drawer. The participants in the meeting remarked that I was a very persistent fellow. I kept on pursuing the matter. Finally I received a reply that the matter had been closed, with the approval of the Prime Minister. The cash of Rupees 90,000 had been returned to the Ambassador of North Korea, and his acknowledgement obtained. Further the offending personnel had been asked to withdraw from the country. I proposed a cash reward of Rs 10,000 for Mahesh Prasad and the appreciation of the government for his high integrity and honesty. The file was turned down, by the successor Secretary of Rao Sahib saying that all government officials were expected to be honest and Mahesh Prasad had only complied with the rules. I again pressed, for recognition of the commendable role played by Mahesh Prasad. Perhaps at some point there might have been some differences between Mahesh Prasad and the then Secretary. The result was that my efforts did not succeed. I was told to put up the file, to the Secretary, at the time of writing of the Annual Confidential Report of Mahesh Prasad. It was done but somehow the Secretary only assessed working of Mahesh Prasad as satisfactory. There was no mention of the incident.

Annual Confidential Report

A confidential report is written on every official at the end of the year. Quite often, the Annual Confidential Report does not give a correct picture of the performance. It is more of an impression or the opinion of the reporting officer over the reported officer. It can and quite often includes the personal prejudices, whims and opinions. There is a constant effort on the part of the government to make the Annual Confidential Report totally objective. But in the bargain, the assessment form has become so lengthy, that people have neither the patience nor the time for filling up the same. One of the colleagues told me that when he was posted abroad he had the misfortune of receiving and putting up the son and daughter-in-law of his boss. Somehow the daughter-in-law, was not satisfied with the hospitality and the personal chauffeuring done by the officer himself, for sight seeing as well as shopping. The result was that he got only a satisfactory report blocking his promotion for the next few years. At the senior level, unless the annual assessment rates you as "Outstanding" or "Very Good", you are not considered "fit for promotion". I am personally aware of the case of another officer who after his posting to Delhi did not call on the Director of an Agency under the Central Government. Unfortunately, that Director was in the Committee, preparing the panel for promotion. So he was graded as "Good" by the Director . The Director at an earlier occasion had warned this officer saying that he had not called on him. He would fix him up, as he was in the critical zone of promotion. Of course, the wrong was amended by the members of the Committee, overruling the Director of the Bureau.

There is a real dilemma before the authorities. Whatever format they prescribe and whatever rules they lay down, unless there is a will to implement these in the spirit in which they are laid down, there are bound to be distortions and deficiencies. Moreover, in some States like Karnataka or even other States if a satisfactory report was given on an officer, it was considered good enough for his future and promotion. The result is that from such States, very few people make it to the Central government jobs, which require you to have "Very Good" reports and records for being accepted in a Central assignment. There is no limit to any performance in the functioning of any individual. Once a Joint Secretary got the following remarks in his annual confidential report recorded by the then Minister of Commerce "Has done well, Could do better". When the matter was examined in detail, it was noticed that this could not be classified as adverse and it was wrong to have communicated it to him. Still, this remark was sufficient to stall his promotion. In fact when he came to know that he had not been promoted he pleaded fervently, and begged, Commerce Secretary Abid Hussain. Abid is and was ever willing to help the needy.

He wrote the confidential report on the officer. This officer did not get on well with anybody, in the organisation he was heading. The officials, in his organisation were keen to see, that he left them at end of his tenure. They were counting hours and days to the 'D' day. Just on the day his tenure was over, I was flooded with requests for relief and assigning his work to somebody else. Abid Hussain told me to wait, for fifteen days, before relieving him. After fifteen days, the Secretary again told me not to relieve him for another fifteen days. When after two months again I asked for orders, the Secretary said that I should hold on for another fifteen days. I was foxed and asked Abid the reasons for holding on to him. He smiled and said that the officer had told him that he will be promoted in two weeks time. He was coming with this request, every two weeks. That is why his relieving orders, were delayed, only for the period requested. Abid said that he wanted to help him. He was sure, that the officer would not be promoted. I said that I was willing to take a bet that the officer would be promoted. Abid Hussain agreed for a small bet. He asked me the reasons, for my assessment that the officer would be promoted. I told him that since I was the custodian of the confidential reports, I had seen the Confidential Reports written by him on the officer. I told Abid Hussian that the way he had recorded his (the officer's) Confidential Reports, the officer should not only be promoted to the Rank of the Additional Secretary, but as Secretary. The Confidential Reports showed that the officer was solely responsible for the efficient functioning of the Ministry and his organisation and without him the Commerce Ministry would collapse. I said the CR was so impressive, that he could skip the rank of Additional Secretary and straightway be made Secretary to the Government of India. I had said it in good humour, without realising that my own Confidential Report was to be written by Abid Hussain. If Abid took my remarks as a reflection on his capability to assess people, my goose was cooked. It must be said to the credit of Abid Hussian that he took my remarks in good humour and did not take offence. There are some people you would walk miles to avoid. But Abid Hussain, who was later on our Ambassador to United States of America is a man, one would walk miles to meet and greet. The helpful nature of Abid Hussain was not only proverbial but universal. One day I was sitting with him for some official discussion . A visitor dropped in to see him with a young man. Both of them greeted Abid very effusively. Abid Hussain was equally warm in reciprocating the greetings. The older man requested Abid Hussian, for a job, for his son, who was with him. Abid Hussain, in turn asked him, to whom should he be recommended. He replied that as Commerce Secretary, he was also holding the charge of the post of the Chairman of the State Trading Corporation, the young man could be accommodated in the STC. The STC had a lot of staff in 1980s and the Government was trying to reduce the flab. Abid said that he cannot be accommodated in the STC. When again pressed that he should be accommodated in STC, Abid merely said, that the boy would be spoiled if he joined the STC. When again pressed to know the reasons as to how the boy would be spoiled, Abid replied that the boy would get used to drawing salary, without working. Obviously the Commerce Secretary did not want to use the office he was holding for providing jobs and be accused of jobbery and favouritism. This was a very nice way of saying "No" without incurring anybody's displeasure or wrath.

Unity of Dishonest People

In 1980's due to the scarcity of foreign exchange, a number of essential commodities were imported through the Government Corporations under the Ministry of Commerce. There were plenty of complaints, about the missing of huge quantities enroute. One such item was the edible oil. The edible oil, Palmolein would be shipped to India in loose form. It would then be packaged in one kg or bigger containers, for sale in retail. Quite often, the tankers carrying the item, would either disappear or come short weighted. There was no fool proof method to check these unscrupulous practices. The only way, the quantity in a tanker, could be measured, was by dipping a stick. Then a rough calculation based on the depth, would be made. Sometimes the stick would be dipped, into the tank, at such an angle that it would show it full, though a few hundred quintals would have been siphoned off. Sometimes the tanker would have less tyre pressure, so that more quantity could be filled up. After selling off a considerable quantity of edible oil, the tyres of the vehicles would again be inflated. Sometimes, tension in the body springs of the vehicles would raise the level of the tanker container. The disappeared oil quantity would be explained as evaporation or some other "miscellaneous" factors beyond human control. During my visit to Bombay, I saw the entire operation of unloading edible oil and in one case the loss was shown due to leakage of the pipe. So many different agencies like the Port Trust, Bombay Police and the Importing Government Company were involved that it was very difficult, if not impossible, to check such malpractices. More than that, there was no will on the part of the local managers to check such malpractices. Even the local officials were mixed up, in malpractices, making a difficult job more difficult. They would lay all blame on the drivers and other junior staff. The lure of the easy money, the lack of any fear of punishment, and mixing of the local bosses, with such malpractices, made the job of vigilance more difficult. The information about the losses and leakages would be kept under the wrap. It continues to be so, even now. Postings of government employees is a gamble for the government. It is not unlike fixing a round peg in a square hole. It is not the government which can always be faulted. Sometimes there is a pre-disposition to post members of a particular service to specific kinds of postings, such as foreign postings. Some take advantage of their proximity to the powers that matter, and manage what they consider plum postings. In Commerce Ministry an absolute novice, was given a foreign posting, in one of the Tea Board offices only on the strength of his "ability" to read palms and make intelligent political guesses and calculations. By the time, he finished his tenure, he had ruined India's exports to that country. He got his plum posting only on the strength of reading the palm of the then Commerce Minister. His successor, D.R Karthikeyan had to work hard in restoring the credibility of the country and his organisation in Australia. In another case, one Swaminathan posted to Germany in a subsidiary of the STC, Handloom and Handicraft Export Corporation, caused losses worth hundreds of thousands of dollars. He made such a mess that the organisation, finally decided to close the office abroad. This was the only way to cut down the losses.

It is quite fashionable to lay all the blame at the doors of the politicians. It is one sided assessment, because it is ultimately the bureaucracy or at least a segment of it, which is equally responsible. When in Commerce Ministry, I was shown 32 letters from important political figures, recommending the names of several officers for postings as Joint Secretaries. A number of sons-in-law, sons and daughters, of a serving Governor at that time, a retired Chief of one of the Defence Services and serving Secretaries were in the Commerce Ministry. I projected my views in an article under the Heading "Making bureaucracy more effective and responsible" it was carried by the *Indian Express* in all its editions published all over the country, in 1987. I said, "it has become almost fashionable to lay the blame for the ills and lapses of administration at the doors of politicians. Is this a correct appraisal of the situation? Or is it a ruse to cover the lapses for all that has gone wrong in the country or is the bureaucracy equally or more, responsible for the problems, of the common man?A lot has been made of the political interference in official matters and it has been claimed that if there were no political interference, the country would be the best administered nation in the world. It is not possible for one individual to run the country and so the government has framed rules of business and delegated powers to its officials at various levels. More than 90 per cent official work of the government is disposed of at the official level and a small percentage of the work, though the most important is put up to Ministers for final disposal.

Experience has shown that sometimes, matters are presented in such a way that Ministers have no choice but to accept the viewpoint put up to them. The "humble civil servant" is actually neither all that humble nor really a servant. The average Minister is unwilling to overrule the bureaucracy. It may be recalled that even some commissions found fault with politicians for not accepting the civil service's point of view, almost reducing the Ministers to the position of ciphers and elevating the civil servant to the infallible wisdom. The Shah Commission found fault with Indira Gandhi, the late Prime Minister, for not accepting the official advice. Since a civil servant is also a human being and liable to err, it is too much to accept that the official advice tendered is always correct. So the view that if the advice of the civil servant is not accepted, only wrong decisions will be taken by the politicians is not correct. If the premise of laying all blame on politicians is accepted, at least the 90 per cent of work which is delegated to the civil servants should be done well to the satisfaction of the general public. Is the general public satisfied with the work within the ambit of the civil service? The other day a friend said that he had been trying to see a senior official of the government for the last three months. He had made three dozen phone calls but could not get an appointment. He was reluctant to complain, lest his otherwise just case might be ruined. In other words, he did not want to invite the wrath of the "humble civil servant". A stage has come in our country where even for getting an interview, a recommendation is required. The main reason why people run to politicians is because of the inertia and inaction of the bureaucracy. It will be totally unfair to brand the whole of bureaucracy as "deadwood and unresponsive". There are some very brilliant exceptions. But such exceptions are microscopic and it is these people who keep alive the faith of the people in the bureaucracy.

As regards political interference, State Governments under 'President's Rule' have been no models of administration, though no politicians interfere in the day to day work of the administration in those cases. I do not know what alibis the civil service can invent to justify inefficiency and delay in such situations. The administration depends on the calibre and quality of the civil servants. Even in the days of worst political interference, I have come across distinguished civil servants who have stood their ground. Why does not civil service as a class stand up? The answer is not far to seek. It is because the civil servants, at least a vast majority of them, would like to have plum postings. They are more than willing, to go out of their way, to oblige anybody who can help them, in achieving that objective. Having accepted favours, they are in no position, to refuse to return the same. So a kind of nexus develops, between the obliged civil servants and the obliging politicians. In other words, political interference is invited by many civil servants, so that they can oblige the politicians and cash the obligation at the appropriate time. The attitude of self-righteousness, adopted by some officials is only a cloak to cover up their weak spots. This is not to say that politicians are less guilty in the whole matter. However, the fact remains that obliging politicians look for the convenient civil servants, willing to carry out their commands, legal and not so legal and this combination suits everybody. Such civil servants, are not in a position, to resist the self-invited interference. This nexus leads to malpractices in the administration, including corruption. The sufferer is, the common man. In some places, nothing moves without some kind of motivation, either financial or a word from the "right quarters". All this has been pointed out by several commissions. Once in a while, some civil servants after their retirement come out, with their recollections, recalling what glorious heights of public administration they achieved during their "golden reign" and what more they could have achieved but for the interference of politicians. These attempts at self-justification are not bought by either their colleagues or the public.

As a nation, we should be concerned with this malaise and ask ourselves why this has happened? Is there any salvation for our country-men from such bureaucrats and such politicians? The remedy has to be drastic and effected quickly, if the country is to progress. The self-perpetuation and self-preservation game must stop. The over protection to the civil servants must end. Today to remove an erring civil servant is just not possible. The only action that the highest in the government can take is to transfer such an official from one job to another. Any number of complaints, against an official, having public dealings, are stone walled. The complainant, who has the audacity to complain, becomes the victim. The civil servant, secure in the belief that nothing can happen to him, carries on merrily in his old ways. The administration has become rule-oriented and not result-oriented. According to present position, action is possible, against the official who takes some interest in his work, but no action is ever taken, against a person not delivering the goods. For instance, not even one Development Officer has been dismissed from service for not completing the development project, assigned to me. No revenue officer as well has been sacked for not implementing land reforms? If the country is to progress, it is time to reconsider whether the excessive protection given to the civil service should be continued. For a result oriented approach, it is necessary to link job performance, with job retention. We have tried the system where the civil servant is almost irremovable. It has proved a failure. It is time to try the other system of "hire and fire". The hiring should be linked with the capacity to deliver goods, and firing to inefficiency and non-performance."

One junior official of Cotton Corporation of India, posted in Andhra Pradesh as a Branch Manager, in charge of purchasing cotton, on complaints of corruption was transferred to Calcutta, a 'dry posting'. He was so influential that he had a memorandum, sent by twenty Members of Parliament, to the then Commerce Minister VP Singh, requesting for the cancellation of his transfer. He also influenced, a Minister of State in the Home Ministry, hailing from Andhra Pradesh to intercede for the cancellation of his transfer. I belonged to the IPS, and this junior Minister in the Home Ministry, felt that it would be only a cake walk for him to get whatever he wanted done from me. After keeping me waiting outside his room for one hour, I was ushered in the Ministerial presence. I realised that it was a ruse to cut me to size and to show me my place before a Minister. The Minister had not bargained, though soft on the exterior, I was firm as steel. The Minister did not even look up, when I entered his room. I kept standing for a few minutes, till invited to sit down. The Minister looked at me and ordered me to cancel the transfer of Shaffi. I kept on listening and told him that I had nothing to do with the transfer, which had the approval of VP Singh. My role was to put up the complaints and vigilance papers to the Commerce Minister. It was the Commerce Minister who had ordered the transfer. It would be better, if he took up this matter with VP Singh. I also said that if he had no objection, I would draw up a note saying that I had been summoned by him for the cancellation of the transfer I would put up a note containing his request and convey the orders back to him. He told me not to bring anything on record. The Minister who started with ordering me, ended up requesting, again and again, that VP Singh should not even be told that I had been called by him for the cancellation of the transfer. V.P. Singh had such a tremendous reputation that the corrupt and dishonest dare not approach him. The Minister of State Mrs Ram Dulari Sinha on getting a similar memorandum had also told me to cancel the transfer of Shaukat. When I told her, that the matter would have to be put to the Commerce Minister, she backed out by saying that she herself would talk to VP Singh and I need not put up any file to him.

Managing Foreign Trips

Under the rules of the Government of India, for any foreign visit, the clearance of the Screening Committee consisting of the Departmental Secretary, Financial Adviser and the Secretary (Expenditure) Finance Ministry of the Government of India is required. During my tenure, the Commerce Ministry had three Financial Advisers. One Gugnani, of the level of Additional Secretary happened to be one of them. He was the king of wangling foreign trips, whenever any proposal for clearance of foreign visits for any delegation, was sent to him. The Financial Advisers or their juniors in the Ministries, have a finger in every pie. For important Corporations and Public Sector Undertakings they represent the Ministry and for less important organisations, the Deputy Secretaries of Directors of the Finance represent the Financial Advisers. He had created an aura around him. He had made an unwritten rule that for clearance of any foreign trip, he had to be consulted whether he wanted to go. In the Corporations like the State Trading Corporation or the Minerals & Metals Trading Corporation, he was a Government Director. No trip would be cleared if the Corporations did not include his name. If it did not happen, the trip would be torpedoed by him.

Calcutta based, *Business Standard*, a financial daily, carried an editorial on his activities. But this still did not deter him, from managing to visit foreign countries, two dozen time, during his tenure. Many junior officers kept him in good humour so that he did not spike their legitimate foreign visits. The office of the Financial Adviser has become a racket. There is no check on any useless expenditure. All the ire of the Finance Division and the Financial Advisers fall on petty items, like the Stationery, telephone and cars. Otherwise, how is it possible that most of the Government Public Sector undertakings are in the red, despite the financial experts being on the Board of Directors.

The *modus operandi* of Financial Adviser was to say "No" first to any proposal. He would clear the same, after repeated visits by the head of the organisation, or the official who had sent the proposal. He followed the same policy in other spheres. This was the only way the people would notice him. His idea was that the more nuisance value you create, the more powerful would you be. Once in the meeting of the Board of the Directors of the Trade Fair Authority of India, headed by Mohammad Yunus, he incensed him by the frivolous objections. Yunus had his objections recorded. He also added that "the Chairman explained that the Trade Fair Authority was not the opposition party." Thereby he implied that the Trade Fair Authority was equally responsible for what it was doing and by implication the observation of the Financial Adviser was not only totally irrelevant but also uncalled for. This was the last time the "Financial Adviser" raised any objection to the proposal of the TFAI. Apart from recording the above in the minutes, the Chairman gave such a dressing down, that all the proposals of the TFAI had a smooth sailing so far as the internal finance was concerned. Trade Fair Authority was set up in the 1970's during the regime of late Indira Gandhi and Mohammad Yunus had been appointed as its first Chairman. Before he could put it on a sound footing the Congress Party lost elections in 1977.

With that, the fortune of persons appointed by Congress regime took a nose dive. The new regime had its own appointees. The Commerce Minister in 1979, humiliated the then Managing Director publicly at a function so much, that the Managing Director preferred to resign than pocket red humiliation.

After the return to power. Congress again appointed Yunus as a Chairman of the Trade Fair Authority in 1980. During my tenure of dealing with the Trade Fair Authority, in less than three years, there were three different Managing Directors appointed. As two of them were very senior officers of the IAS, they found it difficult to work with the style of the Chairman. Both Zaffar Saifullah and Surinder Singh, who rose to be Cabinet Secretary, were failures in getting alongwith Mr Yunus. Of course, if you ask them, they would point out the dictatorial approach and centralisation of all authority by the Chairman. Under the law all authority was vested with the Managing Director. In the Trade Fair organisation, nothing could be done without the approval of the Chairman. This was the main reason of clash. I was a privy to their humiliations and predicament. Both of them were packed off by the Chairman at the end of one year each. It must be said to the credit of the Chairman that he was fully abreast of all the aspects of the working of the organisation, which he had created. No other officer could emulate him. At one stage, the Trade Fair Authority had as many as four senior IAS officers including the Managing Director and the General Managers. One of the General Managers, Vishwanath told me that he did not have any authority even to tell a sweeper where to sweep and when to sweep, as all power had been centralised by the Chairman. So much so, that senior officers would not occupy a chair, unless invited to do so, by the Chairman.

Once a proposal to organise an International Exhibition in London, in 1982 was turned down, by the Finance Ministry, on the ground that the cost was over one crore of rupees in foreign exchange. Orders came from the Prime Minister's office agreeing to the proposal. The Chairman had personally gone and met Indira Gandhi, the then Prime Minister. He had convinced her that India would earn much more foreign exchange than the proposed expenditure. He proved what he said. The exhibition bagged orders, worth fifty crores in foreign exchange. The exhibition was a roaring success. For the first time the British were exposed to the industrial heights, India had achieved since 1947. The pride of Indian Exhibition at Pragati Maidan started developing in 1980's and now almost all the States have their permanent exhibition buildings in New Delhi. The Authority regularly hosts commodity fairs like the Textile Fairs and Food and Electronics Fairs, apart from organising every year an International Exhibition which traditionally commences on 14th of November. It has been regularly organising Indian participation in a number of international specialised fairs in various European and Asian countries. A small nondescript organisation has grown into a popular organisation. It has carved a niche for itself both in national and international spheres.

The Status of Vigilance

Vigilance is never taken seriously anywhere, in our country, though an elaborate set-up exists to deal with corruption, complaints and malpractices. I received a complaint that, an assistant in the Commerce Ministry was a party to a racket of sending people abroad, for jobs. After a thorough inquiry, the Ministry on my recommendation decided to dismiss him. But Advisory body, Union Public Service Commission, which was required to be consulted , under the rules. It did not agree and suggested that the official may be warned only. In another case where an official of the level of Joint Secretary was involved in taking a loan by misusing his position, the Advisory body washed its hands off by saying that the Department may deal with it as it deemed fit. In one case, the Financial Adviser of an organisation was found to be guilty of claiming certain allowances to which he was not entitled. When questioned and confronted with the evidence and the interpretation of the rules from the Finance Division of the Ministry, he had no option but to refund the amount to the government. He tried his best to stay in the Tea Board, as he was getting a number of foreign trips. I did not agree and had him relieved. He went back to his parent department, much against his wishes. During my tenure of nearly 5½ years in the Union Commerce Ministry, I worked with a number of Commerce

Ministers starting from Mohan Dharia, Hitendar Desai, Pranab Mukerjee, V.P. Singh and ending with Shivraj Patil. Some of them supported action to root out malpractices and corruption.

In another case, an officer was continuously bullying the then Chairman of the Tea Trading Corporation of India, P.K. Das Gupta. Despite the completion of his tenure, he had refused to relinquish the charge. He told the Chairman that he could get him into trouble if he insisted on relieving him. The Chairman, despite humiliation and defiance, genuinely believed him. During my visit to Calcutta this was brought to my notice. I advised the Chairman that he should go by the existing rules. If the tenure of the official was over, it was upto him to take action. The Chairman said "What should I do if he refuses to relinquish the charge, does not vacate the office and surrenders the official car?" I said the solution was simple. He had to issue orders saying that "Consequent to the completion of deputation so and so is deemed to have relinquished the charge of the so and so post." I also said that so far as not vacating the office room was concerned, he simply had to order his staff to lock the room with a different lock. It should not be opened, without his permission. If in spite of that, the official concerned tried to barge into the room, it was open to him to lodge a police case. I also told him that getting back the official car was not an insurmountable task. He simply had to order the official driver that from a particular day the vehicle should cease to be at the disposal of the officer to whom it was attached. For any mileage done or petrol spent, the driver would have to pay beyond that day. I assured him that these simple common sense solutions would solve his problems and they did. The officer, who was lionising, over the Chairman, became a tame mouse, the next day, after the above suggestions were implemented.

One of the Acts, entrusted to the Ministry of Commerce for enforcement was the Enemy Property Act of 1968. Under this Act, the properties of Nationals of the Enemy countries, which had been at war with India, were to vest in the Government of India. This was to apply to the properties, business, commerce and trade of the enemy nationals. As a result of 1965 war between India and Pakistan, the properties of the Pakistani nationals were taken over by the Government of India. They were vested in the custodian of Enemy Property under the Commerce Ministry based at Bombay. The Custodian, an officer of the rank of the Deputy Secretary was to administer the properties including shares, deposits and buildings in the best interest of the enemy. He was required to keep a separate account of each property, the profit and loss and the cash, which ran into crores. It was not to be kept or merged in the Consolidated Fund of India. As a Director, it was allocated to me to administer this Act. On visiting the Office of the Custodian, I noticed that a lot of correspondence was being done with the state government for realising the rent of the properties. I personally felt that a lot of staff was deployed in a job which appeared to be endless. Even after nearly two decades there was no possibility of the settlement of the future of the properties in India. I learnt that, Pakistan had liquidated the problem by liquidating the very properties. It was not even willing to enter into negotiations on the subject, despite serious efforts made through formal diplomatic channels. I suggested, that for over two decades, nothing had come out of the overtures made by India to settle the issue. It would be better, if the properties vested in the Custodian of Enemy Property were disposed off and the amount deposited in the Consolidated Fund of India. In the event of settlement, the concerned enemy nationals could be paid the amount realised. I felt that it would be a simplistic solution to the problem. But I had not obviously seen hurdles to any sensible solutions. The fact that enemies of the country have by and large the same legal protection in India, as Indian citizen was a news to me. It was brought home to me by a judgement of Bombay High Court delivered in 1977-78. A building known as Kishori Court was taken over by the Custodian of Enemy property, as a result of 1965 war between India and Pakistan. As Municipal taxes were due from it, Bombay Municipal Corporation auctioned the building, on the advice of the Custodian. It realised its taxes and credited the balance amount, to the Custodian of Enemy Property. The owner of the building was a lady, a former Bombay prostitute, who spread joy, happiness and pleasure migrated to Pakistan. She came to India on a tourist visa, in 1975-76. She filed a writ petition in the High Court, pleading that the Custodian at the best, was a trustee. He had no authority to permit Bombay Municipal Corporation to auction the building. He was to hold the same in the Trust. Holding the properties in trust was to continue, till the two governments resolved the problem. Her advocate also challenged that there was no war actually between India and Pakistan but only skirmishes as there was no notification of India declaring a war with Pakistan. The judge upheld the claim on both counts. His reasoning was that Government of India, had not produced the notification, declaring war with Pakistan in 1965.

One really cannot find fault with the Judge. He has to go by the evidence put up to him. No evidence was put up to him, in form of the Government notification of going to war with Pakistan in 1965. It is a different story that the media was full of war stories and India lost thousands of defence service personnel at that time. Judiciary naturally has to go by what evidence is adduced before it. It is not obligatory for a judge to use his personal knowledge of events. I pressed for going in appeal to the Supreme Court against the judgement of the High Court. But the Law Officers decided that we had no case. The Law Ministry advised that without amending the Act, it was not legally permissible to dispose off the properties of the enemies and credit the proceeds to the Consolidated Fund of India. The Ministry of External Affairs opposed the amendment on the ground that it would equally apply to Bangladesh. Despite my personally seeing and pleading with the then Law Secretary that it was necessary to amend the Act in the overall national interest, the matters did not move. I, in disgust, told the then Law Secretary, one Peri Shastry that we did not need foreign elements to weaken our country. Most of us by quibbling and infighting over petty egos were doing the enemy's work. I understand that the matters remain where they were in 1980s when I had started the move to amend the Act.

I had joined Commerce Ministry on 1st January 1979, so my period of deputation was ending on 1st January 1984. As I had done about a month training abroad, so adding this period I should have finished my period of my deputation on 28th February, 1984. V.P. Singh, who was Minister of Commerce and later on became the Prime Minister of India, called me and said that he would like to give me the job of

Har Prasad Sharma, his Private Secretary. The Commerce Minister was so impressed with my work that he wanted me as his private secretary. The private secretary's job is such that he has to come half an hour earlier than his boss and leave one hour after he has gone. I had no objection to working hard. But I wanted to be fair to him; I told him that my deputation was ending very shortly. My working as his private secretary, would be misunderstood by the Prime Minister, who may not approve of it.

I also told V.P. Singh that he was welcome to assign to me any work he wanted. I was flattered that he trusted me as much as the then Secretary Abid Hussain and Additional Secretary, Vinod Pandey. Vinod Pandey rose to be the Cabinet Secretary, when V.P. Singh became the Prime Minister. When my deputation was about to end, I went again to V.P. Singh and told him that I had come to take leave because in a few days' time I would be leaving the Commerce Ministry. He asked to select a successor and he gave me one or two names. One of the names was that of Prakash Singh, who later retired as Director General , BSF. V.P. Singh rejected his name on the ground that of Prakash Singh was a Thakur, like himself, lest he may be misunderstood for favouring another Thakur from UP. After sometime, in the month of March, I said, "Sir, my period is already over, I have already overstayed. Now let me go back to my cadre." He said that he had already told me that I should continue as long as he was there. I had no option, but to keep quiet. There was no formal request to the Department of Personnel, to continue me, as Director in Commerce Ministry. But you can't go on arguing with a Minister every day. In the meantime, I received a notification promoting me to the next rank of Additional I.G. I had also requested the Karnataka Government to sponsor me for a nine months' course in the Indian Institute of Public Administration. It is used either for getting degrees, or for extended stay in Delhi. It is also used, by the departments, to dump those whom it does not want. I was selected, for the course. Karnataka Government also issued necessary orders deputing me for the course. My interest was to go back to Karnataka and join there in any post, at least for a couple of days. This would show that I had gone back to the State. It would begin my cooling off period, for coming back to the Central deputation. Government of India orders require that there must be a break of 3 years. between one Central deputation and another deputation. I approached the Commerce Secretary on the 22nd June, 1984 for my relief. Abid Hussain was upset. He said when Minister had told me, to stay on, why was I asking, to be sent back. I said that I had got promotion in my State. I was also getting a chance, to stay back with my family, for nine months, when still being in the State. He reluctantly, signed my file, wherein I had sought permission for handing over the charge. I took the same file to VP Singh and told him that I wanted to go back to my State. He was very unhappy. I also told him that, in the event of his moving to a better portfolio, I would be left in the lurch. I may be asked to hand over the charge at 24 hour notice. I urged to be allowed to leave at the time of my choosing, rather than the Government's choosing. V.P. Singh saw the logic and reluctantly approved my request.

After I had finished my tenure with the Government of India, in 1984 in the Commerce Ministry, I had made a request to the State Government to sponsor me for one year course in the Advanced Professional Programme in Public Administration in the Indian Institute of Public Administration in New Delhi. This was a one-year programme, aimed at improving administrative skills. Successful completion of it would also lead to the conferment of M.Phil. Degree in Public Administration. I could also stay in Delhi, for one year more with my family. I approached the then Commerce Minister, Mr V.P. Singh to relieve me, so that I could go back to Karnataka, join there and come back for the APPA course. He said; "As long I am the Minister, you continue". He had such strong faith in me that I could not argue with him any more. Later on the formal orders, promoting me as Additional Inspector General and deputing me for the course were received, when I was still in Commerce Ministry. I approached the Commerce Secretary, Abid Hussain, on 23rd June 1984 to recommend my relief to the Minister. He told me: "Once the Minister has told you that you are not to be relieved, why do you want me to recommend it". I said; "It will be a favour to me". He just signed my file for sending it to the Minister. I told him that I will personally carry it. He replied; "You are a strange fellow. People are willing to give their right hand to stay in Commerce Ministry and you want to go. (It was the regime of permits quotas and licenses.) I said; "I will try my luck". I found that there was green light, at VP Singh's room. Apart from the traffic signals and railways signals, the other places, you can see green light and red lights, is outside the Minister's and senior bureaucrats rooms. Green light means that the concerned occupant is available. Only those can walk in, who are sure of not being rebuffed? I was in that category, being the Director of Vigilance and enjoying the faith of VP Singh. The Minister saw me and said; "What brings you here? Any problems?" I said; "No Sir, I solve most of the problems myself. I will not trouble you. I want a little help and your signature on this file for my relief." He was unhappy and told me: "When I have told you, that you will continue as long as I am here, why do you raise the subject?" I said; "Sir, I am most grateful, for your confidence in me. But allow me, to go at the time of my own choosing, rather than the Government's. My tenure was officially over on 1st January 1984. I stayed on, as desired by you, till my successor was selected. First, you did not accept Prakash Singh on the sole ground, lest you be accused of being a Pro Thakur, as you and Prakash Singh are from the same caste. Later on, the selection of Kiran Bedi fell through, despite your recommending it to the Prime Minister. Perhaps, you will move to a better portfolio and I will be left in lurch. After your departure, I may also have to leave at one hour's notice. By getting selected for this course, I will have a chance to improve my skills. I am at your disposal. But it will be a personal favour, to let me go, before I am thrown out after your departure".

V.P. Singh saw the logic and reluctantly signed my relief order with an offer; "Whenever you want a job in Government of India, please feel free to tell me". After a few months, VP Singh himself went back to UP as the President of Uttar Pradesh Congress Committee.

I left Ministry of Commerce on 25th of June 1984 after a very satisfying tenure of over five and half years. This was the longest stint in my official career in one job. The job had taken me all over the world. It exposed me to a wider world of UK, Europe, USA, Japan and other highly developed countries. It made me realize that notwithstanding the claims, of being an ancient civilisation, we were also technologically and developmentally, ancient. We had to toil a lot to reach anywhere, near those developed countries. It made me humble and level headed. Honesty and integrity, in day to day dealings of most officials at the cutting edge level, was missing. There were no hassles in day to day existence in the developed countries, unlike our country, where even a working telephone or water supply, or electricity or well-carpeted roads are a luxury.

14

Student Again

I joined Karnataka for three days on 27th of June 1984, as DIG Industrial Security. An officer had to proceed, on three days casual leave, to make room for me. It was only a technical posting. I met all my old colleagues in the limited time of two days. Some I met for the last time, as a few of them completed their earthly tenure, sooner than expected. I left for Delhi on 30th June so as to be in time for the nine months course, commencing on 1st of July 1984. As I had joined back Karnataka and was deputed from Bangalore to Delhi for the course, I was treated on duty for the entire course. One invisible advantage which I did not know, before joining back to the State, was to get daily allowance of Rs 50 per day, for entire nine months duration of course. I drew Rs 13,500 for staying with my family. Karnataka rules were and I believe continue to be, liberal.

At IIPA

Indian Institute of Public Administration, (IIPA) had made a student of me again. The one major difference was that I was free from official worries and anxieties. IIPA was a great fun. You could discuss; you could pull each other's legs though some lecturers tried to behave like schoolmasters. We never took them seriously. Very few participants had an ear for fun, joy and taking life as it comes. Some were not only serious, but also serious looking. They gave an impression, as if their existence depended upon IIPA course. I believe in all these training courses, the most important feature, is not the contents, but interaction with the colleagues, friends, and the people you come in contact. It was also an opportunity to study different and contrasting human nature. No participant was less than the level of Director, or Deputy Secretary. Some of them were stingy and down right unfit for the high offices they held. Some others could be just tolerated. Another category of participants were scroungers on everybody. For instance, we used to get contributory tea twice a day. Some would polish off Pakora and Biscuit meant for others also. A few minutes delay meant, that your share of eatables was also finished.

It was a mini India, with people from every State and all Services like the IPS, IAS, Custom, Audit and Economic Services. The best part of the programme was a foreign trip including the visits to Singapore, Malaysia, and Indonesia. One participant was so keen to save every penny, for his shopping. The first thing he would do was to find a place, where he could get cheapest eatable for less than one dollar. It did not matter whether the place was hygienic or not. He returned, loaded with the TV, VCR and other consumer items saved from his Daily Allowance. It is a fact, that most officials, use foreign visits only for acquiring foreign goods not available in India or which carry premium on resale.

Despite all the courses, when the administrators go back, they have to work in stratified, hide bound parameters and atmosphere. This itself can take away all possible initiative. The course, was both fun and an education.

I flew back to Karnataka after completing my course on 31st March 1985. I had requested Government of Karnataka to give me a cadre job for 45 days, so that I could draw my salary in the higher scale, to which I had been promoted long ago. There is a funny rule, that unless you occupy a cadre post, the Accountant General will not authorise you, any higher scale, or increments. You are not considered a regular appointee. My appointment had been made, to the Ex-cadre post of DIG. I did not decide my posting. It was the Government, which did it. The result was, that my juniors were drawing, more salary than I was. Since I wanted study leave, for two years after 45 days, I wanted to be posted to a Cadre job, so that there was no problem with my salary or increments. Karnataka had become totally castesized. One Minister told me; "You North-Indian, why do you come and take our boys jobs. Go back to Government of India who recruited you and ask them for the job." He did not realise that I was in Karnataka cadre since, 1961. It was humiliating, but I was in no position, to hit back at the Minister, or tick him off, that I had been recruited on merit. It was his caste speaking, because caste is a very important factor for important postings in South India, and not only in Karnataka. I realised that I had no future in Karnataka if caste is to count everything. I wanted to proceed on study leave but not immediately. But neither the Police Chief, nor the Government, would agree to give me any other job beyond 45 days. They said you proceed on leave, which you have asked. There was no use of any, argument. I rationalised that, if the Government wanted to give me, full salary, on study leave, I had no reason to be unhappy. Before I returned to Delhi, my family joined me in Bangalore. My wife had taken leave travel concession for coming there. My three daughters enjoyed their stay in Bangalore in the month of May and June. They spent almost all the time, in the swimming pool of Bangalore club. I had become a member of Bangalore club in 1973 and continue to be so even now.

My handwriting is practically illegible. Sometimes, I cannot read what I have written. The ironical fact is that nobody, including myself can read what I have written. I joined a typing school, in Khan Market, to learn typing. It cost me only Rs 30 to know the basic of typing. The rest comes from practice. I used to type one personal letter, every week to my father, late Mahant Kartar Singh at Jalalabad, so that he should know what exactly I had written. This practice ended, with his death on 23rd Janurary, 1996 at Francis Newton Hospital, Ferozpore. My grandfather had also died in the same hospital. I cannot say anything what future holds for me. It must be said to the credit of the Doctors there, that they did their best.When you are on leave or retired, people tend to look upon you, as if you have no work, and no job. I always believe, that your own respect, is in your own hands. You must maintain it yourself. While on leave, I made it a point, not to go to any colleague, or any other person in his office, just to pass time. I made it a rule, to have a strict schedule for myself. I would visit IIPA library and other libraries connected with the Police, for research. The result was I produced four volumes of "*A Blue Print for Police Reforms*" in two years of my study leave. It was a disappointing exercise, to find out that nobody, either the British or Independent Indian Government, had taken any steps, to bring about Reforms in the Police. Mostly, it was a knee jerk reaction, to deal with a particular situation. When the situation became normal, everything was forgotten. In 1977, the Central Government set up a National Police Commission (Third Police Commission). It produced momentous eight reports from 1977-81. They are gathering dust somewhere in the Government, both unsung and unwept. The First Police Commission was set up in 1859-60, and the Second Police Commission in 1902-03. It is true that government machinery moves very slowly. But it is also a fact, that sometime it does not move at all.

The speed of administration, particularly in Police Reforms would be considered, unrealistically slow, even in a community of snails, who are the slowest in the world. This is the kind of approach, we have in the country for improving Indian Police. Every government or individual wants only to temporarily deal with the problem. When it is over, then everything about it is forgotten. Whatever has been promised or whatever is required to be done, is forgotten like an election promise. During the leave period May 1985 to May 1987, I took care of my wife in the house allotted to her in Kaka Nagar. Many people say, that it is difficult to pass time, when you are on leave, or otherwise not engaged. But my problem has been the lack of time. I am very jealous in safeguarding it, so that I can accomplish more and more. The massive work on Police reforms, by me is only a one man's effort, in projecting the reforms needed in Indian Police. I had written, to the Government of Karnataka two months, in advance of the end of my leave.

But when I reached Bangalore, I found there was no indication, of any posting for me. I got a positive impression, that my seniors and perhaps even the government felt that my coming had created a problem for them. I always believe that a government servant neither has respect or disrespect. He is kicked around, by an informal system of pulls and pressures. It is for this reason, that people try to cultivate politicians or senior officials so that they are allowed, to live without humiliation. After a week's waiting, I was posted as DIG Industrial Security, a Closed Shop. I observed that transfers and postings had become an industry both for the politicians and the bureaucrats. The tragedy was, that in this case, the person complained against, or the accused was also the judge. I had also observed, that in unstable and precarious governments, with no majority of their own, both in the state and at the centre, even one legislator could pull strings for any decision.

I asked a Director General of Police as to how much time he spent on the Professional Policing and how much on other work. He replied that he hardly spent any time on Police work. Most of his time was spent on transfers and postings. His main job was to keep politicians happy so that he can retain his job. Transfers though not declared, as an industry, have become a means of enriching oneself. It is perhaps more lucrative than any industry. It is difficult to say, who is more corrupt, the officer or the politician or who taught whom. But there is definitely a nexus between the obliging bureaucrats and dishonest politicians, as it benefits both. I put a question to a politician "Why are you patronising the most corrupt in the Government? Some of these bureaucrats have been, very corrupt and enjoyed cosy postings during the time of previous governments. Why should they be your favourite's now." He replied in Punjabi "They are our Kamau Puttar. (They are our earning sons. They are useful for everybody. They are ones who make the piles for us)." Life does not run in straight lines. Most of us want to avoid trouble. When as a DIG, in the Police Headquarters in Bangalore, I asked my chief, "How about resisting political interference in transfers and postings." He said, "If I resist I will be shifted. There are twenty people, who will be happy to do, what you want me to refuse. I want to retire honourably with my pension. You do, what you want to do, when your turn comes." The pressure comes only on the top man, or the person, who has the authority and can take decisions. It generally does not come, to the middle level people or lower staff, who have no authority. I had been the head of the department since 1973 till 1997. I would receive a number of recommendations, from influential people, including the Ministers and Member of Parliaments and MLAs. I would just file them and forget about them. I would not even read them, because I knew, that they were meant only for the satisfaction, of the person, who had secured their intercession. I was told this fact by a Minister himself, that whenever he sent a recommendation, it did not mean anything. It is only sent to please their constituents. I must also confess, that by following this method, I have been able to ignore recommendations even from the Prime Ministers. Any recommendation is not only meant, to help the person, but also to cause injustice, to somebody. I have never believed, in favouring anybody, at the cost of harming somebody else.

Only after many reminders, I would look at the papers sent to me and find ways to ensure that no injustice was done to anybody. Some experiences are bound to be common, in various jobs, whereas others will always be different.

I found it of utmost importance for the top man, which I had been since 1973 to 1997, till my retirement, to organise his work, in such a way, that he is able to find time for everything. One feature in all jobs has been that of paying homage, to the next Higher Officer, whether one admits it or not. It is a fact of life, both in private and public life. The man above you, wants some homage. But doing your job well, is no substitute for homage. Lack of professionalism, is affecting every branch of administration in our country. Glib talking is sought to be replaced by solid work. There was comparatively more sense of accountability, in the 60s, and 70s than now, when it is almost non existent. You can loot the Government and get away. You can do or not do the job and still be in service, and reach the top. Safety first, has become the criterion.

The Governors do not know how to govern. They have become rules and regulation oriented rather than the result oriented. For instance, I know in various departments, some staff has no work whereas in others, there is overloading. I asked a colleague as to why the surplus staff should not be surrendered. He did not agree, on the ground, that later on, even if required, it will be impossible to get any staff from the Ministry of Finance, despite answering hundreds of questions. The result is everyubody, goes on adding the staff, with or without work. The system itself is responsible for it. Every man seems to be for himself and God is left in peace.

I joined back Karnataka, in May, 1987 as a DIG. It was a completely changed Karnataka, where the caste factor had become predominant in appointments, postings and promotions. I was surprised to see the new face of Karnataka, which was not the familiar old Karnataka, which I had joined in 1962. I was promoted on 18th August, 1987 as Inspector General of Police and posted as Special Home Secretary to the Government of Karnataka. I could feel distance between me and the later entrants, as well in the politicians, There was an undercurrent of hostility and a subtle hint that neither I was wanted there nor welcome to continue. It made me doubly keen to-go back and join the Government of India. I was asked, through Mr P.G. Haralankar, Additional Director General of the Central Reserve Police Force, whether I would be willing to join as Inspector General of Police of CRPF in Chandigarh. I was told that the job was to fight terrorists—a challenging task. I had throughout my life adopted the principle of never asking for any job or never saying "no" to any job I was assigned. I said "yes". This "yes" was opposed by my wife, daughters, parents, relations and friends also. Their rationale was that this job would expose me and my entire family to terrorists. I did not agree with anybody. My logic was that "if I get scared, I will lose respect in my own eyes". For me, once a word is given, there is no going back. The then DG CRPF. S.D. Pandey visited Bangalore, before I had joined CRPF. I invited him for a lunch. He saw me riding a scooter. He was amazed that as an IG, I was driving a scooter. He asked me to sell off my scooter before I left for Punjab. "You cannot drive a scooter in Punjab," he advised me. I protested and said that I did not want to use a government vehicle for private purpose. He replied that it was not I who would like to use the government vehicle. It would be the orders of CRPF, to use the government vehicle wherever I went. "You become a precious commodity the moment you join the CRPF in Punjab. Terrorists would get a lot of mileage by killing you and the country would get a bad name that they could not protect their own IG. It is not that you would be on a pleasure trip. You would have to be available on constant and continuous communication basis. Obviously, the Government will not fit the wireless communication network on your scooter", reasoned Pandey. Reluctantly, I sold my scooter before coming to Delhi.

Heading CRPF

I joined Central Reserve Police Force on January 6, 1988, not realising that I would never be going back to Karnataka. When I drove to Chandigarh, I was surrounded by security vehicles. A jeep fitted with a light machine gun on the top was ahead of my vehicle. Another jeep was covering from the back. The office-cum-residence was in Sector 34. My family had remained at Delhi. I did not want them to join me in Chandigarh. Except for 24-hour work there was nothing else to be done.

One night, I got up to close the door, in the residential portion of my office cum residence at Chandigarh. The door latch was missing. I found that a guard was practically centimetres away from my bed. Another was in the verandah and still another at the entrance gate. This was over and above the heavily armed guard deployed outside. Next morning I inquired, the reasons of guards staying near my bed and in my residential portion. I was informed that it was being done for my security. I was amazed. I said "why should any security man stand on my head, in my bed room". I felt it was unfair to invade my privacy. I ordered, that from then on, no guard would be posted inside my house or in my bedroom.

I was told, that my predecessor, K.P.S. Gill had introduced heavy security arrangements, for his personal security. Gill was the first IG, of the CRPF in Punjab. After he joined Punjab Police from the CRPF, the post had remained vacant for a long time. Another IG from South was holding the additional charge. I was almost the next regular successor of KPS Gill. I explained while I respected the security considerations, I wanted to maintain my sanity and privacy. I had no objection to any security arrangements being made outside the house and the office. A few security drills had to be observed. I was not supposed to talk, on open lines, not to send even wireless messages. I was advised to use a secure line, if possible. My programmes were kept a closely guarded secret. Even the driver of my car was not told of the next programme. The drivers were given standing instructions to keep petrol tanks of the vehicles full. They were to keep their bag and baggage ready. Only after entering the car; I would indicate the destination.

In 1988, there were massive killings of the Hindus by the terrorists. The terrorists, trained by the ISI of Pakistan, wanted to kill as many persons, as possible. They wanted to create an unbridgeable divide, between the Hindus and the Sikhs. Killings in trains, buses, public places, fares, marriage parties clearly showed their thinking and objective. I made it a point to visit all such places, where the terrorists had run amuck. This was to assure the local population, that the CRP would do its best to stop such incidents. I would also take advantage to review the deployment and performance of the Unit. Everyday there would be news of such incidents: 40 killed; 50 killed; 10 policemen killed. Once I attended a funeral of eleven policemen killed in Amritsar District. In one case, 40 innocent persons were mowed down by terrorists in Hoshiarpur.

To make CRPF more determined to fight the terrorists I interacted with all officials including the Constables, in open Sainik Durbars. Sainik Durbar is an institution, wherein the senior most officer, conveys his view to all officials. Attendance for such a meeting is a must for all those present in the Station. I used to explain the Punjab situation and freely invite questions. I personally interrogated a number of terrorists, arrested by the CRPF. and questioned as to why they became terrorists, their candid reply was that they were looking for jobs, for making an honest living. *Ya tay tussi naukari de dayo, ya wo de denge.* (Either you give us the job or they will). They had been trained by ISI in Pakistan. Once arrested, the terrorists spilt out the beans and gave details of their trainers and training camps. What had happened was, that the central paramilitary organisations and the armed forces, had started recruiting people, from different states, in proportion to their population. This was the Policy laid down since 1980 and is continuing even now. The result is that some states are not able to fill their quota, either because the qualified people were not willing, or were not available. But other states, like Punjab, had their intake reduced. The result was discontentment in Punjab, which had traditionally been contributing the maximum number of men to the uniformed forces. As the avenues dried up and the young people had no other means of earning their livelihood, they were grabbed by the ISI for fomenting trouble. When I joined, as IGP CRP in Punjab, J.F. Ribeiro was the DG. After some time, Gill took over, in April 1988. Both Ribeiro and Gill were following the bullet-for-bullet policy. I had been trained in the tradition of strictly observing the laws. But sticking to the rules does not solve the problems always. Sometimes, when the system collapses you have to invent your own rules of the game and break new grounds. I noticed in 1988, that the entire system had collapsed. Nobody was willing to help those who were fighting the terrorists. The police morale had to be boosted. The regrettable situation was that almost all the departments, of the government felt that it was not their job to help and assist in fighting the terrorists. They felt that it was a Punjab police and the CRP problem. The local policemen had their own friends and relations in the state. They became the targets of the ISI trained terrorists. A succession of poor leadership had totally demoralized the police. The Policemen, were ill-trained, ill-equipped and poorly looked after. The first task that any leader had to undertake was to raise the sagging morale of the police force and make them fit to fight the terrorists. And in this, Ribeiro and Gill did exceedingly well. But I personally did not agree with the bullet-for-bullet policy. I did not agree to any killing unless it was a fair fight. My perception was naturally different because of my having remained outside Punjab for so long. Reports were appearing regularly in newspapers regarding the misuse of Terrorists and Disruptive Activities (Prevention) Act (TADA). Punjab Government dismissed about 250 policemen, including some SHOs and Inspectors, for misusing their position, in foisting false TADA cases against innocent persons.

One day, I discussed this issue with Gill. I told him that there were many complaints of corruption against the police and something must be done. He said: "Look, I have opened one front to fight terrorism. I cannot open another. Otherwise, what will happen is that I will lose on both the fronts? It is better that I finish this job and then move on to the next. I am aware of what is happening. But one has to prioritise. There are some police stations where I cannot even find people to head. I have to motivate people. I have to make them work at police stations." In retrospect, probably Gill was right. But mentally I did not agree that anything beyond what law permits should be done. Gill himself never spared anybody if something concrete was brought to his notice. But it was a fact that the Punjab Police was facing a dilemma. When something goes haywire, we ask the police to find a solution. This is what had happened with the spread of terrorist activities. Punjab had become unliveable for an honest and peace loving citizen. I had, a serious difference of opinion on issues. It was because I did not believe in the short cuts and going against the charter of duties laid down for the CRP by the Central Government. I never stepped out of the law nor would I permit any CRP man to do so, for the sake of temporarily pleasing DG, Punjab.

It is universally true that if somebody needs you he will do everything to please you. He will look after you, make you comfortable and see to it that all your needs are taken care of. The same was true of CRPF in Punjab as well as in Jammu & Kashmir. Wherever its need was the greatest, the District Administration went out of its way, in providing the basic facilities and showing respect and accommodation to the senior officers. Wherever they felt that it was imposed on them, they looked at CRPF, not exactly as evil, but something to be put up with, in view of the then prevailing situation.

Some CRPF officers felt uncomfortable in working with the district police chiefs of the Punjab Police. The reason was that some of them, had put in lesser service, than them. But in the prevailing scheme of things, it is the district police chief and the district magistrate, who matter. It is not the number of years one has put in that matters. It is the position one occupies. I had to drill into the minds of my officers that we had to work as a team. Our sole objective was combating militancy and there was no place for personal egos. To set an example, I myself would call on District SPs, DIGs and DM's with CRPF officers. I insisted that we should have a better coordination. We should know them and they should know us. Some CRPF officers used to talk loosely that they were contractors of skilled armed labour. Their job was to provide the manpower, whenever and wherever required, by the District Administration. When senior officers accompanied the CRP units, they would be shown respect and deference. But when junior officers of the rank of Inspectors or Sub-Inspectors, led CRP units, the local Police would order around. CRP units consist of men from different parts of the country. They are a highly disciplined force, and trained never to grumble.

Gill never liked my approach. CRP officers would meet him to plead for my transfer. I was a hard task master and descended very harshly on the malpractices of senior officials. A new post of IG (operations) was created. It was time for me to make a place for somebody else. I continued as IGP CRP, North West Sector, with the Operational responsibility of Jammu & Kashmir in 1989. Most of my time was spent in Srinagar. Gill did not get on well with my two successors and they also had to leave sooner than expected. Whatever be the compulsion, it is a fact that it is the best bet to be within the framework of the laws.

Some time when you cannot handle a situation, then you tend to find scapegoats. In the case of Punjab situation the convenient scapegoats were BSF and CRPF. We used ot have frequent meetings to ensure smoother cooperation. Gill had been IG, CRPF himself so the local commanders were more than willing to carry out at his behest. Some time it would be done at my back. I had made it clear to the CRPF officers that the chain of command would not allow to be broken. The then governor, Siddharth Shankar Roy used to take coordination meeting. One day in such a meeting Gill complained that BSF was not cooperating. Prakash Singh, the then IG BSF told the meeting, of complete lack of co-ordination and cooperation from Punjab Police. He said that Gill had had visited Jalandhar on numerous occasions and not once Gill invited him for discussions or for any other matter dealing with the terrorism. He also said that even if a Constable had told him that Gill wanted to see him, he would have gladly gone and met him. This led to more bitterness between Gill and Prakash Singh. In the same meeting, Gill told the Governor that he had no problem with CRPF. Gill had his own problem in tackling a situation. He himself was and is high on the terrorist list. In a few months, both myself and Prakash were operationally out of Punjab. Kashmir continued to be my charge.

Kashmir was a boiling cauldron. ISI of Pakistan had begun training and infiltrating youth into the valley. Weak kneed policies of local government tried to follow a policy of appeasement. It made this situation much worse. ISI had managed to have moles in the local administration and in the local police. The newspapers have been terrorised to toe their line. A stage came when the All India Radio and TV studios had to be shifted from Srinagar to Jammu.

In December 1989, Rubiya Sayeed, a doctor and the daughter of the then Home Minister Mufti Mohammad Sayeed was kidnapped while returning from duty. Later on the case was detected, it came out that some Kashmir government employees were responsible for the perpetration of the crime. The police had been compromised and demoralised. The terrorists were so strong that any action by the police would invite retaliation. It is a local police who knows the local people, local language and local area. The first task in a situation like this is to raise the morale of the police. Quite often when the situation deteriorates, the paramilitary forces like BSF and CRPF are inducted. There is a misconception that the BSF and the CRPF can do everything. It is not correct. They cannot replace the local police. They do not know the local language. They are not aware of the local people and local customs. Many times they are not even aware of local routes and local geography. Unless the local police guide them, they cannot accomplish anything. One reason for the insurgency in Kashmir was the abysmal poverty of the local population. Rather than pumping in money for investment, the Government has confined it to 500 families of the state. The activities of the terrorists in the valley have led to the migration of 3,25,000 Kashmiri Pandits and Hindus and Sikhs from there. Even some Muslim families had to migrate from the valley. It seems the objectives of fundamentalist and terrorists were ethnic cleansing of non-Muslims from the valley. During my tenure in Kashmir, even the VC of Kashmir University was killed by the terrorists. Gradually the state police was built up. The recovery of the first weapon of AK-47 was done by the CRPF, during my stewardship. In terrorist situations, the important point is to have an upper hand. If terrorists believe that they have an upper hand, then the fence sitters and the local population will show their loyalty to them, if they feel the local police and CRPF are winning they would help them.

When the situation goes bad, we try to find out short-cuts. TADA was in force to deal with the terrorists but it was immediately withdrawn when the situation became normal in Punjab. The legal position is that we have ancient laws to deal with modern crime. There is a need now to have a separate set of laws for dealing with insurgency. Ad-hocism and bending the rules and the laws will not help, whether it is Northeast or Kashmir or Punjab. It should not be forgotten that the discontented elements in any part of the country can be persuaded by the foreign agents, particularly the ISI, to foment trouble. They have been doing this through drug trafficking and arms-trafficking. The free supply of automatic weapons, assault rifles, rocket launchers, grenades which have been seized in huge quantities by the Punjab Police, are a sure indication that our borders are not yet fully secured. If we become careless, we will be doing so at our own peril. What is required is constant vigilance and not running down our own institution.

Just after another 15 months on 10th April, I got my orders promoting me to the Secretary's scale that is Rs 8000 then and now present Rs 26000 per month basic salary. I moved to Railway Protection Force the same day. The DG, RPF is treated as second class Secretary, by the Railway Board. He is not extended the same courtesies and facilities, as members of the Railway Board, who draw the same salary of Rs 26000 per month. The DG shares the same warrant of precedence as other Secretaries to the Government, Chairman and members of the Railway Board do. My approach has been never to stand on formalities and get the work done. I felt that there is no use in begging and pleading. I would discuss my ideas with the then Railway Minister, Mr Ram Vilas Paswan to make sure that nobody came in the way for improvement of the force. Mr Ram Vilas Paswan was very positive and helpful and stood for improving the status, facilities and working conditions of the RPF.

The RPF had no training institutions of its own, worth talking about for its 80,000 strong force. It was treated as an appendage to the Railways. Only the condemned lot, in the Government are normally posted to training institutions. RPF was no exception. The RPF had no vehicles and no communication network of its own. The DG of RPF was treated shabbily. The DG could not even purchase a pin, under his own authority. He had neither the Secretariat's status and was not even the Head of the Department. I initiated a number of proposals for vehicles, computers, separate budget for DG and separate communication set up for RPF. Most of these proposals fructified after three years of my departure from the RPF. I also found time to visit Bombay, Rajasthan, and Punjab during my brief stay in RPF.

The Railway Protection Force

On April 10, 1996, I became DG of Railway Protection Force (RPF). This post had been lying vacant for a number of months. Government is something, which is very vague. You cannot really pinpoint who is the Government. A proposal is floated and it gets lost in the government's labyrinthine structure. It is viewed microscopically at numerous stages, including the Cabinet Secretary, Personnel Minister, Home

Minister and the Prime Minister. Something which should be done overnight takes months instead. It's more so in the case of police officer whose proposals are perused vigorously. But it does not happen in the case of civil services, whose proposals are pushed from hand to hand. In bureaucracy, no posts remain unfilled, whereas police and para-military chiefs' posts remain vacant for months. Though the RPF was designated as the "Armed Force of the Union of India". It did not have even one properly managed Training Institute for 80000-strong force. It was treated more as an appendage to the Railways. Its weaponry was obsolete and its vehicles had been condemned for years together. It did not have any command structure. DG of RPF was reated shabbily.

So something which should be done overnight takes months instead. It's more so in the case of uniformed services, whose proposals are perused vigorously, with a view to rejecting them. But it does not happen in the case of civil services, whose proposals are cleared in no time. In Civil bureaucracy, no posts remain vacant , whereas police and para-military chiefs' posts remain vacant for months.

15

Some More Stints

I had a stint in Central Reserve Police Force, from 1988 to 1993 September. During this period, I had to deal with Punjab, Jammu and Kashmir and Uttar Pradesh. Each was a varied experience. People felt that could get away by saluting and fawning over their seniors. I changed the entire culture, by emphasizing that CRPF had a unifying role to play. The officers were encouraged to forget the metal they carried (Badges of rank) and help the State Government. Petty egos afflicted every rank. One of the senior officers, had rented out his unsuitable house to the CRPF before I joined. The CRPF was paying rent for the unused house. It had been done before I joined. One thing, I have never tolerated, is the wastage of Government money and misuse of Government property. I just cancelled the lease, annoying a lot of vested interests. I sent a clear signal that this country and Nation is our own. No loot would be permitted. Despite all this, petty corruption continued. For instance, when I wanted a pedestal fan in Amrtisar for my camp office, the price quoted was Rs 1100 for an item, which could be purchased for Rs 700. On my further probing, I found out that it would take about 4 months to pay the bill. The Bill had to perform a circuitous route of first to the Battallion Headquarter, which might be in Calcutta, then to its group centre, which might be in Ajmer and finally to the Accounts Section in the office of Director General of the CRP. A single query by any intermediate functionary, would take the bill on its return journey to the place, from where it originated, adding to the delay. Even the issue of a five rupees cheque was centralised and is even now. This is in spite of every body including the

Prime Ministers talking of decentralisation. In reality no body wants to part with the power. The only way you can show down anybody is, by telling him off and rejecting his proposal. It is not that the Chiefs did not know the problem. It is because everybody wanted to pass time, so as to leave the problem to his successors, like what the successive Governments have been doing. There is a heavy s price to pay if you fight with the system. The result is, very few people wish to fight, because nobody wants to face any problem and ultimately be a looser. There will be more problems, if you try to be honest upright and straight. There will be less problems, if you swim with tide. I made it very clear during the terrorism days, we will go strictly by the law of the land though hardly anybody, was willing to admit, that law, if any could be enforced in Punjab, with the guns blazing at you. It was not a very popular move. I said that I would follow the rule of law, as long as, I was there.

Mr P. Chidambaram was the Minister of State for Home. He came to Amritsar in April 1988. I and Raghunandan Lal Bhatia, the local MP received him at the Airport. He said "Welcome Minister and Congratulations". I asked Mr. Bhatia: "What for and why are you congratulating the Minister? He said: "Do you know that he is the first Central Minister to cross Beas, after Blue star operation in June 1984.(At that time the terrorists used to claim that it is their writ, which ran beyond Beas and they called river Beas, the boundary of Khalistan). This only highlighted, the position of how things had gone from bad to worse. Nobody wanted to visit Punjab unless it was unavoidable. The credit must go to Chidambaram that he visited every inch, of the border. He climbed even the rooftop of a house, where once his Dhoti, got stuck in one of the stairs, of the staircase. But he took it good humouresly. I was accompanying him all along. With difficulty, I could hardly conceal, my laughter, at his predicament. He was totally a management Minister, who felt that first inputs had to be made, before outputs could be expected. Whatever modernisation came about in the Central Forces, BSF, CRPF, Punjab Police came only, because of the interest taken by Mr Chidambaram and his intervention. Increase in the Police powers led to unbridled corruption in Punjab. Over 200 policemen were dismissed. It was commons sense, to win the war, first against terrorism, before starting another war against corruption. One should win at one front at a time, before moving on to the next.

Narcotic Control Bureau

There are certain jobs in, the Government of India, which are only sinecures. More and more higher jobs mean less and less, or no job contents. The result is that, people are dissatisfied for being underworked. But every day, the same jobs are being upgraded. After 32 years and three months of service, I on promotion to the rank of Additional Director of Police. I took over, as Director General of Narcotic Control Bureau, on 17th September, 1993. The proposal had been initiated more than nine months ago. But since I did not know anybody in PM's Office or other higher echeleons of bureaucracy, it took ages to be cleared. This is what paid me off, when I took over as Director, CBI. I had not taken anybody's obligation, whether of a bureaucrat or a politician, in my career, I was under no compulsion to oblige anybody. The Narcotics Control Bureau had only 300 people. But it was sufficiently clean, strong, with adequate striking power. I felt that, it is not always necessary to expand the staff. Let me work with the State Police Forces. We started the mechanism of the meetings of the State Police Chiefs, for effective enforcement of Narcotics Laws. The United Nations Drug Control Programme (UNDCP) had advanced $50 million for Drug Control work in India. The Director General had been delegated the powers and functions of the Central Government for drug control work. The result of this was, that a lot of vehicles, computers and other equipments were given to the State Police Forces for drug control work. Like it happens every where, some money spent by the UNDCP was wasted on outdated and non functional equipment. They supplied us computers and communication equipment which were not functional for months and years together. Some imported equipment, supplied by the United Nations Drugs Control Programme remained in warehouses and godowns, still I started bombarding UNDCP, about the wastage of the money by their officers.

During my visit to Vienna, the Headquarter of a number of United Nations Agency, an official told me on strict condition of secrecy, that corruption existed in purchases by UN Funded Organisations, on the pattern, as anywhere else, in the world. My role as Head of the Narcotics Control Bureau was very clear. It was to encourage all organisations including Police, Customs, and Narcotics Department to deliver goods, in the form of effective enforcement. By involving all agencies, with the bait of foreign trips, and huge cash rewards, I was able to enlist their cooperation and enthuse them to take interest. For the first time, during my tenure, rewards of over Rupees two crores, were formally presented by the then Finance Minister, and my Minister, Sardar Manmohan Singh, to the officials and agencies all over the country, who had done outstanding work in the field of Narcotics. I visited every Narcotics Control Bureau Office, all over the country, to make them work and also work as catalyst. I had an opportunity of visiting Pakistan and receiving delegations from there. American delegation also visited India, for bilateral talks. I also received a delegation of German Parliamentarians, for discussing as to how India was dealing with the Drug problem. Most people and Nations have double standards. Once a senior officer from Pakistan came for discussion on narcotics in Delhi. I noticed that he was drinking whisky, at the official dinner, hosted by me. I asked him, Mr Saluhdin, Do you consume whisky in Pakistan also? He said, "No, I do not." I said why? He said "There they are afraid of Mullas. It is a different story that our Mullas themselve take whisky privately".

During my visit to Pakistan to have bilateral talk in December, 1995, I wanted to visit Nankana Sahib, the Holy Birth Place, of our First Sikh Guru Nanak. Due to the constraint of time, a rushed visit was arranged by Lahore office of the Narcotics Bureau. A devout Muslim attendant showed us around. There were no Sikhs doing the traditional prayers every day. For me, it was both a privilege and a treat to pay homage to my Guru of Gurus. A similar visit was arranged to Hassan Abdul, or what Sikhs call Punja Sahib. I had taken visas for visiting these places. The Senior Superintendent of Police and District Magistrate, Peshawar in whose area, that place was located, received me there. The legend is that a stone was rolled on the Guru and his followers, Bala and Mardana, by a jealous Muslim divine. The Guru stopped that boulder, by his hands. The imprint of Guru's hand is still there on the precariously perched stone. I found that Punja Sahib Gurudwara had a lot of Sikh congregation. Most of them were from Peshawar or Afghanistan. I combined pilgrimage along with the official visit to Pakistan, but not at the cost of the work, for which I had gone there. The visit was always after the official work was over.

At Islamabad Airport, the First Secretary of the Indian High Commission, received me at the Airport. There was an invitation, to join the Indian High Commissioner, for dinner along with my delegation. The delegation had a Police officer, Nampoothri from Gujrat and a DRI official Bhattachajee. It was already late in the night. I wanted to be excused from the dinner on the sole ground that it would not be fair to delay Mr Lambhah, the High Commissioner. But a phone call confirmed that the High Commissioner was keen to brief us. We had dinner with Mr Lambah. I explained to him, the stand we were to take.

The Senior Superintendent of Police, Islamabad and the local Head of the Narcotics Bureau of Pakistan along with the protocol officers effusively welcomed us. I was aware that under all that welcome, was the hidden desire to find out our brief. I and my delegation were ready, for the search of the luggage. Outside our rooms, in a five-star hotel, policemen had been posted. They were there, ostensibly to look after our security. But the real purpose was to keep a watch on us and our visitors. With nearly thirty-four years of Police service behind me, it neither surprised nor upset me. It was only a cat and mouse game, in which I was the mouse, and the Pakistani agency was the cat. I could see the tell tale sign of my luggage being rummaged. I had spread a thin line of powder, which had been disturbed. I noticed in the Mariot hotel, very fashionably dressed young women, speaking chaste Punjabi . So I asked my host, how these people are speaking Punjabi. He said that this is a part of Punjab.

I had expected to see Burqa clad women but certainly not in the five star hotel. When I expressed my amazement, to my host and counterpart, General Tarmizi, he replied; "You are forgetting that Rawalpindi is in Punjab". Obviously, the influence of the clergy was confined only to their mosques. The higher classes did not care much for fundamentalist preaching. With money, you can purchase any dispensation all over the world. The bilateral talks went off smoothly. Pakistan promised to cooperate in nabbing drug smugglers. What had happened was that India was being used, as a transit country, by the smugglers in Pakistan? A courtesy call was arranged on the then Home Minister of Pakistan, Mr Babar. He blamed India in the usual politician style for all problems of Pakistan. I promptly hit back. I told him as to how Pakistani smugglers had tried to play hell, in India by smuggling Arms and Narcotics. I also gave him the names of Pakistan Army officials, involved in drug trafficking , as revealed, by the arrested Pakistanis during the interrogation, by us. I told him that as a professional police officer, my job was to fight the crime and the criminals. As a part of sight seeing, we were also taken to Murree, a hill station about one hour drive from Islamabad. There was no war hysteria, against India in the minds of common Pakistani. It appeared to be only the government propaganda, on Pakistan TV and Radio. There was no direct flight to Delhi from Islamabad. We had to come to Lahore and from their take Indian Airlines flight or Pakistan International Airways flight to Delhi. On the return journey we had a few hours in Lahore. We took time to visit Lahore Fort; the Samadhi of Maharaja Ranjit Singh and the famous market called Anarkali. Except for Mall Area, the rest of Lahore was filthy, overcrowded and practically unvisitable.

Despite the Bilateral talks, I had a gut feeling that on ground nothing much would come out. Apart from visiting Pakistan, I also visited Myanmar (Burma) for bilateral talks for fighting drug Mafia. Myanmar was and is under the control of Military Junta. Practically all the ministers including Agriculture Minister were Army Generals and Colonels. The capital Rangoon, now renamed, as Yagoon needed a facelift and lots of cleaning. General San Thein, the police chief of Myanmar was also the head of Narcotics. Their one grouse, privately expressed, was that no Indian Minister, had visited their country from the last over two decades. They promised cooperation but it was very clear that Myanmar Government had no control over the areas controlled by Khunsa. Khunsa was the drug lord till he was killed few years later. The then Indian Ambassador of India to Myanmar, Mr Parthasarthy maintained excellent relations with the Myanmar ministers and officials. After the official work was over. We were taken to see the tomb of the last Mughal emperor Bahadur Shah Zafar, who had died as a prisoner of the British in that country. It had the famous verse, inscribed inside tomb... *Na Kisi Ki Aankh Ka Noor Hoon, Na Kisi Ke Dil Ka Karar Hoon.........*

Other countries visited by me as Director General, Narcotics Control Bureau included Austria, the Headquarters of United Nations Drug Control Programme, Turkey another licit opium growing country. Aruba in Caribbean and Rome, Italy to attend Interpol conference. I also visited Australia and New Zealand for meetings and conferences. New Zealand is one of the most beautiful countries, with no pollution and the purest climate, though windy throughout the year. Integrity wise, it has the highest rating. There is no direct flight, from India to New Zealand. First I travelled to Singapore and from there I took a 10 hours flight to Sydney. At the Airport itself, I had a shower and bath and checked in for the flight to Wellington, the capital of New Zealand. I found a hefty gentleman checking in infront of me. We had adjoining seats and got conversing. He did not disclose who he was. At Wellington Airport, we shook hands and parted. He took a taxi and I travelled in the Embassy vehicle to the Hotel. Later on, in the conference, I found the same gentleman as a keynote speaker. I was told he was the Deputy Prime Minister of New Zealand. For me it was incredible. He had no frills, no security, and no chauffeur driven car. He was checking in and out himself, carrying his own baggage. The same story was repeated when I found the Commissioner of Police (Head of Police of New Zealand) Mr Macleod driving his own car, for the dinner to the Indian Ambassadors House. It was amazing, how a rich and a well-developed country, did not provide any fringe benefits, even to its top people. In India, it is taken for granted that any senior public servant including the ministers and officials will have a large staff of personal secretaries and other handy men to make their life comfortable. It is amazing that poorer the country, the more is the loot. The same story was repeated when New York head of Drug Enforcement Agency, told me that he was to drive his own vehicle and go through the same security check, as others.Apart from foreign travel, I had lot of touring inside the country. India was getting credit for the work done here and not for attending meetings and conferences. I paid equal attention to the enforcement and preventive work.

Foreign travel was also essential to explain the role model played by India in Enforcement. The weaker part was and is the de-addiction work especially in North-East. Enough Government assistance was available for voluntary agencies. But somehow the de-addiction was not making any headway, despite vast funds pumped in. De-addiction programme requires a lot of time and patience. Being unglamorous, it is not given high priority, even by those charged with its responsibility. I was living, literally in suitcases after one foreign trip to another. The drug trafficking yields vast profits. Delhi and Bombay Airports are the favourite haunts for the smugglers. Narcotics Control Bureau in Delhi was successful in nabbing the great grandson of a former British Prime Minister, Edward Heath. He was trying to smuggle Hashish from India to London. When questioned, he said that he could make enough money to live comfortably for two years on the stuff he was smuggling. He was granted bail by the court, which he jumped. The case remains in limbo. African nationals particularly Nigerians, had a lions share in drug trade. One Nigerian travelling in 1st class was carrying 5 kg of Heroin in 5 tins of Pure Ghee (Desi Ghee). It aroused a suspicion, as to why should he be taking five tins of Ghee. He was off loaded. A thorough search, of Ghee tins revealed that he had concealed Heroine in airtight polythene bags at the bottom of Ghee.

I set targets, for enforcement, for every branch. I pulled up all those officials, who were found slack. I did not spare even the senior officers, in the Headquarters. I made it a point to inform our Ambassadors abroad of the involvement of foreign nationals in the smuggling of Narcotics of India. It became a common practice for the visiting Indian Ambassadors to call on me. I moved to Indian Tibetan Border Police as Director General on 31st December, 1995. The only difference was that a new job gives me Rs 200 more as a salary. I had moved to the Pay Scale of the State Director General of Police, that is Rs7600 to Rs 8000 with an increment of Rs 200 to be earned once in two years. As Director General of Narcotics Control Bureau, I was in the pay cale of Rs 7300-

7600, with an increment of Rs 100 to be earned every year, from the bottom of the pay scale. I felt it was unfair to leave Narcotics Control Bureau just after 1 year and 4 months. I would have been happy to continue, and retire from there.

Indo-Tibetan Border Police

The Indo-Tibetan Border Police had an entirely different role. It was a small force guarding the border with China. I was back to uniform, after a break from 17th September 1993 to January 1995. Most of the organisations have become top heavy without enough of file work. I have always believed, that if you want to know the true reality, you must be in touch with the field. The Indian Tibetan Border Police had 30 battalions spread in far-flung areas of Leh, Ladhak, Garhwal and Kumaon. I made it a point, to visit each one of the battalions, to know at first hand, the conditions of troops there. A few battalions were also deployed to Punjab to guard the banks. I decided to visit the areas where no or few Director Generals had gone. For staying at the height greater than 10,000 feet, one has to get acclimatised. Acclimatisation could take weeks. No head of All-India organisation can spare that much of time for one battalion. The Director General of Indo Tibetan Border Police, was permitted the use, of Airforce helicopters, as well as aeroplanes of Central Police Organisations. This made the touring easy, attractive and quick. For instance for going to Auli, Badrinath and Kedarnath and the units deployed that side, I would fly by the Special Aircraft to Dehradun or Rae Bareilley or Chandigarh. From there, I would hop into an Airforce helicopter.

The helicopter would take me to all the forward units. What would take days and weeks, to reach, by almost non-existing roads or mule track, would be covered in one and two hours. The only condition was that the helicopter had to be back, latest by 2 p.m. to the plain. The Helicopters would not fly in the cloudy weather. The pilots had to fly by the sense of direction and by seeing landmarks like rivers, buildings and roads. For the Director General, ITBP, instead of one, two helicopters were deputed. The second helicopter, was acting as the escort helicopter. Neither the CPO Aeroplanes nor the helicopter were pressurized. The noise of the helicopter, was deafening. But the big advantage, was the quick arrival, at the destination easy and quick return, after the work was over. The pilots would never take a chance, if the weather was cloudy or the visibility was poor. During this stint, I paid homage at the shrines of Badrinath, Kedarnath and Hemkunt Sahib, but only from the sky. The helicopters could not land there. The ITBP men were living in the forward area at the heights ranging from 10,000 feet to 17,000 feet. I never stinted in the use of oxygen in the helicopter. For instance, during my visit to Leh, I noticed that my blood pressure shot up to 220/150. I was advised not to worry. It is something normal in hilly areas, if you come without acclimatising. It came back to 120/80, as soon as I reached the plain area of Srinagar. It is for this, that soldiers have to be acclimatised to the weather at heights like those of Kargil or Siachen Glacier.

There is a tremendous lack of oxygen in heights of 10,000 feet and above. Any vigorously executed movement will tire you out. That's why the dances of movements of Ladakhis are very slow. Some ladies privately expressed to my wife that men and women, lose all interest in sex at heights. It is perhaps, for this reason, that the practice of one woman having more than one husband still prevails in some secluded hilly areas. If the children stay too long, there is a danger of their being mentally retarded. Taking all these factors into consideration, I formulated and announced, a policy of rotational transfers, so that nobody stays in soft postings, for too long. I had noticed that some officials had managed to stay for years, in Delhi on one ground or the other, including the frequently used medical ground. One frequent excuse, for a Delhi or other plain soft posting, was on grounds of looking after the aged parents. My reply was that if a person was of 35-40 years of age, his parents could not be below 60-65 years. This will be applicable to 95 per cent force. But to ensure that nobody was unnecessary harassed, I ordered leave should be sanctioned liberally. I had this policy, implemented, without any single exception. I also gave an option to the officials, who could not be given soft posting, all their life, to proceed on voluntary retirement, if they so desired. At the suggestion of Lalit Mansingh now India's High Commissioner to London and then Dean of Foreign Service Institute, I agreed that exposure to ITBP should be an integral part of the training of IFS probationers. This will expose the foreign service officer to the situation on our borders. There ware more than 350 vacancies of drivers in the force. I directed that the recruitment, should be done in all parts of the country, to make the Indo Tibetan Border Police an All India Force, like the Central Reserve Police Force. In six months time, I saw to it, that all vacancies, within my competence were filled up. Promotion examination pending for years together was conducted and promotion ordered against the vacancies, for the Constables, Head Constables and Sub Inspectors. By the time I left the force on 10th April, 1996, the promotion, posting, transfers were streamlined. I visited Joshirnatth, Gowchar, Mussoorie, Auli, Dehradun, Mathli, Mahi Dhanda, Pithoragarh, and Mirthi, apart from Leh, Ladakh, Kinnanor, Sahran, Kullu, and Rekong Peo in Himachal Pradesh. Sitting in Delhi, does not give any idea, of the extreme cold, to which ITBP people are exposed. Once in the month of November 1995, I flew to Sarhan by the helicopter. The weather was unbearably cold. After one hour and forty five minutes of flight, from Chandigarh, deep into Hills in Himachal Pradesh, I had to keep my feet, in the literally blazing fire to get my circulation back. Once, during a visit to a Hot Spring in Ladakh, the helicopter pilot told me not to spend more than five minutes at the post, which was on the border with Tibet, now part of China. There was no oxygen in the air. Helicopter, once switched off may not start again. Hot Spring post, on the border with China, is almost on cheek and jowl basis with Chinese border. It is maintained only with the supplies by air. For medical treatment or for emergencies, the men can be evacuated only with the help of helicopters. There is no motorable road to it. Only one mule track, from Leh exists. It is the place where the Chinese killed CRPF men in October 1959. October 21st is celebrated as a police Martyr Day. I stayed for 25 minutes and talked to each men of the ITBP posted there, then flew back. Having ignored the pilots advice as I thought it was more important for me as the DG to raise the morale of my men, talked with each of them and had tea with them; while the pilot was fretting all the time. Air force pilots having an impression of always being over cautions. There was no way he could leave me behind and fly back. When the helicopters landed at the next post to Chushul for refuelling, the second escort helicopter developed a snag. The single helicopter brought me back to Leh. The engineers were brought from Leh, again by the same helicopter, for repairing it. I have a suspicion that the pilots can lose their way. My pilots had to consult each other quite often to bring me back to Leh. My apprehension that I may not reach back to Leh but land in the Chinese territory, was proved wrong, thanks to the experienced air force pilots. For senior officers like Director Generals or Lt. Generals one spare Helicopter always travels with them. In those heights and in atmosphere where there is no oxygen, one has to depend on outside oxygen supply. I was advised neither to feel apologetic nor try to act big by showing off that I could live without oxygen. ITBP had its Battallion Headquarters or other establishment in places like Kullu, Simla, Dehradun, Mussorie. I observed that men had to fight cold weather or climate, all the time, because they were living, sometime in minus one-degree temperature. It is difficult to exist in places like Leh, where there is very little oxygen in the atmosphere. I flew in helicopter from Chandigarh to Kinnanaur and Rekong Peo in Himachal Pradesh. It was probably the month of October, 1995. In the helicopter and on arrival, I was exposed to extreme cold. I had spent most of my time, in front of the fire, in the officer's mess and the Battallion office. The helicopters are not heated or air pressurised like the aircraft's of the Indian Airlines. This made me doubly firm, in my determination, that minimum comforts should be ensured for the force deployed in inhospitable areas. I made sure, that the force, got the same facilities as defence services and other para-military, forces when working in similar places. We have to have, same facilities, if not better. I did succeed. It is a small well-knit efficient force with good medical facilities. It also had dogs, horses, mules, and yaks which was a new experience for me. My first effort was to make good the deficiencies of animals. It is animals, particularly and mules and horses, which carry provisions, in inhospitable areas. In hilly and in inhospitable areas the roads hardly exist, wherever they exist, it takes days together to reach the deployment post. What I could cover in helicopter in two hours, could be only covered in 3 to 7 days journey by foot on very rudimentary tracks.

16

Role as CBI Director

I was appointed as Director of CBI on July 26, 1996. But did not go to office for three days as I had suffered food poisoning on that very evening. The CBI had been a closed organisation. It avoided the media like plague. But I felt that there was nothing to hide. My conviction was that let the media know to the extent it does not damage a case. So I started a policy of briefing the press on the ongoing investigations. But, of course, care was taken that this media friendly approach was only for helping us and not for damaging a case. The CBI Director does not even have powers to order repairs of the buildings, which I had enjoyed as DG RPF or as DG ITBP. So the first thing, I did was to move the government for sanction of powers of CBI Director on a par with heads of Central Paramilitary Organisations.

The vehicles of CBI were in a ramshackled state. A proposal had been sent to increase the CBI's vehicle fleet by more than 300 vehicles. The proposal had been discussed at various levels, but I took it to the highest level of the Prime Minister. He convened a meeting to discuss the problems of the CBI. Most of the problems were sorted out.

I felt that the most important thing in the CBI was to emphasise on training. More than anything else, in-house watch is very important as the CBI has an enormous clout and undesirable elements indulging in malpractices should be weeded out. I made it very clear that there would be no place for such elements in the CBI. They would be dealt with sternly. A number of cases were registered against CBI officers themselves.

I also started the system of weekly meetings of officers

where general problems would be discussed. Besides, I started convening a meeting of the investigating officers of Dy SPs' and Inspectors' level so that I could interact with them and know problems being faced by them in investigation.

I cleared my intention that I would not tolerate use of third degree method during investigations. Investigators have to work hard and produce results by scientific investigations.

My personal opinion is that in civilized society the old third degree method of investigation being practised by the officers should be stopped and the modern psychological methods should be adopted by us like the western countries.

A number of cases involving the high and the mighty and the prominent people were handled or were being handled before I joined the CBI. These included the cases against former Prime Minster P.V. Narasimha Rao; the MPs' bribery case; the St Kitts case; the Lakhubhai Pathak case; and the Jain Hawala case.

In the Jain Hawala case, the Supreme Court had directed that the CBI Director would not report to the government but to the court itself. In other words, the superintendence of these cases was taken away from the government by the Supreme Court. So, I had two masters to serve.

H.D. Deve Gowda was the Prime Minister when I joined as CBI chief. He was a nice man to work with. He had his own political compulsions. But I had my own official compulsions, too—abiding by the guidelines laid down by the Supreme Court and the various courts.

Honestly I would like to mention here is that anybody who is involved in a case would like to do his best to get out.

It will be futile to say that no efforts were made at interference. Interference does not necessarily come from the political executive. It can come from their relations, friends, colleagues and other sources.

At Interpol E.C.

One feather I added to the cap of India was getting elected to the Interpol Executive Committee. I had gone to attend a meeting of the Interpol in France in June 1997 and when I landed back in New Delhi, I was told at the airport that I had been shifted out of the CBI.

Well, the way I was proceeding strictly in accordance with the law, I knew that this would come one day or the other, sooner or later. That is why I never shifted from my Tilak Lane house, which was allotted to me as DG RPF.

The job to which I was shifted to in the Ministry of Home Affairs was an innocuous one. It required only about half an hour's work in a day. It was only a parking slot which the government had prepared for me till my retirement.

One thing I have always conceded is that the government has the right to transfer anybody. As I had the right to transfer my subordinates, I have never questioned it. But in the context it was questionable. It was challenged in the Patna High Court, the Delhi High Court and the Supreme Court. I retired on October 31, 1997 as Special Secretary in the Ministry of Home Affairs.

The then home Minister Indrajit Gupta was gracious enough to be present at the farewell, which was both for me, and for K. Padmanabhaiah who was the Union Home Secretary.

I made a few points that the Home Ministry's objective was not to help. I also pointed out, that some people did not even have 15 minutes' work, whereas some others were overworked. The Home Minister humorously whispered into my ear: "I hope that they are not complaining about it".

Queries of the Press

I was asked by a journalist, to answer some specific questions, especially on politicians and the CBI. The questions included:

* What do you think of politicians?
* Whether you will join politics?
* Did you get any feelers from any political party to join their ranks?
* Details, if any. If not, any special reasons for that?
* Do you think that you are an untouchable by any political party because of your image as a very tough man?
* Your interesting encounters with politicians. Your critical appraisal of politicians and bureaucrats.
* What ails the CBI? What are your suggestions to improve the working of the CBI?
* What, according to you, were the reasons for your

removal from the CBI Director's post? If you do not break your silence now, when will you?

Well, I think that some questions can be answered. Some politicians are absolutely wonderful. I have seen these politicians from close quarters. Money holds no attraction for them. But unfortunately, the number of this tribe, which includes, Dr Manmohan Singh and Atal Behari Vajpayee is very small. One reason is that we pay our political masters, so little, they are left with no alternatives, except to help themselves, for their existence. For instance, I do not understand why a minister is paid less than a Secretary to the Government. I have worked in the ministries of Commerce and Finance. I can testify, that senior officers, right from Joint Secretaries and above, get one or two vehicles from each corporation, for their and their family's use. Each minister has half a dozen vehicles, which are commandeered by his personal staff in his name. The people close to him use his clout and name to get so many things and sanctions. They live off the accounts of the Corporations under the control of the Ministries. The Heads of the Corporations dare not deny anything, if they wish to survive, and continue in their jobs. Survival is the basic instinct. Politicians are the product of the society. You get the kind of politicians you deserve. Everything is hidden in the government files. It suits the politicians because they can take any colourable decision. Unless somebody is willing to take the risks and challenges it in a court of law, the truth will never come out. Enough has not been done by us, as commoners to expose and ostracise such politicians. A politician is a reflection of the society. A politician today needs about Rs two crore to win an election. And what does an MP get as salary. Not even in five figures. Free travel, yes. Going all over the world, yes. But it does not pay for the elections unless he has some other means. A movement is essential to cleanse the current political system. So when a politician spends a couple of crores of rupees, his immediate objective after winning the election is to make good this amount. It is interesting to note in this context that more than 280 MPs of the 11th Lok Sabha got together, cutting across the party lines and opposed general elections. It was repeated at the time of dissolution of 12th Lok Sabha. As regards my joining politics, nobody asked me and I have not approached anybody. I don't think that I am an untouchable, so far as political parties are concerned. I think they need people of all kinds. You need tough people. You need straightforward people. You need people as showpieces for your political party. You also need partly, unclean people to do unclean jobs. After all, you can't clean a drain unless you get into it. You get dirty alright, but then you can always wash yourself. I am not averse to joining politics. The trouble with most bureaucrats is that, as they rise, they become spineless. They must stand upto the political masters.

What will happen? Worst would be that they would be transferred. If you don't carry out their bidding, be prepared with your bedding. Keep your bag and baggage ready and pack off to wherever you are sent. If a politician or a senior bureaucrat gives some order, let him accept the responsibility. Let him give orders in writing. The trouble arises when these people want to fire the gun from your shoulders. I have always believed that if I have the responsibility, I will have the authority, too. Nobody else will have the authority. There was a senior bureaucrat who used to say "Look, it is your action which may get you into trouble. Your inaction will never land you into trouble. So why act? Let others dispose off the matter and take action." He would never clear a file, which warranted his taking a decision. There was another officer, who even before transferring, a constable, would ask the Home Minister whether he should do that or not. Unfortunately, in the South, where I have worked, the caste factor has become dominant. Politicians want to maintain caste balance in all jobs. Caste has become an important factor even in imposing a punishment. This is the undoing of the country. Far from putting an end to it, politicians have lent their hands to it. Most of the politicians survive only on the basis of caste and creed. We have to de-caste the entire structure. We have to judge a person on the basis of his performance.

What ails the CBI?

Now the question is what ails the CBI? Nothing ails the CBI except that top people would like to use the investigations to settle their own score. It all depends on the top man of CBI, if he is willing to stand up to such challenges, nothing will happen to him except that he may be transferred. The CBI is dependent on the government for everything and it should be freed from the government control. Whether it is a case of engaging a top lawyer or for getting somebody on deputation, the CBI Director has no authority. More delegation of power is required for effective functioning of the CBI. Well, so far as the question of improving the functioning of the CBI is concerned, the government has to have a perspective. They have to have a five-year plan that how much they want to strengthen it. Knee-jerk reactions will not help. It takes minimum of five to ten years to get a trained investigator.

On the question of why I think I was transferred from the post of CBI Director, I have answered this question elsewhere in this book. It was because I did not yield to the pressure of the then Prime Minister Gujral, in fodder scam case. Out of the 17 CBI Directors, I was the only one to be transferred out in 11 months. One thing has to be remembered by every officer. A politician is not here to do any "dharam-karam". He is here to survive. If a patch-up government is there, it would like to see that the patch-up continues as long as possible. I was criticised for calling on P.V. Narasimha Rao. I think that it would be better that I do not say anything on this topic at all, because the Supreme Court has said something on this. My own views on this are entirely different. I accepted whatever the Supreme Court said on that day, because I do not want to get into an argument on this. But I feel that CBI Director should be accessible, should meet people so that he can collect information also. It is not that he is going to be influenced just by meeting a person.

The Bofors Deal: A Sensitive Case

An autobiography of this nature would be incomplete without mentioning a few sensitive cases. One case which comes to my mind is the famous (or infamous!) Bofors deal. This case was registered in 1990. The FIR on the basis of which investigations began runs into over fifty pages. It was a very sensitive case where big names have been mentioned.

One Thing to be Impatient

I felt that this case was like an albatross. This must be cut from the neck of the CBI. The only way to do it was to complete the investigations. I was pursuing this case with the Interpol Chief of Switzerland whom I had met in Turkey personally. I had invited him for lunch also. It was a working lunch, where discussions related only to cases pending in Switzerland. I asked him when would I get the Bofors papers. Rudolph Wyss, the Chief of the Swiss Interpol, told me to expect these papers "either around the Christmas time or may be a few weeks later". He said he would telephone me and I should come personally for taking possession of these papers.The international media was very keen to know the co-operation between the two countries. Wyss said that as soon as I get his call I should leave for Switzerland. He did not know the Indian system where official sanction is required for travelling abroad. This can take some time. As soon as I received intimation through our Ambassador in Switzerland, Bal Krishan, that the Swiss would be handing us the secret Bofors papers on January 22, 1997, I sent a proposal to the Government for permission to go to Switzerland. I debated within myself whether I should go or send somebody else. It may look very silly that you are going to receive a set of documents and for that the Head himself is going. I might be criticised for this. But at the same time, it was the responsibility of the CBI Directors to see that the things moved safely and in time. If anything went wrong, I would be the one who would be blamed and asked that why did I not go myself. It was a trip only for three days. After balancing the pros and cons, I felt that proper security for the papers would be available only if I went myself . I did not even tell which other officers were to accompany me. I kept their names secret. At the last minute I decided that B.R. Dubey, Joint Director, CBI, and Javed Chaudhary, an Additional Secretary in the Department of Personnel, would accompany me to Switzerland. It was a good decision for three of us to go. We travelled on different routes. I travelled to Switzerland via London. Another colleague travelled via Frankfurt and met only in Berne. The idea was to keep the travel plans secret.

The visit of the CBI Director could not be kept secret. This kind of secrecy would come handy for ensuring security of the secret papers. I reached Berne in the evening from London after getting down at Zurich. The Swiss Government had provided the security. Their security is something entirely different from what we have. No gun-trotting policemen, no sirens, no cars. It was a solitary policeman who met at the airport and said he was responsible for my security. He would arrange whatever assistance I required. I Inquired whether journey to Berne would be safe. He said: "Totally safe." He also said there was no need for him to accompany me. We reached Berne, which is about three hours' drive, at about 9 o'clock. My other colleagues had also arrived just then. We immediately went down to the Ambassador's residence for dinner. He briefed about the arrangements. The papers were to be handed over, at a ceremony, to be held in a government building at 9 o'clock next morning. At the appointed hour, the Swiss Police Chief met us and took us to the conference room. The international press was there for covering the ceremony. The Indian Ambassador spoke and thanked the Swiss government for its cooperation and acknowledged the fact that they had changed their laws, for delivering the Bofors papers to us. Probably as a result of the Bofors case, the cooperation of the Swiss with Pakistan government, dealing with the alleged amassing of money in Switzerland by their former Prime Minister Benazir Bhutto had been prompt. The Star Television, had sent its team to Switzerland to cover the event, interviewed me and I told them, as I said in India that the CBI investigations into the Bofors case would be over within three months. Next day, I presented the best Indian watches to the Swiss officials who had helped us in investigation. It was a mark of thanks. The Swiss Police Chief told me that they would report to the government and take permission to keep the gifts given by us. I also told the Ambassador that some more gifts would be left with him and it was upto him to present these to others, who had helped us. The difference was they would report to the government unlike what happens in our country where a gift is just pocketed. These were quite expensive watches. It may look like sending coal back to New Castle, as the Swiss expertise in making watches is world-famous. My idea in presenting the watches to Swiss officials was to prove that India was no longer a backward country. May be some watches, had some Swiss components. The fact that they were made in India, was bound to drive the point home, that India was moving ahead.

Swiss Bank Account

For the return journey, we travelled from Berne to Zurich by the embassy car. I was curious to know how people open bank accounts, in Switzerland for stashing away the ill gotten cash money. I collected this information after talking to a number of important people in the embassy and a number of Indians based there. There is a certain procedure for opening a Swiss bank account. You have to have an introduction from somebody who is acceptable to the Bank. The introducer has to vouch for you. I was told by the people in Switzerland that in all major countries of the world especially in Eastern Europe, no business was ever transacted, unless a huge amount of money is deposited in a numbered account. A numbered account is something, which is top secret. They don't ask you too many questions but you have to pay service charges. There is no question of your getting any interest on your deposits in a numbered account. You can also hire a vault, which is so big that you can conceal a dead body, if you so desire. If you tell them that the vault contains a perishable item, the bank would regulate temperature to prevent or retard decay of the object kept. It is not always the dead body which people keep in a Swiss bank. They keep their paintings, precious antiques, etc., which have to be maintained at a particular temperature. This kind of secret banking works on trust. The numbered account holder can authorise any person to withdraw the deposits from his account, but he would have to give the secret code. Vaults are normally located in the basement as upper floors are used for staff. We devised a strategy to bring the Bofors papers safely to India. I personally carried the seemingly "precious" box, ostensibly containing the secret papers. But actually the documents had already been taken out and kept in the hand-baggage of my colleague, Dubey. My box was just a dummy. When we reached Zurich, we were told that the Air India flight we were to take, from Frankfurt was late by 12 to 14 hours.

Now with the kind of cargo we were carrying there was no question of staying for even one minute longer at the airport. Enquiries revealed that a Lufthansa flight was to be available within 45 minutes. I immediately got our tickets endorsed to the Lufthansa flight. I was travelling in Ist class and my colleagues were travelling in executive class and in different sections of aircraft. If any mischief had to be done, only I was the target. On our arrival at Delhi we were mobbed by a battery of requisitiooning the papers, photographers and television teams. I said wait and see. The documents were the property of the court because the letter requisitioning the papers had been sent by the court. So, the first thing was to produce them in the court and take its permission to keep the documents with us. I kept my word. I saw to it that the CBI investigation in the Bofors case was completed within the deadline of three months set by me and the report sent to the government on 12th May, 1997. All kinds of speculations were rife as to why I don't speak or write about it. There are certain principles which one has to respect.

Politician's Greed Knows No Bounds

My tenure as Director of Youth Services had its political fall out too. Some persons had taken over various Sports Associations and were living off the funds of those bodies, which included Government grants. Their modus operandi was to show double and triple the expenses incurred. With convenient audit statements vetted by friendly accountants, the racket flourished for a long time. A small - time politician, one Ro, whose only qualification was his ability to cringe before the Chief Minister or Chairman of the Sports Council, was appointed the working Vice-Chairman. As the Secretary of the Council, I exercised full authority over its affairs and kept a strict control on the finances. It also included, overruling the working Vice-Chairman, who wanted to treat the Council funds, as his private property. It was something unusual, wherein the Secretary came in the way of a small-time politician, whose perennial argument was that the Government had given the grant. It was upto him and the council to spend it the way it liked. And as the Secretary, I had no rights to come in their way. I told him, "Under the government rules, it is only a Government official who can spend the money. Ultimate responsibility is his. You get a government order stating that you have the authority to spend the money. I will not come in the way. As long as the responsibility is mine, I cannot agree to everything you say unless all the formalities are followed. I cannot go on spending my time in answering audit objections."

The Council had some MLA's and MLC's as members. They often went after my blood, for not passing the grants, recommended by them. In fact I was the only non-official in the Sports Council as Member Secretary. A stage came, when the late Gundu Rao, my Minister advised me that I should pass whatever the members wanted me to pass. I said, "I will gladly comply with your orders, provided you give them in writing. My written advice will be that the expenditure recommended to be sanctioned was based on bogus or incorrect or inadequate documents. It should not be sanctioned. It will not only be open to the audit objections, but also will not pass through the Public Accounts Committee of the legislature".

Much as late Gundu Rao disliked my advice, he never went against me and he never once sought my transfer. (It happened to me only once in my career, as Director, CBI). At one point of time, I was threatened by one of his cronies and a close ally, who had been a member of the Rajya Sabha, for not clearing bogus bills. I took the Minister aside and told him that I will have no option left, but to get his written orders, for passing the Bills running into a couple of Lakhs. I pointed out that it would be the end of his political career. Everybody would know that the Rs. two lakh claimed for transportation charges, from the hotel to the sports venue, could not be justified by any stretch of imagination. The hotel is not even two hundred yards from the venue of the event.

I told the Minister's friend that if he insisted on getting the bogus bill passed by the Minister; he would prove to be his worst enemy. It would finish the career of the young dynamic Gundu Rao. I would personally be very sorry, to see him scarred politically. I have never been averse to using ministerial influence for furthering the interests of the departments I have headed. But I always drew a line and never, ever, in my life I have asked anything personal either from a minister or a chief minister or even the two Prime ministers with whom I have worked.

I would like to mention the following incident in this regard. The CBI had been short of vehicles and a proposal had been sent to the Government to enhance its mobility by sanctioning over 300 vehicles. The file kept on moving from one level to another and would come back to CBI with a fresh query to be answered. On the one hand, the CBI was expected to be totally upright and not to take anybody's obligation. On the other hand, it had no vehicles to transport the accused persons to the Court for facing the trial or for the movement of the investigating officers, for the investigation of the cases. Several units of the CBI, had in their possession a number of seized vehicles, some brand new including imported ones. But they were the case property and could not be used. It is happening, even now in Police Stations, all over the country. Instead of being the Police Stations, many urban police Stations are the graveyards of all brands of cars, truck, motor cycles, buses and cycles. By the time a case is decided, the seized vehicles have rusted completely or somebody has knocked off tyres, tubes and other parts.

Only when I raised the issue, with the Prime Minister H.D. Deve Gowda, reluctantly, the underlings released sanction of 92 vehicles, but without the drivers. This was done purposefully, to spite me for having taken up the matter with the Prime Minister. The vehicles received remained idle, till I ordered the recruitment of constables, who could double up both as drivers and constables. I also sought Government approval to permit the CBI officers, having valid driving licenses to drive the vehicles. But this too, was never agreed.

The work culture in the government is to say "No" for everything. It is not only the politicians, who are responsible for this state of affairs. It is the officer-politician nexus, which has brought the country to the present state of affairs. The bureaucracy has to be made answerable, for the ills of the country along-with unscrupulous political leaders. The job security afforded, to the officers is so much, that nothing will happen, if they decide to say "No" to any illegal order. But this is possible only, if the officer does not have anything, to hide and is clean himself or is not looking for a post retirement job or an extension.

My view is that we have to make the bureaucracy both responsible and effective. It has become almost fashionable to lay the blame for all the ills and lapses at the doors of the political masters. Is it a correct assessment? Is it wholly true? The officers do more than 90 per cent of the routine Government work. Even if we accept the premise of political interference, then at least 50 to 70 per cent work which is a routine work, should be done well for the satisfaction of public. But is the public satisfied with the performance of bureaucracy? Generally not, because the bureaucracy is not only unresponsive for most of the time, but also self-centred in getting or retaining plum postings. This results in a nexus between the obliging politicians and the obliged bureaucrats.

Manipulative civil servants, would never take even ordinary decisions, without consulting political masters, so that they can ascertain and act according to the known or perceived wishes. Obliging politicians look for convenient civil servants (or servant) who can carry out their commands, legal or other wise.

Such people, are not in a position, to resist self invited interference. The remedy, for such a malaise is the need for quick and effective steps in ending, this self-perpetuation and self-preservation game. The administration has to be changed, with emphasis on result orientation rather than rule orientation. Result oriented approach will, and should only lead, to job retention. Hiring should be linked, with capacity to deliver goods. Firing quickly should also be possible, by amending the rules, for inefficiency and non-performance.

Private corporations succeed and make a lot of money, despite numerous complicated laws and cumbersome procedures. This is because; they have a corporate goal, to achieve. Without a set level of productivity profit, they cannot be in the market. The only goal set before the bureaucracy is regulatory in nature. Whether, it is administering the financial laws or for that matter any law in the country, the same approach, is displayed. It is not, that the laws are administered uniformly. The enforcement is not only selective, but also slanted. So much power is vested in the junior functionaries, that the encashment of the power is the rule, rather than an exception. They are either ignorant or are lethargic or are afraid to check malpractices.

For instance, the CBI has found on many occasions, big hauls of cash from those who were in position of power. From the house of a Superintendent of Customs, cash amounting to Rs 38 lakh was seized. From officers of level of Deputy Superintendents of Police in-charge of immigration Rs 42 lakh was recovered. A raid at an Income Tax officer, who had started his career as Upper Division Clerk led to the recovery of Rs 53 lakh. When a former minister's house was raided it yielded Rs 3.61 crore. A contractor, who had accumulated huge amounts of money by increasing the electric bill of residential places and reducing the bills of hotels, had made a neat packet of Rs 5.5 crore. A raid at an Income tax officer's house, who had just seven years of service to his credit, cash and property worth ninety lakh was recovered. I am just mentioning, in passing some of the recoveries, done by the CBI during my eleven months tenure in the CBI from August 1,1996 to June 30 1997. The fear of law or the punishment has just disappeared. There is hardly any social stigma attached, to the corrupt and dishonest, as long as they acquire, enough money to live in a royal style.

It can be safely said that when people occupying high places vitiate the entire moral climate in the country, it permeates to all levels. Allegations have been made against former Prime Ministers and Chief Ministers of having amassed vast wealth by awarding contracts and through nepotism. Why only the ministers, the Chief secretaries and Secretaries to the Government of India, have also been the subject matter of CBI inquiries. Except for judicial officers, in whose case the complaints received are sent to the High Courts or Supreme Court, every wing of the executive has been the subject of CBI inquiries.

Earlier, the Kings and their courtiers lived off the government treasury. The only difference now is that their successors in the form of Prime ministers, chief ministers, ministers and bureaucrats are ruling the roost.

Out of academic interest, I wanted to know the amount of money involved in various scams and corruption in high places just to compare whether it is equal to the figure of the gold and other precious articles taken away by the British during its 150 years of rule.

It is for the researchers to come out with the details and figures. A comprehensive study, I am sure, would make an impressive and interesting reading. Sample this: Bofors 64 Crore, HDW Submarine thrown an another similar amount, Security Scam of 1992 (Harshad Mehta fame) roughly 8000 Crore, Bihar Fodder scam nearly Rs 1500 Crore, Bihar Bitumen Scandal Rs 350 Crore, Bihar Medical Bills Rs 60 Crore, Aryuveda Scam of UP, Rs 32 Crore, Indian Bank Scam nearly Rs 1300 Crore. What I am referring to are the figures of cases with CBI.

Apart from this, Banks' losses, in the form of Non Performing Assets or Non Paying Accounts for three years, as revealed in a reply to a Parliament question, come to nearly Rs 1,20,000 Crore. The term used to cover the bank losses is Non Performing Assets. They are bad loans sanctioned without adequate security or on flimsy grounds.

For a common man, to get any small loan, from the bank, in an honest way, is almost next to impossible. I would like to state my personal experience in this aspect. I was the Superintendent of Police of Bidar District in 1967 when the Government allotted me a car from its quota. The loan sanctioned did not fully cover the cost of the car. It was short by just Rs 1500. I approached the Manager of the Local State Bank for an overdraft of Rs 1600. It was not sanctioned, on the ground that my salary, was not adequate, to repay it in the next few months. It surpasses my imagination, that if a district police chief, cannot be given an overdraft of Rs 1600, how could the banks advance loans to the extent of Rs 40,000 Crore a year which eventually proved to be bad loans. If any action is proposed against the errant banks, the bad loan is sought to be justified, as bad commercial judgement.

In one case, a bank sanctioned a loan of Rs 3 Crore to a company in which a senior officer's wife, was a director. The company went broke or was perhaps made so. The top officer, who had also retired and thought that the bad transaction would be forgotten, was in for a shock when I ordered registration of a CBI case against him. He brought all kinds of political pressure, including from the Prime Minister and a very important MP, who later on became a Minister, to get out of the sticky situation. He requested for a meeting with me, which I agreed on the condition that it would be in the visitors' room of my office. I asked him as to how he could give a loan to a company in which his wife was a director. He had only one reply, "The company had become sick". I asked him; "How is it that only the companies become sick and not its owners or directors?" He did not have an answer. I told him to give in writing whatever he wanted to say. In all fairness, I must say that when I explained the position to some powerful politicians, who had intervened on his behalf, they did not interfere again. Maybe my reputation as a stickler for rules had a lot to do with it.

Writing on the issue of political interference, no serving civil servant will ever admit to its existence. This is because; it means criticism of the politicians, or Government in power. Some bureaucrats would stretch it to mean criticism of the government. They are afraid that disciplinary proceedings, that could be initiated, if he were to admit about the existence of political interference. No political master would give orders for anything covered under the law or the rules in writing. They would like to exercise authority without the responsibility. Law does not contemplate that a Director of the CBI needs anybody's permission to chargesheet any officer or a politician. But at every step, I found hurdles being set up, either for stalling investigation or for not filing chargesheets. This happened only in the investigation of people in high places. In one case, I was castigated by the press, for not opening the locker of a member of the personal staff of an Ex-Prime Minister. And when it was done, nothing was mentioned.

At the back of my mind, I was clear that I could be given marching orders any day for not falling in line. I had overcome the fear of transfer, or being dislocated. So I went full steam, in introducing accountability, in a class which had never been asked any questions before. If a person occupied a public office as MP, MLA or as a Minister, it was taken for granted that he would never be questioned or asked questions about himself, his wealth or influence used for interference.

In all fairness, I must also admit that Mr Deve Gowda as the Prime Minister, generally endorsed steps I took to combat political corruption. Of course, he had his own weak spots. But his interference was totally marginal and you could convince him that the course suggested by him was not in his interest or the country. He would hum, haw, thaw and leave you to do whatever you wanted. If he disagreed with you he would express it in a gentlemanly fashion. But later on when the circumstances proved that I was right, he would never hesitate to admit that he was wrong and compliment me.

I had developed a good working relationship with him. He knew my bonafides and was sure that I would be not be a party to any wrongdoing. I never misused his trust and proximity to me. Once he was unhappy over some press reports. I told him "Sir, the press is free to write anything it wants. I am willing to give you a letter for my transfer, if you so desire."

He was in fact, very sensitive to press criticism to. I told him, "I have issued a standing order that only the Director or the Press officer in the CBI would be talking to the Press. Any news item appearing without being attributed to them would be unauthorised and the organisation does not accept the responsibility for the same". He seemed unconvinced and asked, "Why should you talk to the media"? I said; "If I don't, a lot of misinformation would be published. Your Government believes in transparency. Unless we have something to hide, or sit on cases I see no harm in talking to the Press. Moreover, the Press is told whatever has happened and not what is going to happen. As for my appearances on TV, I have never invited a single TV channel. A few channels have permanently stationed cameras outside my office. The only shot they get of me is either coming out of the car or sitting in the car and a few non-committal statements. The type of cases CBI is handling is of public interest. It is better to tell the public the correct position through the media".

He was satisfied and never raised a word about my meeting the media. Neither he pressed much nor I ever agreed to use the CBI for any political vendetta. I did not accept any suggestion of doing anything wrong. Many a times I pretended not to understand. The result was that CBI functioned with an Independence and support from the Government, hitherto unknown to this agency. This has been the legal position since the 1861 under the Criminal Procedure Code. My role was to exercise the authority vested in me.

My appointment in the CBI as its Director meant the end of easy existence and easy life. The job of Director CBI demanded lot of reading of case files, appreciating fine law points and work of about 28 hours out of the 24 hours per day. There was so much of demand on my time by the CBI, that for the first time, in my thirty five years of service, I stopped going home for the lunch. I had to break old traditions and set up new ones. This was essential to cope with a new type of crimes, which CBI was called upon to investigate. I tried to be as transparent in the functioning of the CBI as possible without affecting the cases.

I found some officials in the CBI, had stayed for too long, in one place. I felt that a comprehensive transfer policy, was a must, before effecting any transfers or laying down the tenure of all ranks. I was told by my senior officers, that by posting out, some officials, I would be raising controversies and creating problems for myself. One of my predecessors, strongly advised me, against such a move. He predicted that a newspaper campaign would be started against me by all those who had been in Delhi for years. Such officials had developed, official, political, and Press contacts. Against all such advice, I announced a transfer policy and then set out to implement it. In the first lot, a senior IPS Joint Director who had completed his tenure and had stayed for over a decade in CBI, was ordered to be relieved. The officer tried his best to stall his transfer order and remain in the organisation for a few more years. I was told by the Home Secretary that a proposal had come from the Department of Personnel – the administrative department of CBI – to retain him. I promptly approached the Prime Minister and told him that holding back a person, who had spent over a decade in the organisation and that too against my wishes, would be detrimental to my position as the head of CBI. Mr Deve Gowda intervened and saw to it that the officer was transferred.

To be impartial, I wanted to start with the transfer of IPS officers lest I be accused of victimising the permanent officers of CBI. Therefore after having said 'good bye' to the officer who had spent over a decade in the capital, I transferred two DIGs who had spent 14 to 24 years in Delhi. The transferred senior officers, were competent and hard working. But what was paramount in my mind, was to reiterate the principle, that no one should claim, the right to be, in one station for a lifetime. Cudgels were taken up, on their behalf by some newspapers, whose reporters had obviously been cultivated by them. For an organisation like CBI, the only way to cultivate, the press is by leaking information. Selective information is the bread and butter of the press. If somebody goes on giving inside information, he is their best friend. I found it strange, when I saw reports, describing how the transferred officers were not only distinguished, but that the organisation had also suffered irreparable loss, because of their transfer. I faced the flake, but after sometime, when the policy began to take shape, nobody took much note of subsequent transfers.

Delays

I have always been impatient with delays. CBI had developed a bureaucratic approach, in which for anything, to reach the top, it could take anywhere between a few weeks, to months together. There is a lot of paper work involved in all cases. The government and its agencies, survive essentially by feeding, tonnes of paper. Delay to some extent was unavoidable, because at any given time there were at least 20 to 30 per cent vacancies in the organisation. It takes about 10 years to produce one good investigator. One investigator is assigned only 2.5 of the cases involving general corruption and 1.75 cases of economic offences per year. By the standards of local police, it may appear, to be too low. But the reality is, that a CBI investigator is a loner. Neither has he the paraphernalia, that the local police have, nor does he enjoy any facilities of transport and help from other staff. Right from sending a letter, to the department, to the carrying of investigation papers, he has to do everything himself. He is investigator, driver, peon, collector of the papers, typist and interrogator rolled into one. When I visited Bangalore, Ecnomic Offences Branch, I was surprised to find that against 10 Deputy Superintendents, there were only five constables. More surprising was, that the organisation itself had asked for that much strength. I decided that I would look into every small problem of administration, myself. It is the small pebble or a grain of sand in the shoe, which pinches and needs to be attended to, lest it disables the wearer. Same is true of administration, in any organisation. Unless the basic facilities are given, nobody can deliver goods. I have been an ordinary person, like millions of my countrymen. The death of my late Father was a great shock to me on 23rd January 1996. I was with him from 20th of January to 22nd of January, 1996. The Doctors attending on him told that there was nothing to worry about him. He will be discharged in a day or two I left Ferozepur on 22nd and was in Delhi on 23rd morning. The Doctors were proved wrong when he passed away on the 23rd of January in the evening. I got the news that he was no more. I along with my wife, Surinder and three daughters, Randeep, Gagandeep and Harveen left immediately for Jalalabad, where his mortal remains had already been taken. I performed his last rites, on the 24th of January in the midst of thousands of mourning persons. The entire town came to a halt and the shops were closed, as a mark of respect to him Well as long as the parental shield is there, you feel that somebody will take care of you. You take it for granted. When that shield is removed, you feel bad about it. I was downcast and did feel bad about it. But time is the best healer. It has not secured my loss. It has not made me forget him. I have come to accept his loss as the wish of God Almighty.

What goes on is my life how has been presented by me as a bird eye view. Best way of doing so was presenting my daily calender happening.

17

Life Goes on

April Fool's Day

Today, my forenoon was spent in meeting Khushwant Singh, the famous columnist, along with Sanjay Jha, the publisher, who presented my Book *Inside CBI* to him. He is too old with an equally aged wife. Khushwant writes from his heart and that is why his writings have a vast audience. He does not mince words and does not believe in sugar coating them. The best thing is that he has 80 titles to his credit and all written in long hand. In his case, the age shows itself. It is a case of spirit is willing, but the flesh is weak. It is true of everybody in sixties and above. We talked about Bhindranwale and his methods of writing. He told me that the only way to treat fundamentalists of any religion is to treat them with contempt. He has a board, which says that do not ring the bell, if you are not expected. In other words, no body without an appointment is welcome. By the time Sanjay, the publisher of my book *Inside CBI* left; I could read Holy Granth for about 20 minutes. Bainshas been bitten by the writer's bug. He wanted to know how to write. Sanjay Kapoor was also invited. Sanjay is an experienced journalist and was the head of *Bltiz* Bureau in Delhi. Now he is a free-lancer. I spilled coca-cola on my white pants of Safari suit and got the same washed so that it does not carry the stains permanently. The guests wanted to linger on. But I literally pushed them out by 3 p.m. so that I could sleep. I do not miss my siesta, unless heavens are falling. Probably on the day of death, if it happens to be after 1 p.m. I may have to tell the Yamraj, please come after I have had my sleep. After sleep, I went for a meeting with Dr. Jain and Chandan Mitra of Pioneer for possible assistance to keep the financially sick paper afloat. It went on till 6.15 p.m. I visited Khan Market for getting the Microwave oven repaired . A visitor, Rajesh Handa, whom I had never met earlier, came for help in getting a job as a Pilot. I had to tell him that he should keep trying. Later on the Garrage Man, who had repaired my Esteem , accidented on 29th March when Surinder was travelling in it, delivered it. I sent the other car for repair for replacement of Mudguard. They left at 8 p.m. By that time, I was too tired. I just saw the news that Jayalalitha would pull the rugs from under Vajpayee. My favourite programme, Chat Show at Movers and Shakers took another 45 Minutes. See I have been busy with nothing. Moral for me is not to have more than one programme per day

Friday, 02 April 1999

Today, it was the usual day to begin with. I read Plain Man's prayers in three volumes. They are the finest set of brief prayers, for each day of the month. There is a separate prayer for morning and evening. By turn each day; I read one Non Sikh scripture in the morning. No non-Sikh religion is left uncovered. I have read Buddhist teachings, Jain's scriptures, Geeta, Quran and Bible. Of course, *Granth Sahib* is read every day and my effort is to have complete reading of the holy book of 1430 on the birthday of my three daughters, Randeep (Born in 1969), First January, Gagandeep and Harveen on 12 th July, (Born on same day but in 1972 and 1977 Surinder on 7th November (Born in 1943) and myself on 12 th October (1939). My late father was not sure of the date. He said that it was just written for the purpose of getting admission to school, as otherwise, I would not have been eligible for the admission to the primary class. There is a rule, which requires children not to be less than five years old before admission to the school. My mother also feels that my age as shown in the records is much more by one year. She is not able to recall the exact date or time. The result is that I do not have any Kundlini or exact date of birth indicating the configuration of stars. It does not affect me. But it foxes all the astrologers. My mother told me that I was born on 15th Magyar or Magh. Since the passing away of my late father when I was the Director General of the Indo- Tibetan Police Force, I have added one Path or full reading of the holy Granth coinciding with the completion on his death anniversary. The reading of the holy Granth is done after bath or whenever I have time.

Saturday, 03 April 1999

Today, I had to spend the entire forenoon for getting money from the Vijaya Bank, located on Barakhamba Road. Fortunately, the driver, Rajesh is there to take care of parking the car, in the overcrowded areas. It is almost impossible to find safe parking for the cars in Connaught Place or other markets like Khan Market or Lajpat Nagar or South Extension, unless one is game for some dents, scratches, mischief's or fights on regular basis, or find another less crowded market, where what you need or want may not be available. Another half an hour was spent in getting the cells replaced in my Palm Top Computer. Awaiting the guests Inderjit Singh, and Om went on till 2 p.m. when I had my lunch of boiled vegetable. I have added at least four kilograms to my weight. This is amply reflected by the tight pants, which were normal, a few months ago. Option for me is either to reduce or face other medical problems. Indiscretions in eating and a lot of free food have bloated me, beyond my own acceptable limits. The fight to keep the weight down has been going on for the last 40 years. Sometimes, I succeed. More often the temptations and the weight win. I have been subscribing to health magazines and buying books on reducing weight. Like millions of fellowmen, I lose in practice. I go on gobbling tempting food, whether hungry or not. One way I try to do is to get rid of all sweets in the house.

I went for the annual conference of Kanadda Sangha in Karnataka Bhavan. Vittal, Central Vigilance Commissioner spoke in English. I had been requested to speak in Kannada. I uttered a few words in Kannada, with Punjabi accent. My feeling is that not many understood my Kannada. So the rest of the speech was a recollection of my pleasant memories of service in Karnataka, and how some kind of system still works, despite all round deterioration in the country. Gokak, Secretary Fertilizer regretted the Anti English Policy of Government Karnataka, which will shut the world window on that State. Editor of Kannada, Samag despite the constraint of the budget and without even a telephone in his paper office or in his house has been able to galvanise

Kannadigas living in Delhi, thereby proving once again that money is not everything. Around 8 p.m. I went for the wedding of Vikrams son of Arun Bhagat, a batchmate in the IPS and a classfellow. All social occasions for me are an excuse to meet people, who otherwise would not be contactable either due to lack of time or inclination. By the time, I returned to the house, it was past 10.30 p.m. hardly leaving anytime except for writing this piece. I was delightfully surprised to find out that the programme "News Break" on Zee India TV starts with my picture at 10.30 p.m. every Saturday.

Sunday, 04 April 1999

My morning, after ablutions and walk started with visit to the Gurudwara Bala Sahib, a shrine built in memory of the 8th Guru Hari Krishan whose mortal remains were cremated. Before my IPS interview on 22 nd December, 1960, I had visited this Gurudwara for Guru's blessings. Since then, if I happen to be in Delhi on a Sunday, I make it a point to re-establish myself with the Guru's blessings. Rarely, if ever I have gone to other Gurudwaras in Delhi, unless they are on my way. I feel that whatever, I have got in life, I owe it to the blessings of the 8th Guru. Not that other Guru's are less important or less holy. It is simply a question of one's inclination in one incarnation of the Guru. Before becoming Director CBI, nobody ever took notice of me in the Gurudwara. It suited me to go anonymously and come back. But the TV Media and newspapers have enabled some people even in Gurudwara to recognise me. It only gives the benefit of a smile from the visitors and the priests. After the visit, I went for the DAV function of celebration of Mahatma Hansraj's birthday. There the best thing was the affectionate welcome from the Governor of MP, Bhai Mahavir, Acharya Swamiji, Sh. TR Tuli President of the DAV Managing Committee and Padam Shri GP Chopra . It was a wonderful function aimed at making you feel that you are proud of being an Indian. I could not stay for long as I had to go to Karnataka Bhavan to receive the honours of having done Karnataka proud to in Administration. I was touched at the honour conferred on me though I had retired more than one and a half years ago. It was also a function to make Kannadigas proud of their heritage, culture and unity of the country. I was mentally, emotionally and physically one with them. Kannadigas are the most liberal and tolerant of people in the country and this has made me have everlasting ties with them till my last breath. Infact, even now I subsist on Karnataka. It pays me my pension of nearly Rs 15000 per month. It has given me a huge lottery from the sale of my house built with a loan of Rs 1,20,000. My contacts are all in Karnataka or from Karnataka. I saw TV for about 45 Minutes while taking tea. In the evening, Mr Sarin and Mr Azad dropped in to discuss about the project of a serial on Kashmir situation. Then afterwards, my nephew Titu (real name Jaswinder) and his wife dropped in. To my horror I find that unless I regulate my time, I will have no time left to write any article or book. My mother, Lajwanti, who had gone to my sister Sarla's house returned along with Titu and his wife Rosy. Anybody who wishes to succeed in any project, must start with his work and not the time.

Monday, 05 April 1999

Today was again an early day. In my dictionary, starting the day's routine before 11 a.m. is too early. Getting up or going for a walk before 7 a.m. is an unearthly hour. While mentally, I am in agreement to get up early as it is said that only the early bird catches the worm, yet in actual practice, I wait to catch the worm late in the day. I went and addressed about 125 prospective entrants to the civil service, who have passed their written examination. It only reminded me of my own interview on 22nd December, 1960 for the IPS. I freely exchanged my impressions and how to go about the job of being interviewed. I told them that in answer to a question as to why I wanted to join the Indian Police Service, my answer was that I liked the service. I was asked on this reply the reasons for my liking the Indian Police Service. It was a tricky query and my selection or otherwise depended on my reply. I said "Liking is something which cannot be explained in terms of reasons. When you look at a flower, you cannot say whether you like it for the colour, or smell or petals". This won me the day. I also had a word of advice for the ladies eager to join the service. I told them that unless they catch or get caught young, with their service colleagues, they might miss the bus and remain discontented "Misses" all their life. On the return journey, I purchased some non vegetarian snacks for use from the Gole Market. It used to be my favourite haunt with my daughters Machu and Choosie, during their non-vegetarian days. Under the influence of their mother, they have become vegetarians. I suppose being the followers of Radhaswami, they are required to be vegetarian. While I am a non-vegetarian, but I can manage being vegetarian most of the time. I suppose, as you age, the food does no longer remain a great attraction. One does not find out the latest Dhabas with the exotic food attractions. Infact, my conclusion is that a chicken or cheese is chicken and cheese only. The rest is the stuffing or condiments sprinkled over it, above it, under it or inside it. There were times when for the sake of tasty food, one went to all kinds of filthy areas to eat unhygienic food in slums. But not now. Even five star hotels serve their food in good vessels by the liveried bearers. Many of them do not have anything to write home about. These days, to compensate for over eating of spiced and fatty foods, I try to eat, totally fat free, only boiled vegetables. Dinner has almost been given up unless it is unavoidable.

By the time, I returned home, it was well past 2 p.m. Just took some vegetables and slept off till 3.45 P.M., when I left for the race club. I am an Honorary Steward in the Club. The word Steward gives the impression of a Head-Waiter. But in the racing terminology, a Steward is both a judge and umpire to ensure that no rigging and no fixing takes place there. I spend about two hours a day on this activity per week. It is amazing how people bet their life's savings on the capacity of one horse to come ahead of others. Probably, the people (Punters in racers language) betting are from the category, who can throw about a few lakhs without feeling any pinch. Running a race club, requires coordination with the horse breeders, trainers, jockeys, punters, judges, local administration and above all bookies who accept the odds and bets on horses.

After returning home, I was feeling tired. The only way I know to overcome tiredness is to take a hot water bath. This is an instant cure for overcoming dullness and tiredness. I have been having bath both in the morning and evening for instant freshness. Ajit, my chum had invited me for dinner. Surinder does not like to go for programmes, later than 9 p.m. She gets up at 2 or 3 a.m. for her Radhaswami routine.

She reluctantly agreed to go to Ajit's place. We were the first to arrive. Ajit was the Defence Secretary, when the former Naval Chief Vishnu Bhagwat lost his job. He has moved now to Industry. A typical bureaucrat, but totally upright and not amenable to any out of the way, recommendations, is the best choice for the Chairmanship of Foreign Investment Promotion Board. His house, thanks to his Foreign Service, Secretary Level wife is a masterpiece of interior decoration. Little delicate items from all over the world give a feeling of delicacy about their entire place. Moses and his wife, both from the IAS, also joined for dinner. There was an instant rapport in the entire group, as Moses and his wife are from my former cadre, Karnataka. Mohan Das Moses, now retired, like me, was in the State Finance Department, when I was the Director of Youth Services. I used to chase him frequently for sanction of sports and youth programme proposals, sometimes to the point of harassment. Ajit, his wife Kamlesh and Achala are 1964 Batch. Their conversation turned to the usually familiar topic of their Mussoorie Academy and training reminiscences. Fortunately, some of the characters dissected and grievously hurt with oral jabs and vibes were also known to me. So I did not feel out of the conversation. Achala, glorified herself as an author and an astrologer. I am not qualified to comment on that because neither have I read her works, no do I believe in the hocus pocus of astrology. I believe, if something good is going to happen to me, let it come as a pleasant surprise. If it is going to be something adverse, why should I know it in advance, to upset my peace of mind. Many a times such dooms day predictions are self-fulfilling. The mind tends to bring about what it believes. By the time, we came back it was 10.45 p.m., too late for me also to work.

Tuesday, 06 April 1999

Delhi Government has constituted a jumbo sized committee of 147 persons to chalk out a programme of Tri-Centenary celebrations of the birth of Khalsa. I as a, invitee being a member of the above Committee decided to attend a programme where Sonia Gandhi, the Congress President was to be present. Being a Special Protection Group Protectee, it is almost impossible to go to any function where she or the Prime Minister of the day, will be present. It took me forty-five minutes to reach near the old Secretariat of Delhi. The Police, as usual overdo everything. They had stopped the traffic at least four kilometres away. People had to foot it out and there was no parking place within a radius of a few kilometres. At the top of it, the strict security checking had generated a half kilometre long queue just for entry to the venue. I felt it was not worth it to go through the hassle. Even if I decided to go through the obstacle course created by the over security, the function was likely to be over. So I just drove back, after having spent one and half hours in my car. Fortunately, Maruti Esteem is air conditioned and I used the time, in reading the Granth Sahib.

One organisation called National Akali Dal sent me a fax message conveying their decision to confer on me the title of Panth Rattan. It is a flattering title, to be conferred in a Gurudwara. I still have to make up my mind on this. There was another function of Sports Goods Industry today. But having spent all the time in the forenoon for journey by car only to the old Secretariat I decided, that I better pack my stuff for going to Gujarat next day.

Wednesday, 07 April 99

I got up at 3.30 a.m. so as to be ready to catch the flight to Baroda at 5.50 a.m. I make it a point to avoid any inconvenient timing while journeying, so that my morning exercise and walk is not affected or ruined . For me, morning walk is just another dose of medicine, so that I can lead a quality life. But as there is no other flight and train journey would take over 13 hours, there appeared to be no option except to catch morning flight. Bleary eyed, and short of sleep, I travelled to Airport by the vehicle arranged by Gujarat Narbada Fertilizer Corporation, Bharuch. An officer Punia, who had attended a seminar addressed by me in Cochin was instrumental in arranging for my address to Bharuch Management Association. I reached Bharuch at about 9.30 p.m. in an Air Conditioned Maruti Esteem Car, the same brand, which I have. With just time to change the dress, I rushed to the Corporate Office of Gujarat Narbada Fertilizer Company to meet and address the senior officers on Management and vigilance. The MD, A.M. Bhardwaj and his team of officers were sharp and brilliant and asked searching questions. I was overcome by tiredness, due to lack of sleep.

After lunch with Mr Bhardwaj, IAS, MD, I slept for 1 hour 38 minutes according to my stopwatch. I make it a point to time every activity, so that I can get the best out of time and regulate my programme. Otherwise, one tends to linger on just to pass time. I do not have any problem of passing time. I have too many irons in too many fires like writing books and writing for newspapers and magazines. I have to write at least two pieces every week. After I got up, there was a horde of local pressmen, wanting to speak to me. My view and verbatim were recorded for the local Bharuch Channel. After them, the local MLA, Iqbal Patel called me for a few minutes. With a quick visit to Punia's house to say "Hello" to his school going daughter and son and his wife, I just rushed to the venue of my address. I spoke for 40 minutes, followed by 80 minutes of question answer session. Question answers session is a battle of wits. I came out as a winner in this. A formal dinner with the Management Committee and a courtesy call to the house of Mr Bhardwaj, ended my visit. Mrs Bhardwaj is a talented lady, who at one time was onto making serials. Now she is busy in promoting a cultural programme of the visit of children to Turkey. I left at 10.15 p.m. for Baroda, called Vadodra in Gujrati to stay for the night so that I could board the flight at 7.45 a.m. on 8th of April. Some people prefer to come from Bharuch in the morning. Sometimes, it can be dicy with a traffic jam or a flat tyre or a recalcitrant vehicle. By the time I could sleep, it was nearly midnight. But all the same, I got nearly six hours of sleep, which is my bare minimum requirement, so as not to feel groggy.

Thursday, 08 April 1999

There was enough work to be done for the defamation case filed against me by Jagannath Misra for publishing the charges against him in a book form. He is trying to avenge my charge-sheeting him in the fodder scam case, so that it deters the future Directors in taking any action against any corrupt politicians having nexuses with the dishonest officers. In the evening, there were two dinners, one hosted by the Dabur Chief Burman, and the other by Dr Madhav Mehra, Chairman World Quality Organisation and Head of the Institute of Directors. At Burmans party, I ran into my batchmate Tejinder Khanna who was unceremoniously removed from the post of Lt. Governor of Delhi, due to the change in the Government at the Centre, to be succeeded by another batchmate Vijay Kapoor. I make it a point to attend all parties, not with a view to eat, but with a view to meet people for getting material for my books and articles. Interaction with fellow human beings is the best reservoir of material for penning one's ideas, reactions and feelings. I time every minute I want to spend and then take leave of the hosts. Nobody minds your disappearing from big parties. In fact some of them expect you to disappear. I make it a point to be back by 11 p.m. so that the delay of one day does not have a snowballing effect on my next day's programme. I make it clear to my hosts the time I can spend and after that I walk out. It enables me to meet and also work as per my schedule. In this way, I can find time for everything and everybody as I enjoy meeting and interacting with people.

Friday, 09 April 1999

There was a fight with my daughter Bibban over her occupying the bathroom for a longer period, delaying my using it. I was clearly in the wrong and so I apologised to her and made it up. She is as headstrong, as I am sometimes. Otherwise a good daughter, but essentially the fights are a reflection of the generation gap. It takes sometimes for the older generation to get used to the ways of younger generation, like their jabbing on telephones for hours together endlessly, wearing shabby and crumpled dresses in the name of fashion or the done thing, late night parties, senseless 'dog music' and taking for granted sometimes, that things will work out for them as desired by them. I had my publisher dropping in to discuss certain matters for *Inside CBI*, my book. He left before my lunch and siesta hour, which I rarely sacrifice, unless it is something totally unavoidable. In the evening, another visitor dropped in to recommend somebody's transfer in the Police and another wanted Police help in recovery of 90 lakhs advanced against documents. I am treated as one-man constituency, as well as recommending agency by ninety per cent of my visitors. Wherever I am convinced, I do try to help. Otherwise it a plain straightforward "No".

In the night, I had accepted an invitation to accept Panth Rattan Award from National Akali Dal, in Mansarover

Gurudwara. It took me over 1 hour and 30 minutes to locate the place. One felt flattered that people recognised my stand in fight against the corruption. I have decided that unless I am totally familiar with the route, I would insist on people inviting me to send the escort, so that I do not waste time in frustrating, aimless and fruitless search.

Saturday, 10 April 1999

This morning I left for Chandigarh with Surinder by Shatabdi Express, at 7.30 a.m. It is a fast train and covers 250 kilometres distance in three hours. Even by car, it takes four and a half-hours. The Executive Class is very comfortable, with free very good breakfast or equally excellent lunch as part of the ticket. The supply of Newspapers is another plus point. The train was late by 50 minutes. We could still reach in time for Bhog for my late mother in law, who passed away last year. The Bhog was a small family affair confined only to the close relatives. It was a wise decision, as nobody either has time or inclination to join anybody's death ceremonies, unless he is a close relation or is under official obligation to attend. After one year, the sting of death is not as sharp as one feels in the initial months. In any case, for old people, which all of us must inevitably become, death is a relief. It is better to die early than to live longer at the mercies of somebody else, both physically and financially. It was pretty hot in Chandigarh. But still after post lunch nap, I and Surinder my wife visited our vacant house in Mohalli. It is a one Kananal or 500 square yard house. It was the initial purchase made by my mother, for Rs 14000 paid over a period of 10 years from 1969 to 1979. It was built as a result of my posting to Chandigarh in 1988. My late father wanted to purchase a new car to replace his 1986 model car. I prevailed upon him to invest the money in building the house rather than in replacing his two year old car, which was doing only 8 to 10 kilometres a day in just going and coming back from the field in Jalalabad. The house had paid for itself during the lifetime of my father. I have not rented it out on the ground that it would be a dead loss, if the tenant does not vacate it when we need or does not pay rent. Then just for getting my own rights, I will have to rush to the Court. Even then , the possibility of justice during my own lifetime would be rare. we returned in the evening by

Himalayan Queen in AC first class coupę. Surinder slept the entire journey, whereas I used the time to write an article.

Sunday, 11 April 1999

It was the hottest day of the season in Delhi with mercury crossing over 41 degree centigrade. Except for visiting the Gurudwara Bala Sahib and buying snacks in Lajpat Nagar market, I stayed at home. Traditionally, I like to rest on Sundays, though every day is a Sunday for me, as a retired person. I spent sometime in working on the computer. In the evening, my daughter Gagandeep and her husband Gunveer dropped in for dinner. Both she and her husband are more computer literate than I am. I always need somebody to help me to press some button or the other correctly. Occasionally computer threatens me that I have performed an illegal action and it will be shut down. I yield to its threat and close it down myself. It forgets and then starts operating alright. For me, it is a constant education.

Monday, 12 April 1999

The standard routine of walking, flushing yourself with tea, bath, prayer and breakfast despite my best efforts consumes four hours of time. At the end of it, one feels tired. In the past, my wife and I would take a nap after a heavy breakfast. Heavy breakfast does not leave you fit for any work for at least two to three hours. I find that if I take a light breakfast, it keeps me fit and I can plunge into my work straightaway. Somehow, I tend to over eat, as if there would be no next meal. A psychologist says that it is an inbuilt instinct from the ancient times, when man used to hunt for his food. Man did not know whether he was going to get the next meal or starve it out. It is true of me in any case. Good food is a magnet. Regretfully, I go on stuffing till I am full to the brim, despite my desire to stay slim and trim. The result has been a constant battle with the bulge. Both sides win occassionally and the fight goes on. Today was no different. After assigning sufficient work to my P, S Jitender Kamboj, I went for inaugurating the upgradation of the of the hospital facilities of Guru Nanak hospital in Roshanara Road headed by M.M. Goldi. The machine had cost Rs 1.45 lakhs. The money was raised in my presence from various transporters, showing that very generous people exist, who care for the underdog. I joined them for lunch or Langar, which was three Tanduri Rotis, Dal and Cauliflower vegetable. It is the same food, which everybody, including my driver partook. This is one universal feature of Sikhism to ensure equality amongst all classes of people. We eat the same food, sitting or squatting, as the place permits. The Roshanara road is a very crowded place, with prayers on almost each one's lips; to spare the new car from dents and bumps. In the evening, I met H.D Devegowda, the former Prime Minister and had a brief chat with him on the political situation. He was worried and was not clear like everybody else, on the election/government scenario. He is also a Prime Ministerial Hopeful. Who knows that he may succeed, and be lucky second time.

Tuesday, 13 April 1999

After the usual routine, I started a simple Paath to be completed on the birthday of my daughters, Bibban and Choosie. Coincidentally their birthday is on 12th July, Bibban in 1977 and Choosie in 1972. They love each other and also have a love hate relationship. Both accuse their mother of being soft to the other. But they make it up quickly and there are no permanent enimities in them. Abassi my eldest son in law was also present at the time of the Paath. Most scriptures of all religions are not in the common man's language, except some portions. But nobody dare say anything for fear of being excommunicated. But in the case of Granth Sahib, the hymns of 9th Guru are not only clear, but are remembered by everybody. Muslim Scripture, The Quran in original form is in Arabic. Result is that very few understand it. My advocate, Vipin Gogia came to see me as yesterday, I had missed seeing him as I was with Mr H.D. Devegowda. We discussed the defamation case filed against me by one of the accused persons in fodder scam case. I have left it to him to take whatever line; he wants to take in the case. The case is of literally the category of "*Ulta Chor Kotwal ko Dantey*". That "It is the thief which reprimands the policeman". Based on the court case and confession of one of the accused, I mentioned the role of one of the influential accused person in protecting the scamsters. He wants one crore for the defamation, which does not exist, as he is already facing a criminal trial, on the same facts, in the Court of Special Judge of CBI, Patna. It has been done, with a view to make sure that nobody, should have the guts, to expose any criminal elements, who are a curse on polity. My book is at the best a minor exposure and my colleague Biswas told me that what I have written is only ' vegetable' and not even 'meat'.

Wednesday, 14 April 1999

Today, it is the three hundredth birthday of the Khalsa or the Sikh religion as it is known and seen in the world. I believe that one's relationship with God is personal. Mostly man is a beggar at the door of Lord Almighty. So rarely, if ever I have gone for any religious festival to any religious place. Moreover, for Sikhs the Holy Book, Granth Sahib is Guru. I have it in my residence since 1968. So I do not feel any need to go to any Gurudwara on any occasion. I do visit Gurudwara Bala Sahib whenever, I am in Delhi on every Sunday. I believe that I owe every thing in life to the incarnation of Guru Nanak in his 8th form, Sh. Guru Harikrishan Sahib. However, when on tour, I do not miss any chance to visit any Historic Gurudwara, if it happens to be nearby. Surinder had a splitting undiagnosed headache. It naturally affects, anybody's outlook on life. I spent my entire day in the air-conditioned room. My Private Secretary, is busy with another book dictated by me regarding corruption and lapses in Police. I had the satisfaction to see my Article on the birthday of Khalsa, as the leading piece in The *Pioneer*, supplement. *Punjabi Digest* and *Punjab Today*, the two leading Punjabi Magazines also carried my pieces on Khalsa.

Thursday, 15 April 1999

When one is in Government service, a few things like prompt service of other Government Departments, like the Municipality, CPWD and others like the hospitals is taken for granted. One does not have to interact with them personally. It is the lair of personal staff, which takes care of the creature comforts one takes for granted. After retirement, I noticed that my wife is occupying government accommodation where it is impossible even to get a leaking tap repaired. Our bathroom's tap has been leaking for the last two months. I have even personally spoken to the Executive and Superintending Engineers. The tap has remained leaking. It will look silly to speak to the Minister or

Chief Engineer to get something done, from the staff for which they are paid. It must be said to the credit of the senior officers, that they are responsive. But at the same time, effectiveness is missing and this is what is wrong with the administration. Another racket is the Maximum Retail Price. I wanted to purchase a ream of paper for my printer. The price varied as printed for the same brand from Rs. 133 to Rs. 180. The mark up on the maximum retail price is not less than 50%. Even the price marking is done by sticking labels and any price can be charged. The ultimate sufferer is the consumer and specially those in fixed salary group. This is one reason for need based corruption.

Friday, 16 April 1999

William Shakespeare said there is divinity, which shapes our ends. Man of course has to continue planning for future development and progress. There is however something called invisible power, which always guides us. Without his guidance and his light, nothing can move, no man can work or do anything. You may call that power divine, the will, intuition or fits of suggestions coming from within.

It happened to me on 16th of April. I went for a walk at 8 o' clock in the morning and I felt uncomfortable for a fraction of a section. I felt it was perhaps due to heat. I asked a co-walker, Gurmeet Singh, if it was really hot or only I was feeling hot. He confirmed that it was actually very hot. I then said from henceforth, I should start coming for a walk little earlier in the morning before it becomes hot. I completed my usual quota of 4 km. of walk in Lodhi Garden in 50 minutes, which comes to a speed of about 5 km. an hour. I had not eaten anything since morning except 2 cups of tea and a glass of juice. On reaching home at about 9.20 a.m. I told my wife Surinder of the discomfort. Both of us attributed it to heat. After my wife left for office, a lingering doubt however remained in my mind and I shaved off my chest to facilitate eventual EGC. I spoke to my wife and she agreed that I should go for a check up. At about 10.30 a.m. I spoke to my batch mate, college mate plus friend, Shri R.K. Takkar. We have known each other, since late 1961 and he is now MD Apollo Hospital. I also rang up my cousin Dr Pradeep Babbar in Faridabad, who said, he will join us in Apollo directly. My wife and I with my Secretary, Jitendar Kamoj, reached Apollo. Dr Pratap C Reddy, Chairman of the Hospital, was not there. His Secretary Raji had been briefed by Takkar, MD to take care of me. She took care of everything.

I was taken promptly to Dr Vipul C Roy, the interventionist cardiologist. I saw again divine hand in going to Dr Vipul Roy. Pradeep later told me that he felt if an Angiography was needed, it should be done by Dr Vipul Roy. But he did not say anything. He was however very happy, how destiny had led me to Dr Vipul Roy, who, he felt was the best interventionist cardiologist. Dr Pradeep is son of my maternal uncle, Jaswant Rai Babbar. Next to my parents, I have been closest to this family. All the children of my uncle are well educated and well placed. What is more important is, they have kept, intact human values. Dr Pradeep presence gave me a moral boost. I was touched by his concern, attentiveness to detail and more so, by his presence. How can one even repay such things, perhaps only by doing good to others. I felt confident that I was in pink of health and after Angio, I would be able to go home. I was however proved wrong. Angio indicated that three of my arteries were blocked, one 100%, other 85% and third 65%. I was told I was carrying a time bomb in my body. There could be heart attack any time. So far I did not have any heart attack. I was therefore advised immediate Heart bypass surgery. Bypass prolong not only prolongs life but improves quality of life. Having been used to an active life and being on tour outside Delhi atleast twice a month, I did not want to live with the fear of having an attack at any time and restrict my mobility. Further any small stomach ache, headache or ache in any other part of the body will give rise to the feeling it must be onset of heart attack. I decided therefore to go for Bypass.

Another factor that helped me to make decision in favour of Bypass, was the story of Dr Vipul Roy. He told me he himself had a hole in the heart. He first had to get his heart operated before he could be cardiac expert. I thought if Dr Roy could survive well after 25 years after heart surgery. Why not I? After decision was made for Bypass, I came in contact with Dr I S Virdi. I was greatly impressed by his cheerful disposition, immense patience and reassuring manner. He put me at ease and I felt I was in good hands.

rather, the best in the country. Apart from good reputation Apollo enjoys, it had three heart surgeons, Dr Virdi and two others. Other two Doctors. had gone to America to attend an important cardiology conference. The result was there was hardly any surgeon in Delhi during the week. Possibly very few operations might have been done, during the week. So divine hand, as per Karma decided the timing of operation, Doctor and Hospital.

Dr Reddy, Chairman, Apollo had told me that they have a system of fast track survey, which was available in Chennai only. I said to myself, life and death is in the hands of God. Nobody can give you one breath more than you are destined. Nobody can make you die earlier than it is due. However, humans beings try as per wisdom given to them and I firmly believe that God helps those who help themselves. God does not come to us personally and say that Joginder Singh, do this or that. He says that I will create conditions which leaves only one option open to you. You have no option but to act in that manner. Here God had beckoned to me and indicated the direction. I was already 59 ½ and any delay to keep the heart in good condition would have been fatal. Bypass means prolonging life and quality of life. It means being independent and not dependent. It means driving yourself than being driven. Dr Virdi told me with all the modern amenities available, the Byepass operation had a success rate of over 95 per cent. But in my case, I was in less than 0. 2 per cent people, who had volunteered to undergo operation to avoid any contingency of a future heart attack. Like all other decisions made in life, I immediately decided within, 10 minutes after the angiography to take the plunge. My wife Surinder, a devout herself was in full agreement. My next request was the immediate operation, though for a few seconds I felt that let it be done on Monday, the 19th of April. It was probably, the inner desire to postpone the operation for two days. Then I reflected on the quotation "Do the things you fear and the death of fear is certain". I did not know anything about the surgeon Dr Virdi. I only felt that whatever will be, will be the best. Dr Virdi dropped into my room and told me to be ready next day to be wheeled into the operation theatre at about 7.15 a.m. Dr Virdi, an endearing, comptent and charming person, had spent over 12 years in Australia and was the elected fellow of Royal College of

Surgeons, a rare honour. Umpteen times, blood had been sucked from my body with several syringes by dozens of technicians, for the tests, I knew or know next to nothing of, even till today. I took it in my stride. and wanted everything to be over soon. It is not the event which affects or scares us, but its waiting or anticipating for it.

17-4-99, Saturday, 18-4-99, Sunday

I got up as usual at 6 A.M and was ready for the 'D' Day. A wheel chair was brought and I had to use it. I volunteered to walk down to the operation theatre, but was overruled. I was wearing an ill-fitting Pyajama and a Shirt, with totally shaved off hair from every part of the body. Even the body had been washed off with disinfectant. An injection was given in my neck at about 7.30 a.m. and that is the last I remember of my earthly existence. When I next got up, in the intensive care unit, the watch showed the timing at 10. I wondered as to how soon the operation was be over. It was pointed out that it was 10 p.m. next day, that is 18th April Sunday. I found my body strapped to all kinds of machines, with innumerable tubes jutting into and jutting out of my body. All thc efforts of the Doctors and nurses were aimed at helping the helpless, paining and aching patients. One does not mind the pain, except the severe backache caused by lying straight. Fortunately, Dr. Virdi said, I could turn sides, though some other Doctors totally forbade it. All bodily functions were being monitored by machines and monitors. It was a miracle that one man could see what was going inside the body of another fellow human being. It was perfect snooping and spying of what was inside the skin and how a particular organ was behaving. It was too complicated for a layman like me. I left it to the better sense, wisdom and medical knowledge of the professional, for giving me as many pricks and concoctions, to join together almost my chest cut across, foot long wound on both legs and one arm, where the blood vessels had been taken out for grafting to replace the diseased arteries feeding blood to the heart. Not that I know anything about the heart and its internal constituents. It is what the Doctors and the medical journals have told me. After excellent care and all efforts at reducing the bodily pain, I was allowed to leave the hospital on 26th of April. My wife Surinder, daughter Harveen accompanied me. It was a nice feeling to be out of even the best of hospital. It immediately made me, forget my worries and pains.

Back Home

I returned Home after spending the time from 16th April to 26th in Apollo Hospital, where I had left my earthly existence for nearly thirty hours to be revived after a triple Bypass Heart Surgery on 18th of April. Home Coming after paying my respects and homage to Eighth Guru Harikrishan's last mortal resting place was itself a moving experience for me. It was an instant decision approved by Surgeon Inderjit Singh Virdi. God only knows, what for and for what purpose. Any surgery, you to lie flat on the bed. In the Bypass surgery it is more so, because the entire chest and collar bone is cut to take out the heart to repair it. This was a major problem. Normally, I do not make any song and dance about any difficulty, as I believe, that if God gives a problem, he gives it solutions also. Only thing is that, as short-sighted mortals, many a time we do not look or see the obvious solution in front of us. It was a case of Spirit being willing, but flesh being weak. There was not enough of energy, to talk on telephone. There were innumerable and tons of medicines to be consumed, at regular intervals, breathing and lung exercises to be done, apart from inhalation to be done three times a day, along with pushing three balls up with the strength of the lungs. Inadequate body strength and no energy even to be able to do the normal things, like being able to get out of bed makes one peevish. Every little activity consumes energy and that is what is required to live well. I had a court case coming up against me, in Delhi High Court, by one of the accused persons in fodder scam. I spoke into the mini tape recorder and asked my wife, Surinder to correct the replies typed by my Secretary. My sister Sarla, my publisher of *Inside CBI*, Sanjay Jha, Inderjit Singh Madan, Om Parkash and Seth Madan Lal, from Jalalabad, dropped in unannounced upsetting my plans to avoid visitors. One has to be civil to anybody, who comes to the house. Some people come for sympathizing, some come for commiserating, some to find out how you survived and how near are you to the death and some come for genuine concern. In any case, some chit chat cheers you up. Quite often, it is also exhausting as the same story as to how it happened has to be repeated. Life after bypass at least for some considerable time is only a story of taking medication and rest so that the incisions can be healed. In my case, both my calf legs and left arm have deep incisions, though fortunately the chest cut where the sternum bone was cut has healed well. One does not know or cannot work out the right ratio proportion, between the rest and activity. Too much lying down gives backache. Too much activity tires one out. One has to muddle along to find the right ration proportion. Life is a long series of lying in the bed, moving in the lawn and ambulating between bathroom, dining room and sitting in the study. Even entertainment on TV does not interest one much, as it is the repeat of old antics, same jokes, same gyrating movements, same violence, where the hero and villain get thrashed regularly. One of my Bombay friend, sometimes, sends me funny videos, which cheer me up. Three dozen or so TV channels are glutted with advertisement. The result is that you cannot enjoy any uninterrupted programme. But the TV Channels, also have to make money to stay afloat. TV, music, exercise are the only activities, which a teetotaller like myself can or would indulge.

I have nothing against the drinks. My grandfather, late Mahant Natha Singh could beat any drunkard, in any competition by miles. My father used to have occasional drinks. I saw to it that whenever, I went abroad, I got the finest Scotch Whisky for him. Somehow, I never liked the stink or smell of liqour or even beer. I also rationalized that with my limited salary, it would be impossible for me to offer drinks. If I accept anybody's drinks, then I would have to offer the same to those, whose hospitality, I enjoy. Of course, some colleagues to whom I posed this question, shrugged off by saying that you do not have to return the hospitality of the rich and famous. You can help them out. When I pointed out that this was nothing but indirect repayment in kind and amounted to corruption, they laughed at me saying "Every body is doing it". I said : " If this were to be accepted as a valid explanation, then God save the uninfluential and unconnected."

Today that is Monday, 03 May, 1999, the *Pioneer* carried my article in the Centre Space, for dealing with corruption. *The Day After*, a weekly magazine, carried two of my articles in today's issue. It is a matter of great satisfaction for any writer to see that whatever he writes is published. A writing is an author's baby. It is good to see it fructifying in the form of a publication. Feeling good cheers you up and makes you forget the constant nagging pain, which must continue till the operation scions are healed. It is a good therapy to keep oneself busy, within the limited energy one has. There are no quick fixed solutions to the healing. Time only has to heal. I was told by my cousin Dr Pradeep that a lot of cholestrol would be used up in my surgery. Cholestrol is what binds the body cells. So I have to alternate between the rest and work period. Even meeting visitors or answering phone calls appears to be a strain some time. Except for 15 to 20 minutes of walk, I generally stay in the house. Only once on the 5th of May, I went for my check up to Dr. Inderjit Singh Virdi. My ECG was taken along with the X-ray. The ECG as interpreted by the machine showed as abnormal. When I asked my cardiologist, he replied that since the sheath (Pericardium) in which the heart is enclosed, was removed, the ECG will always be interpreted by the machine as abnormal. Otherwise, I was in a better shape than was expected within two weeks of my operation.

Again, on 5th I went to a TV Studio for recording of a programme on Doordarshan which was telecast on 6th May,99. The host wanted to know from me, whether there was any political angle in the prosecution, of a former Foreign Minister, for requesting the Swiss Government in slowing down its cooperation in Bofors case. I replied that I had been a professional Police officer for over 36 years. The sanction was in response to a specific request sent by me for a particular offence. It will be incorrect for me to involve myself in any controversy.

As it is the requirement of building body strength on low or nil fat and exercise to the last point before exhaustion, takes all the time. The Doctors had warned that getting conditioned to the "Re-engineered" Joginder Singh would take time. One thing is certain that after a major surgery like the one I had, one has to rekindle one's interest in life. One way is by reading and doing positive things and accept the limitations of the body. It looks as if in a jiffy, I have crossed the threshold of 60. But I still tend to look upon my daughters as small children, needing protection, guidance and help all the time. The style, the process, the method and approach of every generation is the same. I must wait only for the time to heal. Even working on computer tires me out, because for four to six weeks, I cannot sit on a table and work. I have to keep my legs at a higher level, so that the circulation of blood is speeded up. After every work or sitting down of two hours, I must rest for half an hour. But I am reminded that "Even this shall pass away" after a few weeks. Then I would have probably forgotten the trials through, which I am passing now. It is like the sicknesses of the last year, which all of us cannot even recall. The attitude of taking life, as it comes is the only remedy for living well. It is one of the several phases of life, one passes through. In the last few weeks, the daily record has become a combined collection of events and persons. Days and events are merged. Because during the convalescing period, one is only waiting to be fully alright. On the 7th of May, I had my first social outing of the evening to attend a function to honour H.S Nirula, as the Asian of the Year. NRI Institute of which I am the Chairman had organised this function. Mr. Jagmohan Singh, the life behind the Institute and Secretary General of the organisation had an impressive collection of guests. I stayed only for about fifty minutes and did not eat anything. I did the customary presentation of the bouquets and made a short speech.

For me it was only a testing ground, as this outing was done within just three weeks of the open heart surgery. If one does not go out, then one is always thinking of one's operation and becomes peevish. Delhi is getting very hot with mercury touching 44°C. There are ups and down in recovery. There is no solution, except patience for the wounds to heal and energy to be recovered. Even the simple activity of receiving too many phone calls or visitors tires one out. If you lie down, too much rest can cause backache and if you sit too long, then you get tired too early. The trick lies in striking the golden rule. Everybody has to discover his or her own threshold of rest and activity. It is very important to keep yourself busy, so that you get a feeling that you are normal It is impossible to go on watching the TV all the time, as almost the same films are shown on all the channels.

Any channel will present you with shooting, beating or singing of inane songs, which does not happen in real life. Humorous or funny films are very few. May be, it is not the 'in thing'.

From the 22nd of May, I have started going for walk to Lodhi garden. It was my first visit after five weeks. At least, I have been able to do about 2 kms. in 30 minutes. Meeting H.K Dua, top journalist, was doubly useful. He had undergone a similar surgery. His tips and advice was very encouraging. On Tuesday, 25 May, 1999, I had lunch with a young progressive NRI, H.S Nirula, who with his initiative enterprise, starting from $5000 has created an empire of over $500 millions. His business extends over all four continents including India, UAE, USA and UK. He has done his family and the Sikhs proud. When I asked him the secret of his success, he said that the secret was perspiration and some luck. Another thing, was that he never hesitated from trying for fear of failure. He has been adjudged as a top Asian, by the NRI Institute, of which I am the Chairman. Sardar Jagmohan Singh, the enterprising Secretary General of the Institute, was also invited for lunch.

I have been going to Appollo hospital off and on for showing my left arm, which has not healed. Dr. I.S Virdi, a very competent and excellent surgeon and now a friend has been very encouraging. Whenever, the pain becomes unbearable, I remind myself; "Even this shall pass away," like every good and bad thing in life. It is my computer, which is my constant companion. I can let off my joy, my happiness and my frustrations by scripting them.

My daughter, Bibban, a good child, often gets angry at the restrictions I impose on her like not watching movies in the Cinema Theatre from 10 p.m to 1 a.m. Every generation regards the previous ones as ancient and old fashioned. It is basically a generation gap, which is inevitable. The older generation will go by its perceptions. It may not necessarily be the perception of the present generation. There is nothing, which can be done about it except to live with the situations as they arise. My wife, Surinder, that way is more in tune with the modern times. May be, my daughters, share their feeling with her more than they do with me. Surinder, has been more than my wife. She has been support, saviour, my Doctor and my nurse in sickness, health and during and after the heart bypass surgery.

There is a steep decline in the level of energy. It comes back, gradually, may be at the rate of 30 to 40 per cent per month. But by today, that is Sunday, 30 May 1999, I am able to amble around for about 25 minutes in the morning and for a similar period in the evening in Lodi Garden. There is no substitute of patience, for the entire healing process. My food, is bland and totally fat free, unless the cook, contrary to instructions, has been putting the cooking medium. From the day one of the surgery, I have been on sleeping tablet, as the last thing in the night. Doctors recommended this on the ground that undisturbed sleep, accelerates the process of recovery and healing. But even that dose, has been reduced by me to half. The trouble with the sleeping pill, is that it makes you drowsy, during the day time also.

Saturday, 05 June 1999, Today, there is a distinct feeling of being better than in the past. It is also due to the fact that today, it is the end of seventh week, after the operation. Scabs on the two legs and the left hand have fallen off. The healing of the open wounds is nearly 90 per cent over. But the bone part of the chest takes any time between eight to twelve weeks. I am still on half sleeping drug Zopicon or Valium. These drugs act both as pain killer and induce sleep, which may not be easy to come or at the best it may be a disturbed sleep. Sleep plays one of the most important in recovery of health, apart from the medicine. I can walk a distance of over 2 kms. in Lodi Garden. *Day After* Magazine, carried my two articles for June Issue. *Punjab Kesri*, a daily in Hindi, Punjabi and Urdu has been carrying some of my articles, almost every fortnight. *Hindu* carried my Central Piece on 26th of May, 1999. It is a matter of a great satisfaction for me that even when not cent per cent fit, I can write coherently. My Secretary, Jitender Kamboj asked me today, as to why I do not work full time. I told him that my needs in life are so little, that I can manage, very well with whatever, I have earned lawfully plus my pension. I have worked for 37½ years for the Government. I do not want to work for a private person and give him the satisfaction that he has the former Director, CBI working for him. When people hire you, after your retirement, they are not hiring you for your competence. They are hiring you, so that they can trade your influence and former position in the Government. Infact, I had an offer at a fat salary, ten times, more than what I last drew, to work for a company. I politely declined. The head of the company thought that I was declining due to inadequate emolument. He said; "You name the figure for working for us". I said; "Thank you. But I do not wish to work full time. I want to be master of my own time and not be bound by any routine of rushing off at 9.30 a.m. and worrying about getting late due to traffic jam or whether the boss will be annoyed, if on some days I do not come to the office".

He said; "You are the first official to have declined my offer. Otherwise, retired people are running after me for post retirement jobs even at a much smaller salary". I said; "They are not Joginder Singhs", and the matter ended there.

Tuesday, 08 June 1999

I must confess, that despite my handling or mis handling computers, since, 1993, I am still substantially computer illiterate. I had such a low opinicn about the computers, that for years together, I stuck around to good old manual typewriter. Necessity teaches you everything. So, by and by with the help of my daughters and wife, Surinder, I got hooked on to computer. Still, I feel that for me the old models, may be four year old are good enough, for writing Articles and Books. In fact, more complicated the gadget, the more confusing I find it. There are so many functions in modern day computers, that an average user like me, is hardly able to use, or knows how to use, just five per cent of it.

Since my heart bypass surgery, I have been advised to be on sleeping drugs, to dull any pain and to have sound sleep. I follow the doctor's advice, but not necessarily in full. I have cut the sleeping drugs to half, as I do not want to get addicted. The fat free diet, makes me hungry. Lying on the bed for hours together gives backache. So a balance has to be struck, between lying down all the time and the physical activities. In any case, in the post retirement age of nearly 60 and above, the body will have some problem or the other. One has to learn to live with, whatever falls to one's lot.

Thursday, 10 June 1999,

For the first time, I managed to lie down in the bed from 11 p.m. to 6 a.m. without a sleeping pill. I have been on sleeping pill since 16th of April, when I was admitted to the hospital for my byepass surgery. I must have slept for sometime, as I was not groggy this morning when I got up. Lunch was in Oberoi hotel, courtesy of a senior colleague, Abraham Verghese. Verghese has been both my senior, boss, friend, cadre mate as well as a service mate. Now both of us are retired. But I always show deference to him and Mr Haralankar, my other former boss and a friend. Haralankar like Verghese has settled down in Bangalore, a 12 months hill station, with a salubrious climate.

Monday, 21 June 1999

Today, my publisher, Sanjay had fixed an appointment to present my book to the Prime Minister. I called on Atal Behari Vajpayee, the Prime Minister and presented him my book *Inside the CBI*. Vajpayee has spent a life time in the service of his party. It took him 56 years to reach the top. But he is the one Prime Minister, after Jawahar Lal Nehru to whom no scandal has ever touched. Even at the age of 74, he was fresh and alert. An unmarried RSS worker, he brings out the best India has to offer. Unfortunately, he was let down by the bureaucracy, to whom he gave two years extension, by taking the age of retirement from 58 years to 60 Years. He is too good a man to find fault with anybody. He has believed in taking the team with him. Dignified, suave and polished, he asked more in the nature of a question that it was time for me to write another book. I replied that, that also will come. It takes six months to one year to write a book. It was my first visit to number 7, Race Course Road, after 20th June, 1997, when the then P.M. Gujral got annoyed with me for not bailing out the President of his political party, Janta Dal. I was out of CBI, within ten days, for not carrying out the orders or wishes of the then Prime Minister. Despite, whatever happens, there are self imposed restraints on disclosing everything, which passed between me and the former or the present Prime Minister. It is glamorous to be the Prime Minister of the largest democracy, in the world. But the Prime Minister is still not a free agent. He has to carry the Parliament, the party, the coalition partners, press and the country with him for anything he wants to do. Apart from everything, the security staff is hanging around, totally cutting out the privacy of the person of the Prime Minister. I must also confess that I was also equally guilty in telling the Prime Minister what was wrong with the country and how the country should be run. The Prime Minister listened to me patiently.

On 24th of June, I addressed a programme of officers, of Housing and Urban Development Corporation, dealing with Vigilance in the After noon. I noticed that I had recovered about 70 per cent of my body energy level.

Saturday, 24 July 1999

Today, I was conferred the award of 'Delhi Rattan', by All India Intellectual's Conference in the YMCA tourist hostel. Judge Ashok Desai of Allahabad High Court along with Sh. Bhisam Narain Singh and Krishnamurty conferred this honour on me. Earlier, last week, a group of the hosts led by Sh. B.N. Sharma Advocate has called at my house to communicate their decision to confer this award and solicit my confirmation. It was good function, without any Political leanings. Amongst others, I met my friend Karthikeyan. He is a dedicated official, who has literally put his neck on the block, by supervising the investigation actively and effectively of Rajiv Gandhi assassination case. He is a marked man for life. I mentioned to him that Government have a habit of using officials and discarding them. He is the one person who deserves the highest security all his life. LTTE are much more dreaded group than the Sikh or Kashmiri or Naga terrorists. The morning walk to which I have changed from evening, gives me free evening to work on my book. The only danger is that I have to save my time from being used by others or being wasted in dinners and lunches. I force myself to write to discipline myself. The ringing telephone breaks the continuity. Telephone is both a blessing and a curse. With automation, it is impossible to speak to any official with your problem. An automated life less tape gives the answer that you are in the que or the lines are busy or this number does not exist. It is a progress from the 1950's, 60's or 70's, where it was impossible to get across to anybody except on a lightening call basis. One should be grateful in life for small mercies. I have solved the problem of ringing telephones or inconvenient calls. When in service, there was always somebody to take the calls, but after retirement, the telefax with answering machines works as my Secretary. When I am not at home, the caller can always, leave a message for me. My machine can take 40 messages. It also helps me to screen the telephone messages and respond wherever I want and ignore, where I do not wish to reply. In any case there are not more than half dozens calls every day. It also safeguards against mischievous and threatening calls.

Last night I went for a dinner to a Restaurant hosted by Jagmohan Singh. It took my two hours of time and one page of writing in terms of work. But it is good to go out and be in circulation. Spending two hours outside the house on small chitchat means put your article back by two days. In the formal lunches and dinners, for teetotlelers like me, except for inane conversation like the weather or adding to weight or further promotion in service or increase in business, there is nothing much to be done. For those drinking, at the cost of the host, it is a great temptation. Their focus is on the food, and not on the drinks. I avoid dinners, as a late dinner upsets my schedule. I am an early eater and early riser. I avoid dinners and if I have to go I excuse myself early.

Saturday, 07 August 1999

It is sixteen weeks since my heart bypass surgery operation. I feel myself a new man with a new zest of energy at the same level as it was before the bypass surgery. Infact it is much more than at any time in the past. The walk is much brisker. The bypass surgery does not add to the life, which God has given to every body. It only gives you a sound heart, for another fifteen to twenty years, unless one commits indiscretions in food, leading to fresh blockages of the arteries and heart problems. Heart is what sustains life and circulation of the blood. I received an offer from a fellow morning walker to head one of his companies. I told him that I would not like to do any full time job. The temptation of money had no lure for me nor the offer to charge expenses for my staff or the vehicle. I told him that I have enough for my needs during my life time and I do not need anything more. I have been clear in my mind that I would not work for any private person after having worked in the government. He was rather disappointed. Even the offer to be on the Board of Director of the companies was put off by me. I had almost left for London/ Birmingham on the 6th of August, on the invitation of the Indian Cultural Association. Even the ticket had been received. Just one hour before the departure by the Swiss Air, the organiser telephoned, from U.K. to say that they had postponed the function for one month. I myself had declined to accept the invitation and the free ticket. But only on his insistence I had agreed to proceed to London. It was good in a way, as the Swiss Air Flight would have first taken me to Zurich. From there I would have to board another flight for London. The 9 hours journey would have been stretched to thirteen hours. The visit to Europe or England does not have any lure for me, as I have been abroad at least forty times. To me all European cities appear alike. All buildings and departmental stores are the same design with almost the same goods. The only difference is that you pay for the goods in the local currencies. I have engaged a young boy as my Driver. I noticed him not present with the car, when I came out of the bank yesterday. He lied to me that he had a quarrel with somebody over non payment of the parking and that is why he was delayed. In the evening when I went to a function of Ivory Coast National Day at the residence of V.P. Punj, the Honorary Counsel General, I noticed his absence. He again lied that he was there with the car. I myself had taken a round of the parking area. Only when I had almost sat in somebody else's car, I found that the Driver had come. I had to pull him up. He still denied his absence. I found next day from my servent that he had brought the Esteem car home. When I confronted the driver, he said that he had come home to put coolant in the car. I asked him "Is not water, coolant or air checked as first thing in the morning"? He had no answer. I told him that I had lost all faith in him.

Tuesday, 10 August 1999

Considering the conduct of the driver, I have devised my own strategy. Yesterday, I went for lunch at the invitation of a friend to a Taj Palace Hotel. I asked him to park the car and give the key to me. Today, again I went for a function of a film. I made him park the car and pocketed the key. He had taken the car yesterday to sell petrol from it. He did not have much time. About five litres from the full tank was stolen or sold by him. The government drivers sell petrol frequently and also perhaps some other drivers might be doing. One has to safeguard one's own interest oneself. Even the maid servant, who went with my mother last month to my sister Manjit stole Rs. 6500/- from my mother. My mother has very poor eye sight. I make it a point to give her Rs. 1000/- per month to spend as she may like. It is deliberately done, lest the feels that after the death of my father, she has to stretch her hand before anybody. Her income is much more and it is her own money she is getting from me. She is on the last legs of her life, and this is what she has been telling me for the last ten years. I want her to be happy. As long as my father was alive, it was his responsibility to look after her. After his passing away, I want her to feel that she is still cared for. The only trouble is that she has not changed with the time, as my father had changed. It is not her fault. It is only the limited exposure and unwillingness to learn which comes in the way. All of us, including she, feel that our knowledge of men and matters is the best and we know how best to deal with any situation. Nobody and nothing is perfect in life. Even those of us, who claim to be perfect and know all, have their weak points. With minus and plus point we muddle through life. This goes on till the last minute and last day till it is time to call it quits. There is a constant endeavour to improve. But in the eyes of the people, we wish to please we fall short in our achievements. High, low, big and small have their problems, which keeps them worried. The poor have the problem to worry as to from where their next meal is going to come. The rich have the problem to control their weight, diabetes or blood pressure, all the result of over eating. For the rich, it is the constant cycle of over eating, dieting, visiting Health Clubs to shed the excess pounds or kilos. The big hotels and restaurants run on the purses of those who can afford to throw Rs. 500 or more, for one meal. The men earn by their work and the ladies spend. Kitty parties in five-star hotels are a mute witnesses to the bloated, over fed, belching ladies of the super rich in constant search of new avenues of excitement and variety. Many five-star hotels serve meals, which regretfully are the left over of the previous meal.

As of now out of my three daughters, two are married one to an IAS officer in Assam and the other to a banker. The third is still studying. She too will find her own level life partner some day.

Many a time, I have been questioned as to how does one kill one's time after retirement. My answer has been that despite retirement, I have no time to do all the things I wish to do. I decided to write all events, some eventful and some uneventful in my life every day for some period in the form of this back. So that after the sunset of my life, what will be left lehind will be the memories inscribed here. Good Bye and Good Luck.

Index